Daily Power for Joyful Living

Your life is what you make of it.

There is no limit to the power and the joy that can be yours with *constructive* living. This book is your personal "do it yourself" reconstruction kit to build a richer, fuller life.

Start now to clear away the debris of old ideas and habits and build a solid structure of radiant, joyful living! Here are the tools to change your consciousness, and therefore your life, from negative to positive attitudes. Let your mind absorb the powerful ideas in each chapter. Follow these instructions for one month, and you will become an entirely different person—the person you want to be!

These 31 vital chapters—one for every day of the month—cover every important area of your life. Each chapter also contains affirmative verses from the Bible and quotations from the world's great idealists of the past—for each day of the year—all related to the day's uplifting topic. Also, there is the GOLDEN BRIDGE to span each day: a Morning Projection and an Evening Retrospection, enabling you to begin and end the day in the positive frame of mind that all successful people enjoy.

Step-by-step, each chapter gives you a clear understanding of the secret of vital physical and spiritual health . . . how to dissolve fear and guilt . . . how to have financial security . . . a new way to solve old problems . . . seven steps to inner beauty . . . the importance of love, faith and hope . . . how to use your subconscious mind for creative action during sleep . . . and much more.

These techniques will help you discover your purpose in life and how to achieve your uppermost ambitions, desires and goals. As soon as you make up your mind to put the creative power within you to work, you will be on your way to greater health, happiness and success. You will weed out all of the feelings of inferiority, hostility and fear that are holding you back.

Here is ample material for an entire year's program of constructive life building activity that can give you an eternity of happiness. Have fun doing it. Living IS fun! Don't resist it, enjoy it. You are the builder —let's go!

Donald Curtis

An outstanding leader in New Thought and metaphysics for over twenty years, Dr. Donald Curtis is the senior minister of the Unity Church of Dallas where he ministers to thousands in person and through his regular radio and television programs.

In addition to his major books,

Your Thoughts Can Change Your Life

Human Problems and How To Solve Them

Daily Power For Joyful Living

Science of Mind in Daily Living

New Age Understanding

he is the author of many inspirational booklets which are widely read by Truth students everywhere. He has written hundreds of articles which have appeared regularly over the years in **Science of Mind, New Thought Quarterly,** and Unity periodicals. He is a District President of the International New Thought Alliance and speaks and teaches regularly at the INTA Congress each year.

Dr. Curtis speaks and conducts classes at Unity and other metaphysical churches throughout the United States and abroad. His seminars based upon his books are widely attended everywhere.

His writings are used as textbooks in healing, meditation, and spiritual education at many churches and centers. Dr. Curtis' sales and executive and leadership training seminars are popular in the business and professional fields, and he is in great demand as an after-dinner and convention speaker. He appears regularly before service clubs, speaking on his favorite theme, "The Unlimited Potential Within You." He presents techniques for developing this potential, releasing the free, full flow of life through the individual as his consciousness expands and he experiences richer, fuller living. Through the Spiritual Unity of Nations and other organizations throughout the world, Dr. Curtis works tirelessly for human understanding, international cooperation, and world peace.

He carries on a large correspondence with readers, teachers, and students all over the world. An extensive traveler, he has spoken in England, Switzerland, Germany, Ghana, South Africa, Greece, India, Japan, Hawaii and in the Caribbean Islands. A deep student of world religions, Dr. Curtis has studied with the yogis and holy men of India, spending time in their ashrams, as well as seeking out the counsel and instruction of Buddhist monks, and Tibetan lamas. In Japan, he studied Oriental techniques of healing, studied Zen, did research in the traditional older religions, and spoke at the centers of many of the "new religions" there, including an extensive lecture tour for Seicho-No-Ie founded by Masaharu Taniguchi.

Dr. Curtis' broad background and universal approach to spiritual matters make him welcome by religious groups of all denominations.

DAILY POWER
for
JOYFUL LIVING

DONALD CURTIS

1975 EDITION

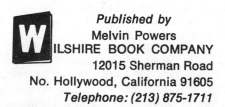

Published by
Melvin Powers
WILSHIRE BOOK COMPANY
12015 Sherman Road
No. Hollywood, California 91605
Telephone: (213) 875-1711

Library of Congress Catalog Card Number:
63–18604

ISBN 0-87980-300-2

Printed in the United States of America

Printed by

HAL LEIGHTON PRINTING CO.
P.O. Box 1231
Beverly Hills, California 90213
Telephone: (213) 983-1105

PREFACE

This book is your personal "do it yourself" construction kit. You are to use it to build for yourself a richer, fuller life. This is the greatest construction job which you will ever have the opportunity to undertake—building your own life. Your life is what you make it:

> "I am the master of my fate;
> I am the captain of my soul."
>
> (*Invictus*, by William Ernest Henley)

For most of us, the task of life construction involves considerable reconstruction. Before we can build a solid structure, we must first clear away the debris of old ideas and habits. That is where this book comes in. It contains the tools by which you change your consciousness, and therefore your life, from negative to positive. When this is done, there is no limit to the power, and the joy of your constructive living.

HOW TO USE THIS BOOK

This book contains 31 vital chapters—one for each day of the month—each one covering an important area of your life, and contains constructive techniques for strengthening each one. Here is the way to use these valuable tools:

1. Read this book completely through to get an over-all grasp of its subject matter. For this first reading, don't study it; just enjoy it.

2. Now you are ready to use the tools in this book for constructive life-building purposes. The first step: Read a chapter a day each day of the month, each month for one year. When you finish the first month, start back at the beginning, and go through it again, studying the references and practicing the techniques given for each day. There is ample material given for an entire year's program of constructive life-building activity. Have fun doing it. Living is fun! Don't resist it. Enjoy it!

3. This book will be your constant companion for the next year, so make friends with it. Be good to it by using it. It will be good to you by helping you become the person that you want to be. Let your mind absorb the constructive ideas in each chapter. This book is really a collection of affirmative ideas. In your tools for each day you will find quotations from the world's great idealists and optimists, including many affirmative statements from the Bible, as well as excerpts from inspiring poems which will lift your spirit to new heights.

   In addition, you will find many references to the author's two previous books, *Your Thoughts Can Change Your Life,* and *Human Problems and How To Solve Them,* both indispensable guidebooks to joyful living. They each contain numerous techniques for developing the affirmative approach. Refer to these books. Along with this one, they will change your life.

4. At the end of each chapter you will find a GOLDEN BRIDGE to span each day: the first part to project your constructive consciousness ahead each morning, and the second to help you review your day before retiring each night. The use of the GOLDEN BRIDGE FOR EACH DAY is an integral part of the joyful living plan for which this book provides the blueprint. This technique is described fully in Chapter One.

   One word of reminder—these techniques will help you to the exact degree that you use them. To make them work you must work them. Just follow these instructions.

5. At the back of the book you will find 366 Constructive Daily Thoughts (one for each day of the year, including Leap Year). Memorize the appropriate thought each morning and repeat it frequently throughout the day. It will keep you on the upward path.

6. Give a copy of this book to at least one person each month. In this way you will be sharing your good with others. It will come back to you many times, because when you give to them and they give to others, the accumulated good is totally active in the life of each individual who is using this approach to the more joyful life.

7. Follow these instructions for one month, and you will be an entirely different person. Live by these suggestions faithfully for one year and you will become the person you want to be. You are the builder. Let's go!

Donald Curtis

I am your friend, and my love for you goes deep.
　　There is nothing I can give you which you have not got;
But there is much, very much, that, while I cannot give it,
　　You can take.

No heaven can come to us unless our hearts
　　Find rest in today. Take Heaven!
No peace lies in the future which is not hidden
　　In this present little instant. Take Peace!

The gloom of the world is but a shadow.
　　Behind it, yet within our reach, is Joy.
There is radiance and glory in the darkness.
　　Could we but see, and to see, we have only to look.
I beseech you to look.

Life is so generous a giver, but we,
　　Judging its gifts by their covering,
Cast them away as ugly, or heavy, or hard.
　　Remove the covering, and you will find beneath it
A living splendor, woven of love, by wisdom, with power.

Welcome it, grasp it, and you touch the
　　Angel's hand that brings it to you.
Everything we call a trial, a sorrow, or a duty.
　　Believe me, that Angel's hand is there; the gift is there,
And the wonder of an overshadowing Presence.
　　Our joys too: be not content with them as joys.
They, too, conceal Diviner gifts.

Life is so full of meaning and purpose,
　　So full of Beauty—beneath its covering—
That you will find earth but cloaks your heaven.

Courage then to claim it: that is all!
　　But courage you have; and the knowledge that we
Are pilgrims together,
　　Wending through unknown country, home.

And so, at this time, I greet you.
　　Not quite as the world sends greetings,
But with profound esteem and with the prayer
　　That for you now and forever,
The day breaks, and the shadows flee away.

CONTENTS

LIVING

Your Golden Bridge to Life

"HAVE you lived here all your life?" the traveler inquired of the hearty old Vermonter.

"Nope, not yet," was the reply as the man continued serenely about his business.

Life is never over, even though many people seem to have very little interest in living.

"Millions now living will never die," is the motto of a certain religious group.

"Yes, but the tragedy is that millions now living are already dead and don't know it," someone observed.

George Bernard Shaw once suggested that an appropriate epitaph for many people might be: "Died at thirty, buried at sixty."

In contrast, however, are those in whom hope—and life—ever spring eternal, and who give every evidence of planning to live forever.

"Dear Father," prayed one old man, "help me to live while I am alive."

Life is inevitable; relax and enjoy it. This is our first step in becoming a wise and mature person and acting like one. Your life is to do with as you will. No one can live it for you. No one can learn for you, grow for you, or express your life for you. Each individual's life is a personal matter. It is up to us what we do with this most precious of all gifts. How are you spending your life? History and reason indicate that the best approach is to live every moment to the fullest and let the results take care of themselves. Life needs no excuse or explanation. It needs only to be lived.

The Golden Bridge method used here has evolved out of my classes and personal counseling work with students over a period of several years. As a result, many thousands are finding it effective in building richer, fuller lives. It is described fully in my first book, *Your Thoughts Can Change Your Life.*[1] Let us review in full the explanation of its use as reprinted from Chapter 11 of my earlier work.

THE GOLDEN BRIDGE—WHAT IT IS AND HOW TO USE IT

The Golden Bridge is the actual completion of our inner identification with the creative process. As we build the bridge in our minds we are constructing a path upon which we travel to completion and accomplishment. The Golden Bridge is a rehearsal for life. By this process we form the invisible structure upon which is built the formation of our lives. It defines where we are going and provides a means for getting there. The Golden Bridge utilizes all of our creative faculties. It takes chance and effort out of our activities. It dissolves the barriers of time and space by building within us an awareness of purpose and completion. The use of the Golden Bridge will enable us to transcend our human failings and weaknesses, and will lift us into a consciousness of our true place in the great scheme of things.

The Golden Bridge will release the power of your magnificent potential, and give you the necessary direction for complete fulfillment. The Golden Bridge has become for me life's most valuable tool. It is a device for bringing divine power into tangible expression. It is tremendous. Let's learn to use it.

Become completely relaxed. Detach your mind from all concerns and random thoughts. Remove all personal effort as you become still and identify yourself with the Indwelling Reality. Visualize light and inner peace and beauty, and let the feeling of power and strength generate within you.

Let yourself become filled with the spiritual fuel which provides the thrust to project you into new and vital experience. Take time to get completely quiet inside. Form the picture of yourself as a whole

[1] (Englewood Cliffs, N.J.: Prentice-Hall, Inc., 1961), pp. 170–78.

person—spirit, mind and body. As you achieve this feeling of completeness you will be ready to build and travel the magic span of the Golden Bridge.

Picture yourself as a magnificent and powerful rocket which is being projected along a beautifully arching trajectory into new spheres of understanding and experience. We span the infinite realms of experience as we traverse the Golden Bridge. We start from where we are. What we are doing in inner visualization looks something like this:

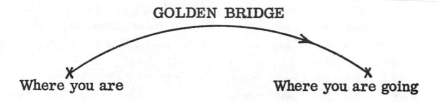

GOLDEN BRIDGE

Where you are   **Where you are going**

The Golden Bridge is the upper path of spirit, mind and imagination. It enables us to reach our destination by rising above the obstacles of ignorance, mistakes and trial-and-error experience which block our way when we fail to use the power within us.

Jesus said, "I go to prepare a place for you" (John 14:2-4). The "I" is your inner creative awareness. Visualization, imagination and realization are its natural capacities. You are this "I." Send it ahead of you and let it prepare the place for you. Identify yourself with it completely in the inner stillness and you will go with it into the glorious realms to which it will lead you. Trust it completely. It is intuition inspired by spiritual realization. It is your real self. Through it you build the Golden Bridge of your life.

This technique may be applied to any section of your experience no matter how small it may be—from a single moment to eternity. The Golden Bridge enables us to know where we are going, because after we have once spanned it in our inner consciousness, we then return and travel it in the action of experience without any peril of losing our way.

Do you see how it works? When the inner consciousness once reaches the destination—even though the outer self may still need to go through plans, problems and worldly actions—the inner self has already reached its destination and achieved its goal. It is a matter of reaching absolute conviction. There is no better way to convince ourselves that we can do a thing than actually to do it. When we travel the Golden Bridge we arrive at our destination first as preparation for starting to go.

Suppose you were to take a trip to a distant country where you had never been. You would arrange the trip with your travel agent, who would help you make plans and would tell you what you could expect along the way and after you got there. You would study travel folders, and learn the language and customs of the place you are to visit. You would provide yourself with tickets and the necessary items to take on the trip. You would make all arrangements. You would prepare yourself completely for a pleasant journey. In essence, you would take the trip many times vicariously before you actually started on the physical journey. You would be there in consciousness long before you ever left home.

So it is with the Golden Bridge. But it is more than just an imaginary journey. It is complete preparation for what is to follow. We both misunderstand and underestimate the true function and power of the imagination. We are what and where we are because we have first imagined it, consciously or subconsciously. The Golden Bridge speeds up the process and makes it easier. The Golden Bridge is the direct path. It avoids the detours, the twistings and turnings, the pain and suffering, the misdirections, the discouragements, and the lost ways. The Golden Bridge looks something like this:

Visualize the Golden Bridge as leading straight up to the summit of a high mountain, which is also traversed by a winding, twisting road. The mountain represents the achievement and enlightenment attained through growth and experience. It represents the distance we travel as we keep moving upward. It may, and undoubtedly does, take many lifetimes to reach the top of the mountain. But the important thing to remember is: We all make it eventually. The Golden Bridge enables us to progress more surely and more rapidly by developing our full inner resources. None of us really knows how far he has progressed up the mountain. We do know that we are on our way upward, and our challenge is to go as far as we can.

The winding road up the mountain represents the long and slow trek upward through experience, trial and error, toil and suffering. It reaches the summit too, but the trip is a long and perilous one, filled with many turnings, backtrackings and detours.

This visual presentation of the Golden Bridge should be firmly fixed in your mind as a master symbol for meditation and inner spiritual work. Even though we may get confused and lost in dealing with life's problems, we can always get back on the right track by visualizing this straight path. We can never get lost when we stay on the Golden Bridge.

The Golden Bridge is a means of co-operating with the creative Law of life. It enables us to use the power within us for the real business of life—growth and accomplishment on every level. It enables us to flow with the tide, the inner resurgence of energy and power which is always seeking expression. The Golden Bridge is one means of making our personal will one with the Divine Will. Constant inner work will enable us to discover what this Will is and will enable us to co-operate with it. An awareness of the larger picture gives meaning and purpose to the adventure of living.

Let's learn to use the Golden Bridge as the path along which we walk hand in hand with our inner partner—the Higher Self.

The Golden Bridge technique may be used to prepare the way for any segment of activity or experience—an hour, a day, a week, a month, a year, or a lifetime. Start by using it to span each day. Mentally cut through any doubts and anticipated difficulties until the path of the day is projected straight and true before you. In this way you arrive mentally at your destination before you actually start the trip.

You have no idea of the freedom and ease with which you travel once you have learned to do this. It will give you the direction and the certainty which will enable you to meet every situation with confidence and power. Once you know everything is going to be all right

—the conviction which you build with your Golden Bridge—you will not be concerned with minor difficulties which may arise. The very fact that you have built your conviction in itself projects an authority and power which keeps difficulties from arising, and causes everything to work out properly.

Golden Bridge for This Day

Construct your Golden Bridge for each day as soon as possible upon awakening. Get perfectly still and travel step by step to the end of the day, progressively building the conviction that you are actually there doing the things which you are visualizing and stating, and that they are completed. Make your statements aloud if possible, for this will keep your mind on a straight track and build a stronger inner feeling.

Here is a model for a Golden Bridge for one day. Adapt it to your own situation.

I am now building the Golden Bridge of this day. I give thanks for this day and the potential of great experience during every moment of it. Throughout this day I am guided and directed by the Inner Intelligence which prepares the way for me and makes straight and true the pathway of my experience.

Everything I do has purpose and meaning. I work efficiently and well. I am in perfect control of myself and every situation at all times. I am free from all doubt and uncertainty as I move serenely ahead. I put my best foot forward at all times. I know that what I plan to do is already an accomplished fact in my experience, and every outer action is a projection of this inner pattern. In this way I can make no mistakes, because I have already traveled the road which I am on. Being sure of myself, I am able to adapt successfully to anything as it arises, being already sure of the outcome. I live joyously, eagerly and expectantly all day long. I love life and I love to live.

Each second of time moves me that much closer to the completion of a happy and successful day. I easily complete my preparations for this day of success. Everything in my home and family is harmonious and orderly. Love and good will bless my relations with my family and all other people throughout this day. I am kind, understanding, and courteous at all times.

Breakfast this morning is a leisurely and pleasurable experience. Good

conversation and sharing of viewpoints grace our table. My family and I
are nourished in soul as well as in body. Everything is wonderful.
I am protected and guided as I journey to my office. I enjoy the trip. I
eagerly anticipate the work which awaits me there. I am on time for
every appointment, and everything is accomplished successfully and is
arranged according to the best interests of everyone concerned. What I
do, I do well. My work is thorough and of high quality. I constantly work
to improve myself and what I do. I am a top-rate person. I do a good
job of being my best self at all times. I take joy in the doing, and I let
results and rewards take care of themselves. I am free from concern,
worry, or fatigue. I gather energy and momentum as I go along. I operate
as a whole person. I get the most out of life today and always. There is
no limit to my potential. I am on the high road at all times. I am a success in every way. *And so it is.*

Continue in this way until you have covered your entire day. Give
special attention to important appointments, decisions and projects.
Take the affirmative approach, and keep at it until the picture is clear
and your conviction is strong. Cover everything, no matter how large
or how small. The results which you achieve depend upon the thor-
oughness of your inner mental work. Refuse to let your mind dwell
upon anything except what you want it to accept.

Spend approximately a half-hour building your Golden Bridge at
the beginning of each day. Be thorough about it, and give it full time.
Doing so will add immeasurably to your efficiency and accomplishment. Once you form the habit of building the Golden Bridge you will
never try to do anything without it. The longer you work with this
technique, the more efficient you will become, and the easier it will
be to do. As you do your inner job well, you will be able to handle
anything that comes up without it throwing you.

Then, too, there are times during the day when you will need to
become quiet and do some repair work on the Golden Bridge, or you
may need to alter the original design. Don't let this upset you; just do
it. Ride with life, be flexible and adaptable, but always work from a
solid inner structure. Nothing is more important than this. The
Golden Bridge is of inestimable value in this respect.

Having completed your Golden Bridge for the day, or any particular segment thereof, release it—forget about it, and go ahead and do

what you have to do. The structure is there, and will automatically provide the pattern for the action which follows. You will be amazed by the results you achieve, and how much more enjoyable life becomes.

The Need of Retracing Your Steps on the Golden Bridge

A technique of retrospection goes hand in hand with the Golden Bridge. Let us suppose that you have built your Golden Bridge and have traveled it—successfully or unsuccessfully—throughout the day. You are now back in bed, where you awakened to start your day many hours before. No matter what the day has been like, get quiet inside and deliberately go back over the Golden Bridge of your day in reverse order. Start from where you are, and retrace your steps through the evening, at dinner, the afternoon, lunch, morning and all the way back to when you awakened. Fix everything so that it is right. Forgive yourself and others. If you were wrong, admit it.

If a situation was handled badly, correct it in your mind and rehearse it visually, with thought, word, action and feeling, until it is right. Erase all unpleasant memories, impressions and confusions and replace them with the corrected ones. Your subconscious mind will retain what you instruct it to retain. Correct your mistakes and fix things that went wrong, giving particular attention to your thoughts and attitudes and what you said and felt.

As you do this you will cleanse your mind, your memory, and your emotional state of everything except what you want to remain there as a permanent and constructive part of your consciousness. You will balance the mental, emotional and spiritual budget. You will sleep better than you ever slept in your life and you will awaken refreshed and strengthened. Remember, the feeling you go to sleep with is the one you wake up with. When your mind is free as you go to sleep, powerful subconscious natural forces are free to work through you, refreshing and instructing your mind, developing your soul, and rebuilding your body.

There are no more valuable life tools than the Golden Bridge and its counterpart, the process of retrospection, by which you go back over the events of your day in reverse order. When you practice these disciplines faithfully you will rebuild your life completely. You will experience health, happiness, success and fulfillment because you will be constantly projecting them mentally, emotionally and spiritually into your world.

DAILY THOUGHTS ABOUT LIFE
From This Chapter

1. Live each moment as if it were both your first and your last.
2. Life is inevitable. Relax and enjoy it.
3. The business of living is to attune ourselves to the free full flow of life which runs through everything.
4. There is no thrill like the thrill of constructive living.
5. The will to live fills us with the energy of life.
6. Life is a personal matter. It is up to each one of us to live fully.
7. Your outer life is the expression of your inner life.

From The Bible

1. Man doth not live by bread only, but by every word that proceedeth out of the mouth of the Lord doth man live.—*Deut. 8:3*
2. A man's life consisteth not in the abundance of the things which he possesseth.—*Luke 12:15*
3. The life is more than meat, and the body is more than raiment.—*Luke 12:23*
4. God is not the God of the dead, but of the living.—*Matt. 22:32*
5. He that soweth to the Spirit shall of the Spirit reap life everlasting.—*Gal. 6:8*
6. He that doeth the will of God abideth for ever.—*I John 2:17*
7. Whosoever will, let him take the water of life freely.—*Rev. 22:17*

From Great Thinkers Past and Present

1. Every man's life is a plan of God.—*Horace Bushnell*
2. If this life be not a real fight, in which something is eternally gained for the universe by success, it is no better than a game of private theatricals from which one may withdraw at will.—*William James*
3. Life is the art of drawing sufficient conclusions from insufficient premises.—*Samuel Butler*
4. The life of every man is a diary in which he means to write one story, and writes another; and his humblest hour is when he compares the volume as it is with what he hoped to make it.—*James M. Barrie*

5. Life is the childhood of our immortality.—*Goethe*
6. The end of life is to be like God, and the soul following God will be like him.—*Socrates*
7. Be such a man, and live such a life, that if every man were such as you, and every life a life like yours, this earth would be God's Paradise.—*Phillips Brooks*

GOLDEN BRIDGE TO LIFE

Morning Projection

My life lies stretched before me in smiling repose. This day I move one step forward toward my demonstration of complete and perfect good. I am guided and directed each step of the way throughout my long and beautiful life. I enjoy every moment of it. I am filled with the joy of constructive living. I thrill to the wonder and glory of Life. I live my life abundantly now.

As I go serenely and purposefully about the business of living, I act from the center of order and purpose within me. My thoughts, feelings, and aspirations are consistent with all that is true and fine. In working for my own good, I am also working for the general good. I construct my life on sound spiritual principles. I am right inside, therefore I can do no wrong. And so it is.

Evening Retrospection

Quietly now, I review today's activities with a calm and introspective eye. I look at myself objectively so that I may interpret my thoughts, feelings and actions intelligently and honestly. I cleanse myself of all unworthiness. I dissolve all negativity. I free myself from all bondage and limitation. I cut through all confusion and congestion. I get my life in order.

As I review this day's activities, I give thanks for this opportunity to grow and learn. I now see all things in their proper perspective. I clean house this evening. As I relax and reflect, I set my house in order so that I am not burdened by any unworthy or unfinished business. As I wind up today's business, I close the office of my mind, leaving everything in perfect order.

As I reflect upon the beauty of life and the glory of God, I quietly and peacefully drift off into deep and refreshing sleep. My mind is filled with pleasant dreams. My house is in perfect order now. And so it is.

2 🖋

SELF

How to Make the Most of Yourself

A Bob Ripley "Believe It or Not" cartoon once pictured a foot-long steel bar worth $5.00. Molded into a pair of horseshoes the same amount of steel was revalued at $10.50. Recast into a piece of machinery it was worth $3,285. In the form of fine steel springs for watches its value increased to $250,000. The same pattern of upgrading applies to our lives. *Our* value basically depends upon what we make of ourselves.

Take that important step forward—the step toward honest self-evaluation. Ask yourself these questions: "Who am I? Why am I here? Where am I going? What is my purpose in life? How can I do a better job? Am I living up to my full potential?"

PERSONAL EVALUATION

The average person uses barely a tenth of his tremendous inner potential, content to settle for mediocrity. King David sensed the measure of man more clearly when he sang, "What is man that Thou art mindful of Him? . . . Thou hast made him a little lower than the angels, and hast crowned him with glory and honour" (Psalm 8:4, 5).

Shakespeare wrote: "What a piece of work is man! How noble in reason! How infinite in faculty! In form and moving how express and admirable! In action how like an angel! In apprehension how like a god!" (*Hamlet*, II, ii)

12

DOMINION

If such heights are to be attained, man must first establish dominion over himself. Man must search within until he finds the key to his personal dominion. There is an Eastern saying: "He who conquers a city is great; he who conquers himself is mighty." It is a matter of self-conquest of our worries, anxieties, inferiorities, hates, guilts, and all other inner negativities. But, rather than accent the negative aspects of consciousness, let's dissolve them by releasing them from our consciousness, and promptly build more constructive attitudes of mind.

MAN'S RELATIONSHIP TO GOD

It is said that every cell within the body is a Universe in miniature. We have billions of cells, each one of them a unit of intelligence, each one of them receptive to the guidance and control of a Superior Intelligence. This direct control comes from the human mind, but the human mind is in turn a cell within a Larger Consciousness. As we control the cells of our body by our thinking and feeling—with our minds—we in turn are receptive to the influx of a Higher Intelligence: the One Mind which is God. Thus is defined man's relationship to God. Man has been described as having his head in heaven and his feet in the mud, and living in the area between. Man is both human and divine in his nature. He has the potential to discern God directly, but he also has the negative potential to outdo the beasts of the field in their ignorance and lack of development. This divergence in our nature brings about the inner conflicts which cause most of our problems.

THE "WHOLE MAN"

Always think of yourself as a whole person, a balanced triangle made up of spirit, mind and body. *We are spiritual beings, using mind, living in a physical, material environment.* Unless we learn how to use our minds intelligently, the Spirit will not have an opportunity to flow through and make us whole and happy individuals. The concept of the "whole man" is now being accepted by all enlightened people. *Religion, psychology and medicine join together in a unity of view-*

point as they minister respectively to the souls, the minds and the bodies of men. The Science of Mind combines all three in a unified philosophy of integrated and sensible living. This consciousness of wholeness is our answer to the world's negative thinking—the selfishness, aggressiveness and greed of people and nations, and the many false ideologies of every kind.

ONENESS

It seems to me that Oneness is what Jesus had in mind when he said, "If therefore thine eye be single, thy whole body shall be full of light" (Matt. 6:22). Let your eye be single; see yourself as a whole person—an integrated person. The law of cause and effect says that what we think and feel, what we are inside, is what we experience outwardly. Let your eye be single and see your Oneness with the Universe. What is the Oneness that we see? Call it God if you like, call it Principle, call it Life, call it Science, call it Philosophy, call it Religion, call it Spirit—but whatever you call it, it is Truth. Jesus said, "Be ye therefore perfect, even as your Father which is in heaven is perfect" (Matt. 5:48).

This Father is the Creative Power of Truth, the Universal Law of Right Action, the Infinite Healing Presence, the way God works. It is the Universal Subjective Mind; It is the subconscious mind in man. Jesus said: "The Father that dwelleth in me, he doeth the works" (John 14:10). He meant that you will know the meaning of Oneness when you can say with him, "I and my Father are One" (John 10:30). "He that hath seen me, hath seen the Father" (John 14:9). Jesus taught us how to make the most of ourselves when he said, "Ye are the salt of the earth . . . Ye are the light of the world. . . . Let your light so shine before men, that they may see your good works, and glorify your Father which is in heaven" (Matt. 5:14–16).

Here are five steps which show us how to get the most out of ourselves:

—1—

TAKE PERSONAL INVENTORY

Find out who you are, what you are, what you need to get rid of, and where you are going. An anonymous student at one of my lectures recently delivered himself of this poem. It humorously points up what we are talking about.

ME, MYSELF AND I

My life is becoming more hectic,
It's due to that ego I bring.
It's awful I know but wherever I go
I go, too, and it spoils everything.

With people I'm fairly contented
My life is as gay as a song.
But in spite of good health, when I'm with myself,
I make myself sick and that's wrong.

A change of surroundings was mentioned,
The doctor said it would be fine.
I started anew, the train came in view
But the face in each window was mine.

I've traveled from nation to nation
By land, by air and by sea,
But try as I may there's no place to stay
Where I can get rid of that "Me."

If you have the slightest suggestion
Please tell me what it is about.
My case may seem strange but I'll make any change
So my "Inner" can live with my "Out."

—2—

FIND OUT WHAT YOU CAN DO BEST

Some of us undertake too many projects; we waste our energy by spreading it too thin. Let's seek to discover the real talents latent within us. If you possess musical talents, why not develop them wholeheartedly? If you are a wonderful mother, that is your particular point of expression. If you are a good grocer, a good nursery man, a good salesman, a good waiter, a good practitioner, whatever it is—be it with all your heart! Stop playing at life, and begin to live life in full expression of what you do best. Are you an actress? An actor? A director? Be a good one. You are not in competition with others. Just use your talent, your gifts, your ability, and your training to make yourself the very best that you can be.

The tragic ones in life are those who try to get by as second- and third-raters. The world isn't too kind to second-, third-, fourth- or fifth-raters. But there is always room at the top, and everyone can be a first-rater at something, if he wants to be. *Find out what you can do, and do it to the best of your ability.*

—3—
USE YOUR ABILITIES TO MEET THE NEEDS OF MANKIND

"How does what I can do contribute to the needs of mankind?" Ask yourself that question. Don't worry how you are going to do it. Ask searchingly, "How can I use my ability to help other people?" Find out. Are you a teacher? Then teach. Are you an actor or actress? Then act. Give more laughter, more entertainment, more joy.

Are you a salesman? Use your talent to bring people together with the things that they need. Good salesmen are needed in this world. Do you work in television? What was television developed for? To sell soap and cigarettes? No, it was developed to bring beauty, information and entertainment into the lives of people. Help to adapt this medium to people's needs.

No matter what your place is in life, ask, "How can I use my talents, my body, my emotions, my mind—my soul? How can I use what I am to meet the needs of other people?

—4—
FIND FULFILLMENT IN SERVICE

The only way we can have anything is to share it, give it away, direct it for the service of others. When we so enrich the lives of others, we find our own greatest fulfillment. If we are willing to surrender the false ego—the little self—and lose ourselves in a dream, a goal, an ambition, in love and in service to others—then the Kingdom of Heaven will be opened to us.

—5—
FORGET ABOUT YOURSELF

Jesus said, "Your Father knoweth what things ye have need of, before ye ask him" (Matt. 6:8). Forget self. When we do what we are here to do, the Father takes care of his own. As we give, so shall we receive. Use common sense and God will take care of you. The great Prayer of St. Francis of Assisi instructs us further:

Lord, make me a channel of Thy Peace
That where there is hatred—I may bring love,
That where there is wrong—I may bring the spirit of forgiveness,
That where there is discord—I may bring harmony,
That where there is error—I may bring truth,
That where there is doubt—I may bring faith,
That where there is despair—I may bring hope,
That where there are shadows—I may bring Thy Light,
That where there is sadness—I may bring joy.

Lord, grant that I may seek rather
To comfort—than to be comforted;
To understand—than to be understood;
To love—than to be loved;

For it is by giving—that one receives;
It is by self-forgetting—that one finds;
It is by forgiving—that one is forgiven;
It is by dying—that one awakens to eternal life.

DAILY THOUGHTS ABOUT SELF
From This Chapter

1. Our value depends upon what use we make of what we are.
2. The first step in making the most of yourself is self-evaluation.
3. We need to look within ourselves to find the key to personal dominion.
4. God can work for us only by working through us.
5. We are spiritual beings, using mind, living in a physical and material environment.

6. The soul is what we are when we are all put together.
7. Stop playing at life, and begin to live life in full expression of what you do best.

From the Bible

1. I am fearfully and wonderfully made.—*Psalm 139:14*
2. God said, Let us make man in our image.—*Gen. 1:26*
3. God hath made man upright; but they have sought out many inventions.—*Eccles. 7:29*
4. Jesus answered them, Is it not written in your law, I said, Ye are gods?—*John 10:34*
5. In Him we live, and move, and have our being.—*Acts 17:28*
6. There is a spirit in man, and the inspiration of the Almighty giveth them understanding.—*Job 32:8*
7. Know ye not that ye are the temple of God, and that the Spirit of God dwelleth in you?—*I Cor. 3:16*

From Great Thinkers Past and Present

1. Oftentimes nothing profits more than self-esteem, grounded on what is just and right.—*John Milton*
2. Self-approbation, when found in truth and a good conscience, is a source of some of the purest joys known to man.—*Edward C. Simmons*
3. Be displeased with what thou art, if thou desirest to attain to what thou art not; for where thou hast pleased thyself, there thou abidest, and if thou sayest I have enough, thou perishest.—*Saint Augustine*
4. The superior man will watch over himself when he is alone. He examines his heart that there may be nothing wrong there, and that he may have no cause of dissatisfaction with himself.—*Confucius*
5. Never lose sight of this important truth, that no one can be truly great until he has gained a knowledge of himself.—*Johann G. Zimmerman*
6. "Know thyself," said the old philosophy.—"Improve thyself," said the new.—Our great object in time is not to waste our passions and gifts on the things external that we must leave behind, but that we cultivate within us all that we can carry into the eternal progress beyond.—*Edward G. Bulwer*
7. He who reigns within himself and rules his passions, desires, and fears is more than a king.—*John Milton*

GOLDEN BRIDGE
TO YOURSELF

Morning Projection

As I move out into this day I express myself at my highest and best at all times and in every way. I put my best foot forward and keep it there. I am on the pathway toward self-discovery and self-unfolding. I know who I am and where I am going. I travel the Golden Bridge from self to Self. I am constantly moving out of the lesser into the greater. I am evolving from the human into the divine. I am becoming my true self.

This day affords me countless opportunities for developing myself. I learn priceless lessons today. Each experience is a tremendous opportunity for growth and self-discovery. There is no limit to how far I can go today. There is no restriction on what I can accomplish on this day.

This is my day. I live it fully and abundantly. I dedicate this day and myself to the service of God and man. And so it is.

Evening Retrospection

In the quiet of the night I survey my day's activities. I find out how I handled myself today and how I could have done better. I look at myself clearly and incisively. I correct my faults. I repair the damage of my mistakes. In my mind I redo everything that was less than my best today. I revise the entire script if necessary. I play every scene of this day's activities over again until I get it right. I leave no stone unturned. I do a thorough job of making my peace with this day.

As I retrace my steps for this day, I savor each action of good. I enjoy this day all over again. I change everything that needs to be changed by co-ordinating my will and my imagination. I do a thorough job on myself tonight. I am serious about wanting to grow. I am growing.

In sleep now, I release the cares of the day, and let the Infinite Healing Presence have its way with me. And so it is.

3 ✐

PEOPLE

*"...all the World Art Queer Save
Thee and Me..."*

THERE are all kinds of people: short ones and tall ones, thin ones and fat ones, young ones and old ones, smart ones and dumb ones, kind ones and mean ones, beautiful ones and ugly ones, white ones and colored—many different-colored ones—all quite wonderful, all basically the same but individually varying, and all "made in the image and likeness of God."

"God must be a funny-looking character if we all look like him," you may observe. Not at all. Since God is Infinite, there is no limit to the variety of expressions that can come from the One Source. God is not a Being, but a Beingness. Many of our problems arise because we limit our concept of God.

" 'God created man in His image and likeness,' and man, not to be outdone, returned the compliment," someone astutely observed.

We have a greater understanding and love for people when we think of ourselves as brothers and sisters of everyone, because we all have the same parents—God and Life—the Father in heaven and his creative Self-expression.

We are often distressed by the conflicts which take place within the human family. Mankind's history is pretty much the record of the conflicts and struggles in our efforts to get along with each other. Ironically, in past ages, religious or so-called holy wars resulted in the slaughter of untold numbers of people. Enlightened as we are, our civilization still spends too much of its time, money and energy either in getting over a war, fighting one, or preparing for the next. It is far too high a price to pay because of differences between people—the way they think, the way they worship, or the difference in the colors of their skin.

Racial prejudice and discrimination continue to be our national shame. The white-Negro conflicts in Little Rock, Arkansas and in Oxford, Mississippi, and those which occur in other racial hot spots continue to reveal this cancer in our society. Integration programs are progressing but final success cannot come without the subconscious switch-over to common sense, understanding and love. We haven't made it in this generation. The next generation is still too close to ours to be free from this inner disease of hate. Jesus clearly taught that love alone could cure our human ills. This message to the millions has gone largely unheeded for nearly two thousand years. Many of us now realize that we have no choice but to accept the constructive approach of love. Since we have the potential for nuclear destruction, the survival of civilization hinges upon our firm resolve to get along with others. We have no other option.

Prejudice and discrimination can reach alarming proportions. Germany in the thirties is a classical example. Yet the seeds for a program of growth and improvement are within the individual. Happily, we are making progress in these matters. Each year, the second Sunday in February is designated "Race Relations Sunday" by the National Council of Churches. On this day many predominately white congregations invite Negro ministers as guest preachers, and many Negro congregations hear sermons by white clergymen. Microscopic though this may seem in the face of the over-all problem, it is certainly a step in the right direction. In time it will undoubtedly lead to the acceptance of the position set forth by laymen at the close of a conference on race relations called by Rt. Rev. Oliver J. Hart, Episcopal Bishop of Pennsylvania. At the conference, Episcopal laymen urged prompt action to "break down un-Christian barriers" in all areas of life, especially in religion.

It was then resolved: "Any division of humanity by race is blasphemy against our faith. When this separateness enters into the household of faith, it is a heresy with which we cannot compromise."

That lays it right on the line. Separateness in "the household of faith" or any place else is merely a projection of separation within

ourselves—separation from God, Truth, Faith, Oneness. We have some
fence-mending ahead of us, if we share the attitude of the old Quaker
who mused: "Martha, all the world art queer save thee and me, and
methinks at times that even thee art a bit queer."

The elimination of hostility and prejudice in favor of love and
understanding is necessary for self-preservation. It was estimated that
there were 47,000,000 more births than deaths in the world in 1960,
and that there will be 75,000,000 more in the year 2000. At this rate,
according to Athelstan Spilhaus and Earl Cros in the Los Angeles
Times for June 12, 1960, "by the year 2900 every bit of dry land in the
world would be covered by humans standing shoulder to shoulder in
one vast subway rush." That kind of proximity will require a fresh
look at our concept of brotherhood, of getting along together. Co-
existence and togetherness will have to be more than slogans. They
will have to become a way of life.

We live, share, work with and depend upon people. People are
wonderful.

1. Be interested in people.
2. Love people.
3. Encourage people.
4. Help people.
5. Bless people.

This ancient proverb gives further instruction about our attitudes
and actions where others are concerned:

> He who knows not and knows not
> that he knows not,
> He is a fool. Avoid him.

> He who knows not and knows
> that he knows not,
> He is simple. Teach him.

> He who knows and knows not
> that he knows,
> He is asleep. Wake him.

> He who knows and knows
> that he knows,
> He is wise. Follow him.

The Golden Rule—"Do unto others as you would have others do unto you"—is the basic guide for establishing our attitudes and actions toward others. Every one of the ten world's great living religions embraces its universal truth:

THE GOLDEN RULE
In Ten of the World's Great Religions

CHRISTIANITY: "All things whatsoever ye would that men should do to you, do ye even so to them."

CONFUCIANISM: "Do not unto others what you would not they should do unto you."

BUDDHISM: "In five ways should a clansman minister to his friends and familiars—by generosity, courtesy and benevolence, by treating them as he treats himself, and by being as good as his word."

HINDUISM: "Do not to others, which if done to thee, would cause thee pain."

ISLAM: "No one of you is a believer until he loves for his brother what he loves for himself."

SIKHISM: "As thou deemest thyself so deem others. Then shalt thou become a partner in heaven."

JUDAISM: "What is hurtful to yourself, do not to your fellow man."

JAINISM: "In happiness and suffering, in joy and grief, we should regard all creatures as we regard our own self."

ZOROASTRIANISM: "That nature only is good when it shall not do unto another whatever is not good for its own self."

TAOISM. "Regard your neighbor's gain as your own gain and regard your neighbor's loss as your own loss."

DAILY THOUGHTS ABOUT PEOPLE
From This Chapter

1. People are wonderful.
2. Since we are in constant contact with people, the best way to get along with them is to be interested in them, love them, encourage them and bless them.

3. If we love God, we will love ourselves. If we love ourselves, we will love people.
4. We have a greater understanding and love for people when we think of ourselves as brothers and sisters of them all.
5. Since we have achieved the means for total destruction, we must learn to get along with others or there will be no one left to get along with.
6. Separateness in our relations with others is evidence of separation within ourselves.
7. Friendship is the crowning achievement of personal relations.

From the Bible

1. Inasmuch as ye have done it unto one of the least of these my brethren, ye have done it unto me.—*Matt. 25:40*
2. He that loveth his brother abideth in the light.—*I John 2:10*
3. As the man is, so is his strength.—*Judges 8:21*
4. Lord, what is man, that thou takest knowledge of him! or the son of man, that thou makest account of him!—*Psalm 144:3*
5. Jesus answered them, Is it not written in your law, I said, Ye are gods?—*John 10:34*
6. The Lord will not forsake his people.—*I Sam. 12:22*
7. Be strong, all ye people of the land.—*Hag. 2:4*

From Great Thinkers Past and Present

1. The most indisputable fact about man is that he is a union, and not a disjunction, of . . . contrasted aspects, which are complementaries and not mutually exclusive alternatives. Man is both lower and higher, both body and spirit, both outer and inner, both mechanical and purposive.—*Ralph B. Perry*
2. A man's ledger does not tell what he is, or what he is worth.—Count what is in man, not what is on him, if you would know what he is worth—whether rich or poor.—*H. W. Beecher*
3. Man himself is the crowning wonder of creation; the study of his nature the noblest study the world affords.—*William E. Gladstone*
4. Man is greater than a world—than systems of worlds; there is more mystery in the union of soul with the body, than in the creation of a universe.—*Henry Giles*
5. Show me the man you honor, and I will know that kind of a man you are, for it shows me what your ideal of manhood is, and what kind of a man you long to be.—*Thomas Carlyle*

6. One cannot always be a hero, but one can always be a man.—*Goethe*

7. It is not the situation which makes the man, but the man who makes the situation. The slave may be a free man. The monarch may be a slave. Situations are noble or ignoble, as we make them.—*F. W. Robertson*

GOLDEN BRIDGE
TO OTHER PEOPLE

Morning Projection

Today I turn my attention to other people. They are important to me just as I am important to them. There is nowhere where they leave off and I begin. We are one with each other. People are wonderful. I love them. I live with them. I work with them. I talk with them. I help them and they help me. I rejoice in being a part of the human race. We are one big happy family. We are brothers and sisters on earth because we have the same Father in Heaven.

Everyone I meet today is helped and inspired by his contact with me. I am a channel of love and blessing through which good flows out into the lives of other people. Today is a masterpiece of effective human relations. I respect and love all people. I understand them and they understand me. No one is ever alone. I revel in the fellowship of my fellow man today. And so it is.

Evening Retrospection

I am thankful that people have filled my life today. I am grateful that I have been part of them and they of me. We have helped each other and have profited from our mutual contact. I forgive where forgiveness is necessary, and I know I am forgiven in return. I am at peace with myself and with all people. My heart is filled with love and compassion.

I have enjoyed this day. I have found it easy to get along with people. As I have given everyone the benefit of the doubt today, no one has disappointed me. We have all been good for each other today.

I am at peace with God and mankind because I am at peace with myself. As I embrace deep and healing sleep I provide the inner structures of love and understanding upon which the Creative Law builds magnificent mansions in my soul. And so it is.

4 ✑

WORK
Thank God for Work!

MAURY WILLS, Los Angeles Dodgers shortstop, stole 104 bases during the 1962 baseball season, breaking Ty Cobb's record of 96 which had stood for many years. This was no accident. Maury worked at it. Baseball is more than a game to professional players. They play as if their very lives depended upon it. They do.

Maury first worked on himself by using the power of positive thinking. Sid Ziff, sports columnist for the Los Angeles *Times*, quoted Maury as follows: "Stealing bases is a matter of confidence and even conceit. It's more than getting a good jump, a big lead. It's being in the right frame of mind. I run with the thought that the pitcher will make a perfect throw, and the catcher will make a perfect throw, and I'll still beat them. I don't have a doubt."

Maury developed such control over his mind that he made it work for him at all times. Pitchers went all-out to catch him off base, but rarely succeeded. Why? Maury explains it:

"Once the pitcher has made a throw to first, that particular attempt is done with. I don't give it another thought. I wipe it out of my mind. If I began to think back then I wouldn't get as big a lead the next time. I don't ever let myself get on the defensive."

"I don't ever let myself get on the defensive." Here is perfect proof that our attitudes largely determine how successful our work will be. In addition to his record-breaking base-stealing, Maury is proficient at bunting. He spends countless hours practicing laying the ball down

27

the line until he can control it completely. He does this before each game, studying the condition of the basepaths and taking every factor into consideration. It is no accident that Maury Wills, ballplayer par excellence, is a success at his work.

Success depends upon learning how to:

1. Work *on* yourself.
2. Work *with* others.
3. Work *for* a purpose.

We have seen how Maury Wills works *on* himself by controlling himself—his mind and his skills. Naturally, he follows through by working *with* his teammates *for* the purpose of winning. When we learn how to work *on*, *with* and *for*, we will be champions also. We win with work.

Jess Mortenson, the late great track and field coach at the University of Southern California, used the "Five I's" in developing the many fine athletes who established records under his direction. The formula provides the necessary steps for any worthwhile work or activity:

1. Imagination
2. Intelligence
3. Industry
4. Integrity
5. Initiative

Develop these ingredients and your work will pay off not only at the paymaster's window, but with the satisfaction which comes from a job well done. The two essential attitudes toward work are *joy in the doing* and *pride in the result*. There is no substitute for these constructive attitudes.

WHY DO WE WORK?

Most people work just to make money to provide the essentials for life. To such a person, work becomes drudgery and unbearable bondage.

"I have nothing to look forward to for the rest of my life except to sit in an office and pound a typewriter," wept the disconsolate young widow who sat in my office pouring out her despair. "There is nothing left for me now that John is gone. I have to work to provide for my children, but I hate the very thought of it. What am I going to do?"

"Glad to see you back, Jimmy," sang out several passengers in an elevator in one of New York's tallest buildings. "How was your vacation?" They were greeting the familiar operator who had had his "ups and downs" in that same elevator for many years.

"Oh, the vacation was all right," Jimmy answered glumly. "The vacation was fine—but now I don't have another single thing to look forward to until next summer." The doors closed, Jimmy pressed a button, and we shot upward, enveloped in the gloom of this little man who hated his job and had nothing to look forward to except his vacations.

How tragic! And how senseless! These two are typical examples of millions who live lives of not-too-quiet desperation. Fortunately, I was able to help them to learn the joy of constructive living.

JOYFUL ATTITUDES TOWARD WORK

The young lady found meaning and purpose in her job and in her life by applying the affirmative principles of the Science of Mind. Through counseling and prayer treatment, she developed a fresh approach to things. Thereafter she progressed from typist to secretary and then to office manager.

"You know, Doctor Curtis," she marveled. "I actually enjoy working. When John died, I dreaded the prospect of making my own way but now I know it is essential that I do. I'll be a better person as the result of the experience. Thank you for helping me see that work could be more than just a monotonous job."

The young widow married her boss, a widower with children of his own. Now she has much more to look forward to than the typewriter for the rest of her days. When her thoughts, feelings and attitudes toward her work changed, her entire life became different.[1]

With Jimmy, the elevator operator, my approach was considerably less formal. I deliberately set out to change his attitude. At this time I was an enthusiastic beginning student of the Science of Mind, eager to use it on everyone I met. I went to work on Jimmy by riding in his

[1] Read Dr. Curtis' *Your Thoughts Can Change Your Life* (Englewood Cliffs, N.J.: Prentice-Hall, Inc., 1961).

elevator daily. This made it possible to maintain steady contact with my captive audience. I succeeded in getting him to talk and even to laugh. He started enjoying people.

"You know," he confided one day, "I didn't realize how much fun people are. I love these people I see every day. I'm going to miss them."

"Why, Jimmy," I asked. "Are you going away?"

"Yup, for two weeks. It's that time again. My vacation is due. You know, I kind of hate to leave this year." Jimmy actually became glum again—for the first time in months. This time it was at the thought of *taking* his vacation.

Jimmy took his vacation, but never returned to his elevator. He was promoted to elevator-starter in the lobby of this large office building. He had developed a love for people, and was promoted to a job where this could be expressed—for both his benefit and others'. Jimmy received further advancements and is now an executive in charge of personnel.

There are no lowly jobs. You may have to start in one, but you don't have to stay there! "There is always room at the top!" Adopt a joyful attitude toward work, and your job will change—for the better.

THE GLORY OF WORK

"Work is love made visible," sings the poet Kahlil Gibran.[2]

Work is many wonderful things. Work is an outlet for energy. Work is God in action. Work is life in circulation. Work is self-expression. Work is the means by which we serve. Work is the means through which we find ourselves. Work is the way we assist the creative process. Work justifies our existence.

"Don't you get worn out from all this hard work day after day?" asked a well-meaning friend of the cheerful Negro washerwoman.

"No, I don't," the washerwoman laughed. "I suppose I could. Maybe I should even. But every time I get weary, I think of my boy, Bill, up there in medical school—holdin' his own with all those other fellows, gettin' good grades and gettin' ready to help people. I feel like I was right there with him, and I plunge into another tub of clothes—for Bill—to pay his tuition. I can't let Bill down now, can I? No, I don't get tired. You see, I've got a glory!"

2 *The Prophet,* by Kahlil Gibran (New York: Alfred A. Knopf Inc., 1923).

WORK

A Song of Triumph[3]

Work!
Thank God for the might of it,
The ardor, the urge, the delight of it—
Work that springs from the heart's desire,
Setting the brain and the soul on fire—
Oh, what is so good as the heat of it,
And what is so glad as the beat of it,
And what is so kind as the stern command,
Challenging brain and heart and hand?

Work!
Thank God for the pride of it,
For the beautiful, conquering tide of it,
Sweeping the life in its furious flood,
Thrilling the arteries, cleansing the blood,
Mastering stupor and dull despair,
Moving the dreamer to do and dare.
Oh, what is so good as the urge of it,
And what is so glad as the surge of it,
And what is so strong as the summons deep,
Rousing the torpid soul from sleep?

Work!
Thank God for the pace of it,
For the terrible, keen, swift race of it;
Fiery steeds in full control,
Nostrils a-quiver to greet the goal.
Work, the Power that drives behind,
Guiding the purposes, taming the mind,
Holding the runaway wishes back,
Reining the will to one steady track,
Speeding the energies faster, faster,
Triumphing over disaster.
Oh, what is so good as the pain of it,
And what is so great as the gain of it?
And what is so kind as the cruel goad,
Forcing us on through the rugged road?

[3] From *The Hour Has Struck* (The John Lane Co.), used by permission.

Work!
Thank God for the swing of it,
For the clamoring, hammering ring of it,
Passion and labor daily hurled
On the mighty anvils of the world.
Oh, what is so fierce as the flame of it?
And what is so huge as the aim of it?
Thundering on through dearth and doubt,
Calling the plan of the Maker out.

Work, the Titan; Work, the friend,
Shaping the earth to a glorious end,
Draining the swamps and blasting the hills,
Doing whatever the Spirit wills—
Rending a continent apart,
To answer the dream of the Master heart.
Thank God for a world where none may shirk—
Thank God for the splendor of work!

—Angela Morgan

DAILY THOUGHTS ABOUT WORK
From This Chapter

1. Our attitudes toward our work determine how successful it will be.
2. Success depends upon learning how to work *on* yourself, work *with* others, and work *for* a purpose.
3. The two essential attitudes toward work are joy and pride.
4. Change to a constructive attitude about work and your job will change for the better.
5. Constructive work depends upon the "Five I's": Imagination, Intelligence, Industry, Integrity, Initiative.
6. Work is the means by which we find ourselves.
7. Work justifies our existence.

From the Bible

1. Seest thou a man diligent in his business? He shall stand before kings.—*Prov. 22:29*
2. Study to be quiet, and to do your own business.—*I Thess. 4:11*
3. Whatsoever thy hand findeth to do, do it with all thy might.—*Eccles. 9:10*

4. Be strong, all ye people of the land, saith the Lord, and work.—*Hag. 2:4*
5. If any would not work, neither should he eat.—*II Thess. 3:10*
6. The labourer is worthy of his hire.—*Luke 10:7*
7. What doth it profit, my brethren, though a man say he hath faith, and have not works?—*James 2:14*

From Great Thinkers Past and Present

1. Without labor nothing prospers.—*Sophocles*
2. The fruit derived from labor is the sweetest of all pleasures—*Luc de Clapiers Vauvenargues*
3. There is a perennial nobleness and even sacredness in work.—*Thomas Carlyle*
4. Excellence in any department can be attained only by the labor of a lifetime; it is not to be purchased at a lesser price.—*Samuel Johnson*
5. I have no secret of success but hard work.—*Sir Edward Turner*
6. A man is a worker. If he is not that he is nothing.—*Joseph Conrad*
7. As a cure for worrying, work is better than whiskey.—*Thomas Edison*

GOLDEN BRIDGE TO WORK

Morning Projection

Joyously, I go forward into my day—exulting in the privilege and opportunity of doing constructive and creative work all day long. I release all of my energies through my work. I am a channel through which limitless power flows. I move mountains. I perform mighty deeds. I am a worker. I am a builder. I am constructing monuments to God for all eternity.

"Whatsoever my hand findeth to do, I do it with all my might as unto the Lord and not unto men." As this is my attitude, of course all people profit from my endeavors. I am now in my right job, doing pleasant, constructive work which expresses me, helps others, and which offers progressive advancement with abundant and steady income.

I power-glide into high gear today. I cruise easily and effortlessly through all tasks and assignments. I give thanks for my work. I do it well because "I of myself do nothing. The Father that dwelleth within me; he doeth the works." And so it is.

Evening Retrospection

Quietly now, I look back over my day's work. It has been a good day. I have done good work. I have made constructive and noteworthy contributions to the world's work. I work for God. I work to express the glory within. I do the very best I can at all times. I am an artisan of living; I am an artist of Life. I turn out only masterpieces.

I give thanks for the use that has been made of my time, my talent, and my energies today. I give thanks for the constructive good that has come from my creative efforts. I give thanks for the abundance of fulfillment which is mine.

As my mind and body relax and prepare for sleep with the delicious fatigue of constructive tiredness, I am completely at peace. I refill from the Great Source of all energy. My soul and my body are strengthened as I sleep. I let sleep refill and renew me. I rest. I sleep. And so it is.

5

FAMILY

The Keystone of Society

"I'VE never belonged anywhere," the distraught young woman sobbed. "That's the trouble, Doctor Curtis. No one has ever wanted me. All I want is to belong to someone and have them belong to me."

"But your father—?" I asked. "He loves you, doesn't he?"

"Oh yes, in his way. I'm not blaming Daddy. He's done the best he could. I guess you'd call him my family—anyway he's all I have. But whenever I've needed him most, he wasn't there. I never had what other kids had. I didn't even have a home to go to at Christmas."

Again my patient broke into uncontrollable sobs. This was the real key to her problem—*she didn't even have a home to go to at Christmas.* She had been denied the most important of human needs—love, security, acceptance, belonging—that only home and family could give her.

Her mother had died when she was a small child, and her father, busy with the things of the world, packed her off to boarding school "where she could have proper care." She got the care all right. That is, she was fed, clothed, kept clean, taught manners and how to read and write. But the love and sense of belonging she craved were denied her.

With no place else to go, the little girl turned within herself. *She had to go somewhere.* She did, and that was where she stayed. Now, in

35

her early twenties, she was forlorn and lost. After years of introspection, she was bored and frustrated. Having felt rejected by others for so long, she inevitably began to reject herself. Now she was overweight and ill-groomed. Although she had a pretty face, she could hardly be called attractive. Her personality was anything but endearing. She was resentful, rebellious and trusted no one.

Her father had brought her to me for counseling because, as he said, "I can't do a thing with her. I give her everything, but nothing seems to matter to her at all. She's just not normal."

Of course she wasn't! She had not experienced those emotional experiences commonly shared in normal family relationships. It was now necessary to supply her emotional needs in some other way. At first she rebelled against my efforts to help her, but when she came to understand the constructive approach she became a different person.

She forgave her father, and with co-operation from him, the two became friends rather than mutual concerns. The young lady became hostess of her father's home, and in the first semblance of family living she had ever known, she blossomed into a beautiful woman. She took pride in her appearance, lost weight, learned the essentials of dressing and grooming, and consequently had no shortage of suitors.

She continued to study and counsel with me for nearly three years, during which time she was able to strengthen within herself those qualities which normal family life would have given her, but which now, with guidance, it was necessary for her to provide for herself. So marked was her improvement that her father started coming to me also, and continued his personal visits for several years.

Through affirmative spiritual guidance and understanding counsel, both these "unfamilied" family members found emotional maturity. Marriage followed for both the father and the daughter. The young lady now has two children of her own which she vows "will not have to go through what I did," and her father is happy and secure in a mature marriage which provides all those needs that only family life can give.

These two people found happiness within themselves and are able to give and sustain it in the normal atmosphere of family life. Many, however, are missing out on this most important factor in growth and living. The family has always been the keystone of civilization. Its structure and customs have varied in different ages and cultures, but its one essential function has never changed—*the procreation and rearing of children*. Since by its very nature the family involves more than one person, organizational, government, social, economic, spiritual and educational functions all come into play. The family is society in miniature. Nothing can take its place. The solution to personal and world ills lies in the strengthening of the family.

"Honor thy father and thy mother: that thy days may be long upon the land which the Lord thy God giveth thee," is the Fifth Commandment (Exod. 20:12). Psychologists have discovered the importance and necessity of loving and balanced parental relationships in the emotional life of the child. There would be no juvenile delinquency if there were not first parental negligence. It is obvious where our first line of defense—and offense—lies. The future of the human race depends upon mature men and women who will form, sustain and maintain mature family relationships so that their children may grow up with roots of love, security, dignity, respect and discipline.

The incidence of divorce and the broken home has increased alarmingly in recent years. Many of our personal and social problems result from this breakdown in the family unit, but divorce itself is an effect before it becomes a cause. What causes divorce? We recognize that it should not and would not be necessary if we could develop constructive attitudes and plans which would lead to maturity in personal and family relationships. Divorce may still be the solution in certain individual instances, just as it has been since ancient times. But, the modern *disease* of divorce must be cured, lest the insecurity of future generations victimized by it form a vicious circle which will destroy the family unit as we now know it. This cannot be allowed to happen.

There is no place like home and family. Robert Frost said, "Home is a place where when you go there, they have to take you in." It is commonly conceded that "home is where your heart is." Families provide experience in living. The enduring and noble qualities of the individual first emerge and try their wings in the permissive atmosphere of the home. The family is mankind's incubator. It is the garden plot of greatness. There is no substitute for home and family. The family is the soil in which are anchored the roots of what we are and do. A healthy family is a generator from which we recharge our batteries.

Love, security, peace, protection, guidance, comfort, inspiration, joy, discipline, sharing, understanding, fair play, dignity, respect, reverence, wisdom, strength, courage, dedication, and all noble and necessary qualities and ingredients for personal growth are provided and nurtured in the family. The father is the head of the family, the mother is the heart, and the children are the body—the three elements which make up a complete unit of anything: thought, feeling and experience; spirit, love and action. The family is the fountainhead of the soul.

Family strength and beauty emerge from the strength and beauty of the individual, and vice versa. Father Peyton's great affirmation, "The family that prays together stays together," points up the importance of worship in family life.

Here are some affirmative prayer treatments for you to use for yourself and with members of your family:

LOVE

I am loved as I love. Through love I learn the meaning of life. Through love I am reborn into new and transcendent experience. Through love I express what I really am, and through love I attract into my life that one right person who loves me as much as I love him (or her). Our love fulfills us both. In love we are one. Through love, all separation, pain and loneliness are healed as we walk together along life's pathway, loving every moment of it. Tenderly, we express our love for each other in every moment of life. Love makes our world go around. We are in love forever. *And so it is.*

MARRIAGE

I give thanks for my marriage (or my marriage which is to be). In marriage my soulmate and I are complete. Spirit and Soul are One. Male and female are one. Man and woman are married. In marriage I am my complete and total self. I give everything I have to my marriage, and I receive everything in return. In marriage I experience perfect happiness. Two halves form one whole. We are one today and forever. We are partners in God's supreme Plan as we consummate our marriage with love, dedication, blessing and beauty. Thank you, Father, for our perfect marriage. *And so it is.*

To My Wife (or Husband)

God is blessing you, my beloved. You are the sum of all loving things to me. I adore you. You are the soul of all things to me. You are the very meaning of existence. In you I live and move and have my being, because in you I find God. You are beauty, warmth, tenderness, strength—all the virtues and blessings together. You are precious and pure. You stand ever in the pure white light of the Spirit. I look upon you and find you good—very good indeed. This is my beloved in whom I am well pleased. I am that which thou art; thou art that which I am. *And so it is.*

Home

Home is where the heart is. Thank you, my beloved, for making our beautiful home. Thank you for making it ever a haven of security and peace. Thank you for being the heart (or the head) of our home, because you are the center of my life. All things come to rest in our home. Here we reside in the secret place of the Most High. It is our temple, our altar, our shrine. We worship Life here. We open our doors, our arms, and our hearts to all who enter here. We are grateful for the privilege of sharing our love and our home with others. *And so it is.*

Family

Thank you, Father, for our family. Thank you for our wonderful children. Thank you for the privilege of living, of learning, of just being together. Thank you for these images and likenesses of ourselves. May we ever be worthy parents. May we ever remember that we are merely the channels through which our children came. May we ever add wise and enduring counsel to our love. May our children ever be strengthened by the closeness of our family as they go forward into the world to do God's great work. God is blessing our beautiful family. We belong to each other because we belong totally to Him. *And so it is.*

Joy and Happiness

All this and heaven too! Joy and happiness fill my heart. I am the most blessed of all God's creatures. Together we live happily ever after, because the joy and happiness of our life together is more than enough to sustain us throughout all eternity. You make my life complete, beloved. I awake with you each morning and go forward into days of continued joy and happiness. My heart sings with the joy of you. You have made my soul happy. My cup runneth over. Surely, goodness and mercy follow us all the days of our lives, and we do dwell in the house of the Lord forever. Amen.

DAILY THOUGHTS ABOUT FAMILY
From This Chapter

1. The family provides for the important human needs: love, security, acceptance and belonging.
2. Emotional normality and maturity grow out of normal family relationships.
3. The family has always been the keystone of civilization.
4. The family is society in miniature.
5. The solution to personal and world ills lies in strengthening the family.
6. Loving and balanced parental relationships are necessary to the emotional life of the child.
7. Juvenile delinquency can be eliminated by eliminating parental negligence.

From the Bible

1. Honour thy father and mother; which is the first commandment with promise.—*Eph. 6:2*
2. He shall turn the heart of the fathers to the children, and the heart of the children to their fathers.—*Mal. 4:6*
3. Train up a child in the way he should go: and when he is old, he will not depart from it.—*Prov. 22:6*
4. Children, obey your parents in the Lord: for this is right.—*Eph. 6:1*
5. I have no greater joy than to hear that my children walk in truth. —*III John 1:4*
6. Hear the instruction of thy father, and forsake not the law of thy mother.—*Prov. 1:8*
7. Whoso findeth a wife findeth a good thing, and obtaineth favour of the Lord.—*Prov. 18:22*

From Great Thinkers Past and Present

1. Happy are the families where the government of parents is the reign of affection, and obedience of the children the submission of love.— *Roger Bacon*

2. Woman is the salvation or the destruction of the family.—She carries its destiny in the folds of her mantle.—*Henri F. Amiel*

3. The happiness of married life depends upon making small sacrifices with readiness and cheerfulness.—*John Selden*

4. Marriage is the mother of the world, and preserves kingdoms, and fills cities and churches, and heaven itself.—*Jeremy Taylor*

5. Our home joys are the most delightful earth affords, and the joy of parents in their children is the most holy joy of humanity. It makes their hearts pure and good, it lifts men up to their Father in heaven. —*Johann Pestalozzi*

6. A hundred men may make an encampment, but it takes a woman to make a home.—*Chinese proverb*

7. He is the happiest, be he king or peasant, who finds peace in his home.—*Goethe*

GOLDEN BRIDGE
TO FAMILY RELATIONSHIPS

Morning Projection

I give thanks for all things today. I give thanks for myself. I am grateful for my life. I give thanks for my family. I give thanks for my close relationship with those I love and who love me. I give thanks for our close relationship with each other. I give thanks for the love and understanding which we give to each other. I am grateful for my place in my personal family and for my place in the great human family. God is our Father, therefore we are brothers and sisters of all who live.

I am grateful to my earthly father and mother for their love and guidance. I gratefully accept all good that they have given me, and I forgive them the rest. I give thanks for my family heritage. I give thanks for the privilege of passing it along. There is order and harmony in my family. There is security and beauty in my home. Balance and peace are established in my home. I draw strength and inspiration from my family. I love my family. And so it is.

Evening Retrospection

I give thanks for another beautiful day spent with my family. I give thanks for the closeness. I revel in the joy of sharing happy experiences with them. I luxuriate in the healing happiness which envelops us.

As I review this day, I correct all family matters. My family is the most important thing in the world to me. I forgive all who may have been wrong, and I accept forgiveness in return. I help all who need it, and I accept help in return.

Love flows from me, synchronizing my heart with that of everyone in my family. We are in tune with each other. We are one with each other. Freedom and trust characterize our relationships. We find security and peace in each other's love and company.

All is well. God dwells in the midst of us. "Where two or three are gathered together in my name, there am I in the midst of them" (Matt. 18:20). *Thank you, Father, for my family. And so it is.*

6

TODAY

The Best Day You Have Ever Had

> Look to this Day!
> For it is Life, the very Life of Life.
> In its brief course lie all the Verities
>   and Realities of your Existence:
> The Bliss of Growth,
> The Glory of Action,
> The Splendor of Beauty.
> For Yesterday is but a Dream,
> And Tomorrow is only a Vision;
> But Today well-lived makes every
>   Yesterday a Dream of Happiness,
> And every Tomorrow a Vision of Hope.
> Look well therefore to this Day!
> Such is the Salutation of the Dawn.
>
> *—from the Sanskrit*

We can make this day whatever we want it to be. It exists as a page, neither good nor bad. The day awaits the dawning of ideas within our own mind.

Our day is like the close play at second base in a World Series baseball game some years ago. The base-runner came sliding in like a locomotive just as the catcher's fine throw was taken, and the tag was put on the runner. Boy, it was close! The umpire was peering closely at the runner hugging second while the second baseman pressed the ball against him. Players of the two teams clustered around waiting for the call, but even though the umpire's hand was raised, he didn't say a word. Finally, unable to stand the suspense any longer, one of the players asked hoarsely, "Well, Mugsy, what is it?" Without losing his composure, the umpire turned disdainfully on his questioner and thundered, "It ain't nothin' until I call it!"

And so it is with our day. We have to call the shots. This always means that we have to make a choice.

Grandpa was 97 years old—hale and hearty, and quick of mind and body. When asked the secret of his health and longevity he drawled, "Well, you see, it's this way: I wake up every morning with two choices. I can either be happy, or I can be miserable. I always choose to be happy, and more often than not, that's the way it turns out. Anyway, I know that when I think happy thoughts, I feel better. That's good enough for me."

That speaks volumes for all of us, doesn't it? An affirmative attitude toward life makes us feel good; a negative attitude has the opposite effect. It's up to each of us. Which do you choose? One of my students told me that ever since he could remember, he waited until he went to the window to observe the weather before deciding whether he was to be happy or miserable. During our counseling, he discovered that the weather had absolutely nothing to do with his happiness or lack of it. Of course not! Neither does the rising or falling of the stock market, the time of year, the political party in power, what other people say, your state of employment, your condition of affluence or poverty—or anything else. We alone control our happiness by controlling our minds. Each day is a unit of time to be used in creating happiness and good for ourselves and others.

After a restful and restoring night a wonderful day is opening up and life's picturesque show is starting to roll by. There may be problems to be coped with but they are challenges and yardsticks on our way to perfection. Life is so thrilling because it connects us with the eternal.

Thinking is the most essential for by thinking we form and are formed. *Think* today only of what you like and desire to be expressed in your situations and circumstances. Consciously turn away thoughts popping up that bring fear, worry and misery, and replace them by thoughts of goodness. It takes some effort but you will be amazed how the scenery has changed at the end of a single day.

—Anonymous

Today is the son of yesterday; the father of tomorrow. It is the most important day we have because it is now. Live in the here and now. Jesus said, "Take therefore no thought for the morrow; the morrow shall take thought for the things of itself. Sufficient unto the day is the evil thereof" (Matt. 6:34).

Sufficient unto each day is the experience of that day—the good and the evil, the pleasant and the unpleasant, the successes and the failures. We can't do it all in one day. Rome wasn't built in one day, and neither is a life. It is the long pull that counts. Live one day at a time, but live it well.

It's the way we carry through the business of the day—that makes and moulds the character, the things we do and say; the way we act when we are vexed; the attitude we take, the sort of pleasures we enjoy; the kind of friends we make.

It's not the big events that make us what we are—Not the dizzy moments when we're swinging on a star—It's the things that happen as along the road we plod. The little things determine what we're really worth to God.

—Esther Baldwin York

A constructive approach to each day, and the efficient handling of the events of that day are our assurance of happiness, health and prosperity.

Think on these things:

Just for today, I will try to live through this day only, and not tackle my whole life problem at once. I can do something for twelve hours that would appall me if I felt that I had to keep it up for a lifetime.

Just for today, I will be happy. This assumes to be true what Abraham Lincoln said, that 'Most folks are as happy as they make up their minds to be.'

Just for today, I will adjust myself to what is, and not try to adjust everything to my own desires. I will take my 'luck' as it comes, and fit myself to it.

Just for today, I will try to strengthen my mind, I will study, I will learn something useful. I will not be a mental loafer. I will read something that requires effort, thought and concentration.

Just for today, I will exercise my soul in three ways: I will do somebody a good turn and not get found out; if anybody knows of it, it will not count. I will do at least two things I don't want to do—just for exercise. I will not show anyone that my feelings are hurt; they may be hurt, but today I will not show it.

Just for today, I will be agreeable, I will look as well as I can, dress becomingly, talk low, act courteously, criticize not one bit, not find fault with anything, and not try to improve or regulate anybody except myself.

Just for today, I will have a program. I may not follow it exactly but I will have it. I will save myself from two pests: hurry and indecision.

Just for today, I will have a quiet half-hour all by myself, and relax. During this half hour, sometime, I will try to get a better perspective of my life.

Just for today, I will be unafraid. Especially I will not be afraid to enjoy what is beautiful, and to believe that as I give to the world, so the world will give to me.

—Anonymous

DAILY THOUGHTS ABOUT TODAY
From This Chapter

1. We can make this day whatever we want it to be.
2. We alone control our happiness by controlling our minds.
3. Each day is a unit of time to be used in creating happiness and good for ourselves and others.
4. Today is the son of yesterday and the father of tomorrow.
5. Today is the most important day we have because it is now.
6. Live one day at a time, but live it well.
7. A constructive approach to each day, and constructive handling of everything in that day is our assurance of happiness, health and prosperity.

From the Bible

1. On Thee do I wait all the day.—*Psalm 25:5*
2. The day is Thine, the night also is Thine.—*Psalm 74:16*
3. Every day will I bless Thee.—*Psalm 145:2*
4. Thou knowest not what a day may bring forth.—*Prov. 27:1*

5. Jesus answered, Are there not twelve hours in the day? If any man walk in the day, he stumbleth not, because he seeth the light of this world.—*John 11:9*
6. Every man's work shall be made manifest: for the day shall declare it, because it shall be revealed by fire.—*I Cor. 3:13*
7. Weeping may endure for a night, but joy cometh in the morning. —*Psalm 30:5*

From Great Thinkers Past and Present

1. There is nothing more universally commended than a fine day; the reason is, that people can commend it without envy.—*William Shenstone*
2. Every day is a little life, and our whole life is but a day repeated. Therefore live every day as if it would be the last. Those that dare lose a day, are dangerously prodigal; those that dare misspend it are desperate.—*Joseph Hall*
3. Count that day lost, whose low descending sun views from thy hand no worthy action done.—*Charles Stanford*
4. Enjoy the blessings of the day if God sends them: and the evils bear patiently and sweetly; for this day only is ours: we are dead to yesterday, and not born to tomorrow.—*Jeremy Taylor*
5. Do today's duty, fight today's temptation; do not weaken and distract yourself by looking forward to things you cannot see, and could not understand if you saw them.—*Charles Kingsley*
6. Look upon every day as the whole of life, not merely as a section; and enjoy and improve the present without wishing, through haste, to rush on to another.—*Jean Paul*
7. Every day is a gift I receive from Heaven; let us enjoy today that which it bestows on me. It belongs not more to the young than to me, and tomorrow belongs to no one.—*Mancroix*

GOLDEN BRIDGE TO TODAY

Morning Projection

Today is my day. I live it fully. I awaken with joy in the new day. I go forward into life joyously and enthusiastically. I don't know what is ahead for me today but I know it can only be good. I live this day from the center of inner awareness and power. Nothing is too wonderful to happen; nothing is too good to be true. This day offers me the potential of all good and wonderful things. I give thanks for this day.

As I build the Golden Bridge of this day, I travel forward into tremendous experience. The surge of life is in free, full flow through me. The mainstream carries me ahead. I assist the process of evolution. I strengthen and amplify my own growth. I live my entire life in miniature today. I approach each moment as if it were both my first and my last. I do a good job living today. And so it is.

Evening Retrospection

In the quiet of the night I review this beautiful day. I have come to the end of a perfect day. I am alone with my memories of it. I revel in the glory of it. I give thanks for the privilege of living it. It is mine forever. I can never lose the wealth of this day. Magnificent treasures have been stored up in the kingdom of heaven within me today. I am a better person because of this day. Each experience has been a blessing. I am truly blessed.

Quietly now, as I prepare for restful sleep, I carry all the good of this day forward into eternity. My deeper mind amplifies and expands my inner good throughout the night. My soul grows as I sleep. I am refilled, refreshed and renewed. The infinite pours its wisdom and wholeness into my being throughout this night. I sleep in peace and I awaken in joy and anticipation of tomorrow's new day. Thank you, Father, for the magnificence of life. And so it is.

7

THE WORLD

This Great Big Beautiful World

Our world is what we make it. The conscious thought that this is a great big beautiful world soon invades our actual experience. We are in this world to enjoy it and contribute toward its betterment. We have the ability to make this world the kingdom of heaven. When we find fault with our world, we can improve it in direct proportion to our self-improvement.

ESTABLISH PROPER PERSPECTIVE

A man gave his son a jigsaw puzzle, telling him, "This puzzle when put together properly will form a picture of the world. Let's see what a good job you can do." In a short time the boy had completed it and his father was amazed, because it was a very difficult puzzle. He asked the boy how he had done it so rapidly. The boy answered, "Well, Daddy, there was a picture of a man on the back of it, so I worked on that. I knew if I got the man right, the world would be right." When we are right inside, our world will be right outside.

We are not worldly beings, we are spiritual beings. When we discover our spiritual nature, the material world is no longer of first importance to us. We virtually live in two worlds: Heaven and Earth.

When we learn to appreciate, to enjoy and to make the most of our environment we will be using our minds and emotions to bring about better results in our world. As Jesus said, "Ye are the salt of the earth;

but if the salt have lost his savour, wherewith shall it be salted?" (Matt. 5:13) Unless you and I get our savour back—which means our taste, our zest and love of life—unless we have the dedication and enthusiasm which will follow an idea through to its conclusion, unless doing good for others takes priority over selfish interests, and unless personal enthusiasm, self-improvement and sincere concern for others become a part of us, we will lose our savour. All too many people have lost their savour. They are reaping the dubious reward of mediocrity. This world is our garden. Ours is the privilege to live in it, enjoy it and improve it.

STRIKE IT RICH

Jesus said, "Lay not up for yourselves treasures upon earth, where moth and rust doth corrupt, and where thieves break through and steal: but lay up for yourselves treasures in heaven . . ." (Matt. 6:19, 20). All of us need and desire the things of this world. They are produced by our physical labor, our attitudes, our abilities, and our talents. Material things of the world are ours to use as good stewards. But, we can't take them with us. They are merely the treasures of earth. There are the treasures of heaven as well: love, faith, truth, an appreciation of the good and the beautiful, a desire to be a little better each day, a desire to give to others, a sense of wholeness and unity. The business of life, of course, is to make heaven out of this world.

This world is here for our delight. Have you ever really thought what deep inspiration and guidance can come just from observing the beauty of nature? Have you ever felt the deep peace of being one with nature? When we identify ourselves with it, we make its beauties our own because they are all symbolic of the things that are going on within our hearts.

A large part of this great big beautiful world is water. Often, when the waters, rivers and oceans are mentioned in the Bible, they represent the creative power of the Mind, the undifferentiated substance of Spirit, the great creative potential. This is why Jesus said, "Except a man be born of water and of the Spirit, he cannot enter into the kingdom of God" (John 3:5). This is why people are always refreshed when they go to the seashore, or to a lake in the mountains. Subconsciously we yearn for this great refilling from the reservoir of the Mind. Whenever we swim, fish, wade or bathe in it we feel a tremendous refreshment.

If the waters represent the great expanse of Mind, the great creative potential within, the mountains represent the higher aspects of the mental activity or the higher aspects of experience. They are still here in this earth, but they challenge us and make us aspire to great heights. The wonders of the mountains are staggering.

What is this little spinning ball of mud in the universe, this world of ours, where we have been born for a purpose? Emerson said we may own our little plot of ground, our home, our farm, but the horizon belongs to no man. It belongs to all men. Set your horizon into the awareness of larger experiences. Keep walking toward it and see this world as an experience. You are in it, but not of it. Don't sell your soul for the things of the world. Many times there seems to be an advantage in equivocating or compromising to get something material, but always remember who you are and sustain your integrity. In the Bible it says, "For what is a man profited, if he shall gain the whole world, and lose his own soul?" (Matt. 16:26)

The world and the things in it are made up of four basic elements: earth, fire, water and air. We have within ourselves these various aspects. Earth is the body, the material self. Fire is emotion, feeling and energy. Water is the mind. Air is the spirit. We are one with nature, one with life, one with everything there is. A Hindu friend walking through the forest may be heard to say, "My brother tree, my brother rock." In the tree and the rock he senses the same current that stirs in the plant, awakens in the animal and has sprung forth into full God-consciousness within himself. This is why at the beginning of any treatment we say, "There is one life, this life is God, this life is whole, this life is perfect, this life is my life now. I am living it, I am expressing it, I am enjoying it, I accept it."

If we would seek help, happiness, or abundance, we must first develop a consciousness of greatness and beauty within our own hearts. How can we expect the world to give back to us unless we give to it? The smallest expressions of it—the rock, the bush, the tree—are our brothers. They combine within them the elements of earth, fire, water and air. The life-stuff stirs; the atomic action is there. The energy of

Infinite Mind is stirring—asleep perhaps, but stirring—within everything that has ever been created. To see deep meaning in everything in life, in every natural thing, is to experience a renewal of faith and wholeness.

When we see this as a great big beautiful world, we become integrated and healed inside. We then benefit by a constant cleansing, vitalizing, creating action that can overcome any difficulty that may assail us. We get into difficulty only when we trust in the physical senses alone, when we judge by outward appearance and believe that the world of matter is stronger than we are. The world has been created by us. The earth was given us "and the fullness thereof," but the world that we have made out of the earth is the accumulation of all the generations of consciousness that mankind has brought to it.

What are we to make of it? We stand at the crossroads. Are we going to let our own ignorance, greed and neglect destroy this beautiful place? Or are we going to get quiet and go within, and discover some things for ourselves? As we look inward as well as outward, we become integrated and we expand the horizon so that good and beauty and truth are with us at all times.

There were four angels contemplating the world. The first angel asked, "Why did God make it?" The second angel wondered, "How did God make it?" The third angel demanded, "Give it to me, it is mine." The fourth angel said nothing, but hurried off to make a better world.

We all have these four viewpoints. The angels are aspects of consciousness within ourselves. If we would truly enjoy our world, we must realize that we create it. If we do not like the world we see, then we clearly have the duty to change it.

What is your attitude toward your world? Do you love it? Do you accept it? Do you express it? Do you enjoy it? Do you live in it fully? The world is all around us, teeming with energy, good and beauty. How much of it have you absorbed, contemplated and filtered through your consciousness? This world can be the kingdom of heaven.

If we would have a great big beautiful world, we must become great and big and beautiful in consciousness. The only way we can do this is to strive toward perfection—to put the higher motives first; learn the laws of love; set apart moments for reflection; experience the inner action of life constantly flowing through us, and expand the width and height of the soul. These inner dimensions are the basic form and structure of our outer world.

DAILY THOUGHTS ABOUT OUR WORLD
From This Chapter

1. Our world is what we make it.
2. When we are right inside, our world is right outside.
3. The world that we have made is the accumulation of all the generations of consciousness that mankind has brought to it.
4. If we would have a great big beautiful world, we must become great, big and beautiful in consciousness.
5. When we learn to appreciate, enjoy and make the most of our environment, we help to bring about better results in our world.
6. This world is our garden, and it is for us to live in it, enjoy it, and make the most of it.
7. The dimensions which we have within us are the dimensions, the aspects and the appearances that show in our world.

From the Bible

1. The earth is full of the goodness of the Lord.—*Psalm* 33:5
2. Sing unto God, ye kingdoms of the earth.—*Psalm* 68:32
3. He hath set the world in their heart.—*Eccles.* 3:11
4. The care of this world, and the deceitfulness of riches, choke the word.—*Matt.* 13:22
5. The children of this world are in their generation wiser than the children of light.—*Luke* 16:8
6. The pillars of the earth are the Lord's, and he hath set the world upon them.—*I Sam.* 2:8
7. In the world ye shall have tribulation: but be of good cheer; I have overcome the world.—*John* 16:33

From Great Thinkers Past and Present

1. The only true method of action in this world is to be in it, but not of it.—*Madame Swetchine*
2. It is a beautiful and a blessed world we live in, and while life lasts, to lose the enjoyment of it is a sin.—*Talbot W. Chambers*
3. The world is God's epistle to mankind—his thoughts are flashing upon us from every direction.—*Plato*

4. The only fence against the world is a thorough knowledge of it —*John Locke*
5. We may despise the world, but we cannot do without it.—*Baron Wessenberg*
6. The world is seldom what it seems; to man, who dimly sees, realities appear as dreams, and dreams realities.—*Thomas Moore*
7. The world is a comedy to those who think, a tragedy to those who feel.—*Horace Walpole*

GOLDEN BRIDGE TO THE WORLD

Morning Projection

My world is what I make it. My world is created of my thoughts, feelings, attitudes and actions. I am the channel through which my world is formed. I decide to be the creator of a better world today. My world has no power over me. I alone have power over my world. "In the world ye shall have tribulation: but be of good cheer; I have overcome the world (John 16:33)." I am sitting on top of the world. The world is my oyster. I am in the business of world-building today. I enjoy my life in this world. This world is an extension of myself. I see this world differently than anyone else because my world is different from everyone else's. I make my world; they make their world. As I get myself in order, my world is in order. When I am right, my world is right. I love this world. I make it the kingdom of heaven today. As I am happy and whole in my world, I help others to be happy and whole in theirs. This world is a good place now. And so it is.

Evening Retrospection

I am grateful for my journey through this world today. It has been a wonderful day. This world has taught me many lessons today. I am grateful for every one of them. Every experience, good and bad, has been useful to me. As I turn them to my advantage, I do a better job of living in this world. I have reached an important conclusion: The world itself is neither good nor bad. It just is. It is what I do with my world that counts.

I turn everything toward good—toward God. All day I have been busy with the things of the world. Now I turn my attention inward. "My kingdom is not of this world (John 18:36). The world is the kingdom of experiences, actions and things. Tonight I dwell in a higher kingdom. I seek "first the kingdom of God and His righteousness" (Matt. 6:33), and all these things are added unto me. The kingdom of heaven is within me. I am a native of eternity. I see my world in perspective tonight. I live in it, I bless it, and I release it. Now I have business in the realm of greater experience. I bid my world good night as I lie down to pleasant dreams. And so it is.

8 ✍

COUNTRY

"My Country 'Tis of Thee!"

THE heritage of America is great. It is not by accident that we are called "the land of the free." The history of man is the story of his striving for freedom. The United States of America came into being as a direct result of man's need, right, and determination to be free. Our country is the aggregate of nearly 200,000,000 people whose freedoms are guaranteed by the Constitution.

The purpose of our democratic government is clearly set forth in the Preamble to the Constitution:

> We, the people of the United States, in order to form a more perfect union, establish Justice, insure domestic tranquility, provide for the common defense, promote the general welfare, and secure the blessings of liberty to ourselves and our posterity, do ordain and establish this Constitution for the United States of America.

Throughout the Constitution, which defines the duties, powers and responsibilities of the legislative, executive, and judicial branches of our Government, and on through the first ten Amendments—known as the Bill of Rights—it is the rights of the individual that are of primary interest and concern.

The United States did not come into being by accident. It evolved from the great dynamic of freedom inherent in man's inner nature. The Declaration of Independence heralds the philosophy of freedom in these words:

We hold these truths to be self-evident: that all men are created equal; that they are endowed by their Creator with certain inalienable rights; that among these are life, liberty, and the pursuit of happiness.

Thomas Jefferson, Benjamin Franklin, Robert R. Livingston, John Adams, and Roger Sherman, who framed the Declaration of Independence, were remarkable men representing a remarkable people. The American colonists—our forefathers—placed human dignity and freedom above everything else. Today, we would call them rugged individualists. Aggressive, strong, independent and imaginative, they were the prototype of a new nationality—the American. They were unafraid to voice their views, and to accept full responsibility for their actions.

The Declaration of Independence and the Constitution of the United States are unique because they place so much importance and responsibility upon the individual. We Americans glory in that tradition. We thrive under challenges and responsibility. We support free enterprise and initiative. We believe that each man's destiny is pretty much up to him. If he doesn't like the way things are going, it is up to him to do something about it. We honor and support our form of government, bearing in mind the words of the Declaration of Independence, which further states: "that to secure these rights, governments are instituted among men, deriving their just powers from the consent of the governed."

Our political system is so constituted that if we don't like what is going on in government, we can change it to conform to the will of the majority. This right of ours entails great individual responsibility. If we are to continue to enjoy the freedom which our forefathers established and which we have constantly fought for, individually, politically, domestically, internationally and militarily, we must realize that the entire responsibility rests upon the individual—that is, upon you and me. Our Government is the projected image of our collective selves. We must, individually, assume the responsibility whereby we and others of like mind will preserve and develop our heritage of freedom.

The only way we can be fit for liberty and continue to enjoy individual and national freedom is for each of us to develop his own personal code of constructive living. The individual is God's highest creation. As we accept this evaluation of ourselves, and establish physical, mental, emotional and spiritual disciplines to attain and maintain it, we will make possible the fulfillment of our destiny as a free people, in a free country, in a free world.

Our heritage of freedom and the individual's responsibility in protecting it are strongly emphasized in one of the most stirring of American utterances, Lincoln's Gettysburg Address, already well known to most of us.

In modern times, even though our individual and national problems are more complex, the same challenges confront us that confronted our forefathers. The Inaugural Address of President John F. Kennedy on January 20, 1961, has a stirring individual message for every American. The President-elect on his inaugural day said, in part:

We observe today not a victory of party but a celebration of freedom —symbolizing an end as well as a beginning—signifying renewal as well as change. For I have sworn before you and Almighty God the same solemn oath our forebears prescribed nearly a century and three-quarters ago.

The world is very different now. For man holds in his mortal hands the power to abolish all forms of human poverty and all forms of human life. And yet the same revolutionary beliefs for which our forebears fought are still at issue around the globe—the belief that the rights of man come not from the generosity of the one state but from the hand of God.

We dare not forget today that we are the heirs of that first revolution. Let the word go forth from this time and place, to friend and foe alike, that the torch has been passed to a new generation of Americans— born in this century, tempered by war, disciplined by a hard and bitter peace, proud of our ancient heritage—and unwilling to witness or permit the slow undoing of those human rights to which this nation has always been committed, and to which we are committed today at home and around the world. . . .

In the long history of the world, only a few generations have been granted the role of defending freedom in its hour of maximum danger. I do not shrink from this responsibility—I welcome it. I do not believe that any of us would exchange places with any other people or any other generation. The energy, the faith, the devotion which we bring to this endeavor will light our country and all who serve it—and the glow from that fire can truly light the world.

And so, my fellow Americans: ask not what your country can do for you—ask what you can do for your country.

My fellow citizens of the world: ask not what America will do for you, but what together we can do for the freedom of man.

Finally, whether you are citizens of America or citizens of the world, ask of us here the same high standards of strength and sacrifice which we ask of you. With a good conscience our only sure reward, with history the final judge of our deeds, let us go forth to lead the land we love, asking His blessing and His help, but knowing that here on earth God's work must truly be our own.

DAILY THOUGHTS ABOUT COUNTRY
From This Chapter

1. The history of man is the story of his striving for freedom.
2. The primary concern of our Constitution is to protect the rights of the individual.
3. Human dignity and freedom come before everything else.
4. We are free when we speak up for what we believe and assume responsibility for what we do.
5. Our destiny is up to each one of us, and if we don't like the way things are going it is up to us to change them.
6. Our Government is the projection of the consciousness of the sum total of the individuals who are governed.
7. The individual human being is God's highest creation.

From the Bible

1. The Lord will give strength unto his people; the Lord will bless his people with peace.—*Psalm 29:11*
2. Open ye the gates, that the righteous nation which keepeth the truth may enter in.—*Is. 26:2*
3. Dwell in the land which the Lord your God giveth you to inherit.—*Deut. 12:10*
4. All nations shall serve him.—*Psalm 72:11*
5. And hath made of one blood all nations of men for to dwell on all the face of the earth.—*Acts 17:26*
6. Let every soul be subject unto the higher powers. For there is no power but of God: the powers that be are ordained of God.—*Rom. 13:1*
7. Blessed is the nation whose God is the Lord.—*Psalm 33:12*

From Great Thinkers Past and Present

1. Better the occasional faults of a government that lives in a spirit of charity than the consistent omissions of a government in the ice of its own indifference.—*Franklin D. Roosevelt*

2. You can't run a government solely on a business basis . . . Government should be human. It should have a heart.—*Herbert H. Lehman*

3. The less government we have the better—the fewer laws and the less confided power. The antidote to this abuse of formal government is the influence of character, the growth of the individual.—*Ralph Waldo Emerson*

4. Man well governed should seek after no other liberty, for there can be no greater liberty than a good government.—*Sir Walter Raleigh*

5. The best of all governments is that which teaches us to govern ourselves.—*Goethe*

6. Only free people can hold their purpose and their honor steady to a common end, and prefer the interest of mankind to any narrow interest of their own.—*Woodrow Wilson*

7. A State to prosper, must be built on foundations of a moral character; and this character is the principal element of its strength and the only guaranty of its permanence and prosperity.—*Jabez Curry*

GOLDEN BRIDGE TO COUNTRY

Morning Projection

What a glorious country I live in! I am proud to be an American. I thrill to all it means. I do everything possible to be a good citizen. I am thankful that I live in this country. I know that the United States of America is "the land of the free, and the home of the brave." I know that my America is what I help to make it. I assume personal responsibility for being fit for liberty. I strive to understand all personal, community and national issues. I serve whenever I am called upon to do so. I know what a priceless heritage is mine. I am an American!

In whatever I do, I do it for the glory of God, of myself, and of my country. I am a projection of the dream of our founding fathers. I am a free citizen in a free land! By doing the best job I can in constructive daily living, I help others do a good job of being good people and good citizens. I accept personal responsibility for protecting my own freedom, and I help to preserve the rights and freedom of others. And so it is.

Evening Retrospection

Tonight, as I rest upon my own bed in my own home, I am free to let my thoughts blend with the infinite majesty and inspiration of Divine Mind. "I know the truth, and the truth makes me free." I am a citizen of God's Universe. I am part of an Infinite Plan. I am man—"made in the image and likeness of God." In God is my trust. I am free and whole because I live in America, that "one nation, under God, indivisible, with liberty and justice for all."

As I reflect upon these things, I feel the thrilling, stirring determination of the Pilgrims. The fierce determination of the early American colonists pounds in my heart. The genius of our early leaders elevates my mind. I am strengthened by the pioneers. I am closer to nature and nature's God because of the Indians who first owned this mighty land. I am sanctified by those who have died in the defense of our freedom. I am elevated by the great ones who have guided our destiny. I have faith that the great dream of this free land is an enduring fact. God is blessing my fellow citizens. God is blessing America. And so it is.

9

MIND

"As a Man Thinketh..."

EMERSON said, "There is one mind common to all individual men." There is actually no such thing as your mind and my mind. What we designate as our personal mind is the individual use each of us makes of the One Mind. In other words, Mind is not individual, but *individualized*. It isn't a matter of one person's having a better mind than someone else; it is just that he is making better use of the One Mind which is available to all of us.

In the Science of Mind teaching, we often describe God as Mind, and capitalize it accordingly. We use such phrases as "One Mind," "Divine Mind," "Infinite Mind," and "Universal Mind," as synonyms for God. The concept is that God is a great intelligent Beingness, functioning objectively as Spirit and subjectively as Creative Law.

The Bible teaches that man is created in the image and likeness of God, so we must assume that we function similarly, i.e., objectively and subjectively. The objective function is performed by the thinking, or conscious mind. The subjective function is performed by the feeling, or subconscious mind. Of course, we don't have two minds; we have one mind which works in two ways. Both activities are integral to the functioning of our thought processes.

Your mind is not as complicated as you think. It is a magnificent instrument, but its operation is really quite simple. Within itself, it does two basic things: it acts and it reacts. This is what happens: When your conscious (or surface) mind thinks, your subconscious (or deeper) mind receives the imprint of your thought and acts accordingly, thereby setting creative power into operation. When this process is completed it produces an experience or object which is the visible manifestation of the original thought. Hence, "Thoughts are things," or "Things are thoughts made visible."

The subconscious mind responds by corresponding to the action of the conscious mind, hence, action and reaction. As we are concerned here with the constructive aspects of thinking and living, it is essential that we understand this basic structure of our intellectual and creative processes.[1] It is easier to understand ourselves when we understand what happens in our minds. Everything originates in the mind. We are born into the world with a complete set of mental, emotional and physical equipment. Then we are left on our own. What we do with what we have to start with depends upon how we use our minds.

The more we think about a thing the more real it becomes to us. The energy flows to the focal point of our attention. What we think and feel is what we become. "As he thinketh in his heart, so is he" (Prov. 23:7). As we *think* in our *hearts*. This means that action takes place when thought and feeling come together.

Our thoughts reflect our heart's desire. How we feel about this choice—our desire to experience it—is what gives it power and causes it to happen. If you don't want something, don't give it houseroom in your mind and heart. Thoughts are things in their invisible form. Things are thoughts made solid. Thoughts and feelings are the cause of experience and manifestation, while the things and happenings of our lives are the effect of these same thoughts.

Once we learn how to think constructively, everything works out better, and we have the key to turn defeat into victory, illness into health, and failure into success. Look at it this way: You can't play in the dirt without getting some on you. Similarly, we can't spend time in worry, criticism, resentment and destructive thoughts and attitudes without being hurt by them. The choice is ours, isn't it? Today—right now—let's direct our attention to thoughts of good will, love, peace, well-being, and the expectation of good. Do this, no matter what the outer situation may be, and all will be well.

[1] See also "Your Technique of Alignment" in my book, *Your Thoughts Can Change Your Life* (Englewood Cliffs, N.J.: Prentice-Hall, Inc., 1961), p. 114.

The phrase, "It's all in your mind," is literally true. Outer circumstances and physical conditions appear in our factual experience, but they have their origin in the mind. Since everything can be traced back to mental causation, we can control ourselves and our world by controlling our minds.

The key to mental control is quite simple. It just takes awareness and discipline. It is all a matter of *what thoughts you admit into your mind*. Your mind can be a cesspool or a cathedral. It depends upon you; you must choose what you think about at any given moment. Your conscious mind entertains countless thoughts—they flow through the mind with lightninglike rapidity—*but you can think only one thought at a time*. So your job is to determine and control that single momentary thought. By organizing the sequence of these moments, we gain control of our thoughts. Remember these two basic principles of the scientific use of the mind:

1. The conscious mind selects.
2. The subconscious mind responds to suggestion.

We are constantly making suggestions to the subconscious mind by our thoughts, words, feelings and actions. Think constructive thoughts, say constructive things, feel and act constructively, and your subconscious will produce constructive experiences for you. Be a strict custodian and disciplinarian of your mind—condition it constructively—and you will find happiness, health, success, and harmonious adjustment to life. Train your mind to see only the good in every situation:

Whatsoever things are true,
Whatsoever things are honest,
Whatsoever things are just,
Whatsoever things are pure,
Whatsoever things are lovely,
Whatsoever things are of good report;
If there be any virtue,
And if there be any praise,
Think on these things. (Phil. 4:8)

"*If there be any virtue, and if there be any praise, think on these things.*" That is all there is to it. Establish your conscious selection and judgment as the permanent custodian of your thoughts, set up a constructive standard, and think only of those things which are constructive and praiseworthy. In this way, you make your life what you want it to be. Have nothing to do with the cheap, shoddy and sensational. Eschew violence, gossip and criticism. Avoid the negativities which constantly bombard us from newspapers, radio, television, and the irresponsible "they say" everyday small talk of individuals. Of course, we are constantly exposed to these influences but the conscious mind, with its powers of choice and discrimination, can refuse to accept them. Make it a habit to dwell only on those things which you want to, and which you know are constructive. In this way you determine your experience.

The subconscious mind never fails to obey any order given to it clearly and emphatically. As you learn the science of constructive thinking which we have just been describing, your inner creative machinery will have a steady flow of good, clean material out of which to produce the "issues of life." Think of your subconscious as a great meat-grinder. When you feed good round steak into it, good ground round steak comes out. If you put in cheaper chuck and scraps, you get ordinary hamburger. If you put in sawdust, sawdust comes out. There is no escaping the mathematical certainty that we can only get out of our deeper mind what we put into it. Just as we can not expect ground round from sawdust in the meat-grinder, we cannot expect constructive experiences from inferior mental and emotional ingredients.

As you form these new constructive habits of mental control and discipline, do not be discouraged if the old patterns and experiences continue for awhile. Stick to the constructive approach, and your life will change. What goes in must come out. Be concerned about what you admit into your mind, and everything else will take care of itself.

There is one further step. We have been talking about conditioning your mind to the constructive approach. Considerable *reconditioning* may be necessary before this can be fully accomplished. This entails a process of self-examination and personal inventory to see what negative habits, ideas, attitudes, responses and reactions need to be changed. Not only does the subconscious respond to suggestion, but it continues to respond to a suggestion once given until that suggestion is removed or replaced. This means that we have considerable excavation and repair work from the past to take care of.

Follow this program of self-repair and self-discipline without delay.

Follow the suggestions here, and remember that you alone are responsible for the contents of your own mind, conscious and subconscious. Break the bondage of the past by affirming:

Everything unlike the nature of good is removed from my inner mind. I cleanse my consciousness of everything other than constructive thoughts, attitudes, ideas, habits and feelings. I break up old pattterns and make way for new and affirmative thoughts and ideas. The free, full flow of constructive mental, emotional and spiritual wholeness is surging through me now. My mind is a willing instrument for the expression of all good things in my world. *And so it is.*

DAILY THOUGHTS ABOUT YOUR MIND
From This Chapter

1. Mind is not individual, but individualized.
2. God is a great Intelligence, functioning objectively as Spirit, and subjectively as Creative Law.
3. The more we think about a thing, the more real it becomes to us.
4. You can only think of one thing at a time.
5. The conscious mind selects; the subconscious mind responds to suggestion.
6. Train your mind to see the good in every situation.
7. The subconscious mind never fails to obey any order given to it clearly and emphatically.

From the Bible

1. Wisdom is the principal thing; therefore get wisdom.—*Prov.* 4:7
2. Through wisdom is an house builded; and by understanding it is established.—*Prov.* 24:3
3. A fool uttereth all his mind.—*Prov.* 29:11
4. Apply thine heart unto my knowldege.—*Prov.* 22:17
5. Be ye transformed by the renewing of your mind.—*Rom.* 12:2
6. I will pray with the spirit, and I will pray with the understanding. —*I Cor.* 14:15
7. Be renewed in the spirit of your mind.—*Eph.* 4:23

From Great Thinkers Past and Present

1. Whatever that be which thinks, understands, wills, and acts, it is something celestial and divine.—*Cicero*

2. A man's mind is wont to tell him more than seven watchmen sitting in a tower.—*Rudyard Kipling*

3. The immature mind hops from one thing to another; the mature mind seeks to follow through.—*Harry A. Overstreet*

4. There is nothing so elastic as the human mind. Like imprisoned steam, the more it is pressed the more it rises to resist the pressure. The more we are obliged to do the more we are able to accomplish. —*Tyron Edwards*

5. The mind is its own place, and in itself can make a heaven of hell, and a hell of heaven.—*John Milton*

6. It is the mind that maketh good of ill, that maketh wretch or happy, rich or poor.—*Edmund Spenser*

7. The mind ought sometimes to be diverted that it may return to better thinking.—*Phaedrus*

GOLDEN BRIDGE
TO YOUR MIND

Morning Projection

My mind is eager, alert and awake. I am receptive to new and fresh ideas. I think only upon those things which are true, honest, just, pure, lovely, and of good report. My thought is constructive at all times. I eliminate any tendency to dwell upon the negative, unhappy or depressing. I see through each experience into the good which indwells it. I look for the best in every one and in everything. I watch every thought. I choose them wisely and discriminatingly. I select only those thoughts and ideas which will produce good in my world. I train my mind to do my bidding. I am a strict disciplinarian. My mind is the watchdog of my soul. I am transformed by the renewing of my mind. The energy of life flows to the focus of my attention. The true and the beautiful command my attention. I select the ingredients of my life with interest and care. I give thanks for my magnificent mind within which originates all the issues of my life. And so it is.

Evening Retrospection

As I turn within, I cleanse my mind of any negativity which may have accumulated during this day. I attune my consciousness to the constructive standard which has been established for it. I dissolve all limited and unhappy thoughts. I replace them with expansive and happy ones. I forgive myself and others for any destructive misuse of the Law of Mind. I turn my attention to the correction of this day's mental and emotional activity. I completely control my thoughts. My mind is open and receptive to the inflow of Divine guidance and inspiration. During my sleeping hours, my mind is filled with God's Mind. Spirit cleanses and heals me. I am filled with good. I lay up treasures in heaven. Throughout this night I am purified and strengthened. My mind is one with the One Mind. As I select this path, and give these orders, I slip quietly and peacefully out of the external world into the subjective realm of deep sleep, refreshment, and fulfillment. I am at peace. And so it is.

10 𝒟

BODY

The Temple of the Spirit

In *Human Problems and How to Solve Them,*[1] 1 presented an explanation of the human body in terms of its spiritual correspondences. Listed there were the major organs and functions of the body, and what they stand for in terms of spiritual reality. Ever since the publication of that book I have had many requests for further explanation of this approach. Since complete understanding of the structure and care of our bodies is vital to constructive living, let's explore its mysteries and wonders.

YOUR SPIRITUAL REALITIES

The miracle of being a human being is magnificently apparent when we study the structure and meaning of our own bodies. Truly, we are "fearfully and wonderfully made," and as Walt Whitman said, "There is more to a man than that which lies between his hat and his bootstraps." Plato taught that there are perfect patterns for all things in the Infinite Mind. This theory certainly applies to the human body. Every part of it has a spiritual significance and correspondence. As Paul said, "There are . . . celestial bodies, and bodies terrestrial" (I Cor. 15:40). Our physical bodies are but the outer form of bodies of much subtler essence. Let's look at the spiritual meaning of our various parts.

The following table will help you understand how to treat an indisposition in any part of your body by affirming, strengthening and stimulating the spiritual correspondence of that particular part.

[1] (Englewood Cliffs, N.J.: Prentice-Hall, Inc., 1962), pp. 163–64.

Spiritual Correspondences of the Human Body

Head

Head	Awareness
Mind	Reason
Nerves	Communication
Brain	Thought
Face	Recognition
Eyes	Perception
Ears	Understanding, Balance, Faith
Nose	Direction
Teeth	Analysis
Mouth	Praise and Thanksgiving
Tongue	Appreciation
Skin	Protection, Individuality
Voice	Communication
Throat	Expression
Breath	Life
Neck	Flexibility
Hair on head	Vitality, Strength

Body

Back	Support
Body	Manifestation
Chest	Potential
Hand	Attention, Grasp
Fingers	Persistence
Fingernails	Examination
Thumb	Comparison
Wrist	Freedom
Arm	Action
Elbow	Movement
Shoulder	Power
Leg	Forward movement
Knee	Variety
Ankle	Ease
Foot	Understanding
Heel	Conviction
Toes	Concentration
Toenails	Detail

Organs and Functions

Lungs	Inspiration
Liver	Assimilation
Heart	Love
Abdomen	Soul
Kidneys	Purity
Generating organs	Life
Stomach	Receptivity
Bladder	Retention
Bones	Permanency
Womb	Creativity
Bowels	Elimination
Backbone	Righteousness and Inspiration
Blood	Life and Joy
Veins and Arteries	Circulation
Muscles	Power
Touch	Selection
Glands	Distribution, Order, Maintenance
Solar Plexus	Feeling
Joints	Unity

If you would understand the spiritual symbolism of any part of the body, observe its physical function and see what it actually does. Then realize that in back of the physical function is the spiritual function which is carrying on a parallel activity in the invisible. The physical activity is merely the visible, factual expression of the inner reality. The real care of the body is done on the spiritual level. In spiritual mind healing, we bring the mental and emotional factors into focus with the spiritual reality, thereby healing the condition at the point of cause. The effect—body and physical function—automatically is healed.

No part of the body is isolated from the whole. Our body is the physical expression of an integrated and unified organism which includes the other levels mentioned. Malfunctioning on the physical level indicates imbalance or conflict on one or all of the other three— the mental, emotional and spiritual levels.

Of course, there are many purely physical causes for disease, but these are invariably accompanied by inner causes as well. Proper diet and exercise are important in the care of every part of our bodies, but equally and sometimes even more important is similar attention to the inner factors.

THE HEAD

Head. The head itself, which contains so many separate parts and functions is a marvelous outpicturing of our inner being. The very fact that the head contains the brain, the headquarters of the central nervous system, makes it of special interest and significance. The head represents our capacity to know God, and every part of it is integrated to assist in that function.

Mind. The mind is not really contained in the body. The body lives in the mind. Our mental processes are not confined in the head or the brain. The mind actually operates throughout the body and extends beyond it. The one individual personal mind is an individualized use of the One Mind, as we discussed in Chapter 9, and its capacity is limitless. However, the headquarters of the human mind is certainly in the brain, and therefore, of course, the head.

Nerves. The nerves carry messages from various parts of the body to the brain where they are interpreted. The processes of thought, reason and selection originate in the brain itself and are carried as orders to various parts of the body.

Brain. Even though we exist *in* mind, which has no exact location, the brain is the physical instrument of thought and reason. It coordinates and interprets the messages from the nervous system. It is the organ of consciousness.

Face. It is largely by our faces that we are recognized. What we are shines forth from the face. The face is a direct reflection of the inner life. The face is the means by which we project our image of God.

Eyes. "The eyes are the windows of the soul." We see *through* our individual eyes, but *with* God's eyes.

Ears. Just as with sight, hearing is both an inner and an outer sense. The ears represent receptivity to guidance—listening to the "still small voice." Just as the ear is symbolic of the faith which balances the consciousness, so the small bones within the ear provide the leveling device which maintains the equilibrium of the body itself.

Nose. Metaphysically, the nose represents the capacity to select an idea and follow it through to completion. It indicates the ability to pursue a train of thought through to its conclusion. The nose is also symbolic of the wisdom of minding one's own business.

Teeth. The teeth represent the capacity to break up God's ideas so that we can examine and swallow them. The physical teeth break up the material substance of our food and prepare it for swallowing and assimilation. If the teeth decay or break down, good dentistry is essential, of course, just as expert medical attention is often necessary for other parts of the body, but the condition should also be treated at the mental, emotional and spiritual levels.

Mouth. "Let the words of my mouth, and the meditation of my heart, be acceptable in thy sight, O Lord, my strength, and my redeemer" (Psalm 19:14). Jesus said, "Not that which goeth into the mouth defileth a man; but that which cometh out of the mouth, this defileth a man" (Matt. 15:11). The mouth is for the purpose of projecting constructive words of joy and praise.

Tongue. Symbolically, the tongue represents appreciation and enjoyment. As it helps us taste and savor our food, so there is within us the spiritual capacity to appreciate "the bread of life," the ideas and inspiration which flow from the Mind of God. The tongue is also the organ of clarification and articulation, both of which are steps in spiritual understanding.

Skin. Our external skin gives us definition and protection. It is symbolic of our individuality as a complete unit of expression. Lack of love or any threat to our identification as an individual may result in skin problems.

Voice. "The still, small voice" which we intuitively hear within, is God speaking to us. Our human voice represents the capacity to communicate this inner awareness into outer expression. Verbal communication is one of the distinguishing characteristics of the human being. The voice is the instrument by which spiritual ideas are expressed.

Throat. The passage through which air, food and liquid enter in, and from which sound emanates, the throat represents expression, and the free, full flow of God's ideas entering in and issuing forth. Any interference with the complete expression of the individual may result in throat problems. Treat for expression.

Breath. Breath is life. The process of respiration—inhalation and exhalation—is one of receiving, using and releasing the life force.

Neck. The neck represents the freedom to move freely in awareness so that we may receive ideas of Truth from whatever direction they may come.

Hair on Head. The story of Samson in the Bible is a dramatic presentation of the symbolism of hair as representing vitality and strength.

We will continue with our discussion of the spiritual correspondences of the human body in Chapter 11, which deals with health.

DAILY THOUGHTS ABOUT YOUR BODY

From This Chapter

1. Every part of the body has spiritual significance.
2. Our physical bodies are but the outer form of bodies of much subtler essence.
3. An indisposition in any part of the body can be healed by affirming, strengthening, and stimulating the spiritual correspondence of that particular part.
4. Regularly and systematically stimulate the flow of life through every part of your body by repeating affirmative statements of blessing.
5. If you would understand the spiritual symbolism of any part of the body, observe the physical function and see what it actually does.
6. Bodily care must start with the inner consciousness.
7. The body is the physical expression of an integrated and unified organism which includes the mental, emotional, and spiritual levels.

From the Bible

1. Know ye not that your body is the temple of the Holy Ghost.—*I Cor. 6:19*
2. The body is not one member, but many.—*I Cor. 12:14*
3. God hath tempered the body together.—*I Cor. 12:24*
4. There are also celestial bodies, and bodies terrestrial.—*I Cor. 15:40*
5. There is one body, and one Spirit.—*Eph. 4:4*
6. The body without the spirit is dead.—*James 2:26*
7. In the beginning was the Word. . . . And the Word was made flesh.—*John 1:1, 14*

From Great Thinkers Past and Present

1. Can any honor exceed that which has been conferred on the human body?—Can any powers exceed the powers—any glory exceed the glory with which it is invested?—*John Pulsford*
2. Our body is a well-set clock, which keeps good time, but if it be too much or indiscreetly tampered with, the alarm runs out before the hour.—*Joseph Hall*
3. It is shameful for a man to rest in ignorance of the structure of his own body, especially when the knowledge of it mainly conduces to his welfare, and directs his application of his own powers.—*Philip Melanchthon*
4. God made the human body, and it is the most exquisite and wonderful organization which has come to us from the divine hand.—It is a study for one's whole life.—*Henry Ward Beecher*
5. Every man is the builder of a temple, called his body.—*Henry David Thoreau*
6. The human body is an instrument for the production of art in the life of the human soul.—*Alfred North Whitehead*
7. All are but parts of one stupendous whole, / Whose body Nature is, and God the soul.—*Alexander Pope*

GOLDEN BRIDGE TO YOUR BODY

Morning Projection

Blessed be my head, which represents my capacity to know God.

Blessed be my mind, with which I think of the wonder of God.

Blessed be my nerves, which carry God's messages through my body.

Blessed be my brain, with which I develop my awareness of God.

Blessed be my face, through which shines my recognition of God.

Blessed be my eyes, through which I perceive the beauty of God.

Blessed be my ears, with which I hear and understand the word of God.

Blessed be my nose, which keeps me on the path to God.

Blessed be my teeth, which enable me to break up God's ideas so I can understand them.

Blessed be my mouth, with which I praise and sing the glory of God.

Blessed be my tongue, with which I savor and appreciate the nourishment of God.

Blessed be my skin, which protects my individual expression of God.

Blessed be my voice, with which I communicate God's ideas.

Blessed be my throat, through which God's ideas come and go.

Blessed be my breath, which is God's life circulating through me.

Blessed be my neck, which turns freely to God's ideas from whatever direction they may come.

Blessed be my hair, which represents God's vitality and strength in me. And so it is.

Evening Retrospection

I give thanks for my magnificent and healthy body. As I relax and breathe deeply, the cleansing flow of life circulates through my body, healing it and renewing it. As I release the cares and pressures of the day, all fatigue is washed away and the poisons and toxins are dissolved. My blood stream is pure and vital, joyously nourishing the tissues of my body, and giving me abundant life.

Every organ and function of my body is in harmony with the perfect pattern within. My body is the physical expression of God's idea for me. My body is the manifestation of my consciousness. My body is my soul made visible. I bless my body, knowing that every cell is a unit of intelligent expression of the One Mind which is God.

My body is in tune with the spirit, mind and substance of the universe. The currents of divine energy are restoring my body and maintaining it in perfect health. God is blessing and rebuilding my body as I release it into His care and lie down to pleasant sleep. And so it is.

II ✐

HEALTH
The Secret of Vital Health

IN this chapter we will continue the discussion of the spiritual correspondences of the human body.

In this discussion of the body and its care it is important to remember that the body was made to function and last. Its formation, metabolism, growth and operations are automatic. It actually works more efficiently when we leave it alone. Our self-abuse through faulty care, underexercise and overeating, as well as our abuse through discordant and neglected spiritual, mental and emotional factors, is what disturbs health. The purpose of these two brief chapters, "Body" and "Health," is to provide greater understanding of the relationships between our visible and invisible "selves" and to bring about better co-ordination between them.

While any discussion of health is usually assumed to be about the body, it must also, of necessity, be about the other factors which go to make up the whole person. As we continue the discussion of our spiritual realities, we will include the whole person.

BODY

Back. The back represents uprightness, strength and support. The alignment and balance of our spiritual, mental and emotional attitudes have a great deal to do with the health of the back. Such heavy and depressing attitudes as worry, burden-bearing, weariness and discouragement affect the back in the many aches and pains associated with it. Pressure about money matters is often a cause of backache.

Body. As we have said, the entire body is the visible manifestation of our spiritual reality. Since the spiritual person is perfect, the body is in reality perfect. The potential is there. All we have to do is let the cleansing power of spirit heal our minds and hearts, thereby establishing inner health, which in turn, will produce bodily health.

Chest. The chest represents our potential to express our spiritual reality.

Hand. The physical function is an outpicturing of the spiritual reality. The hand represents man's capacity to grasp God's ideas and do something with them.

Fingers. The fingers are the instruments of our persistence in dealing with details.

Fingernails. A further extension of the hand function, the fingernails assist in our grasp, attention and persistence, and our ability to deal with small details.

Thumb. The opposed thumb, symbolic of the faculty of comparison, represents the ability to hold on to ideas, plans and projects until we complete them.

Wrist. As part of the action symbolism of the hand, the wrist represents the capacity of taking hold of ideas no matter where they come from and to turn them, examine them, and activate them in the proper direction.

Arm. As the hand with its multiple faculties is the instrument of action, the arm represents action itself. It is the symbol of strength, work and accomplishment.

Elbow. Just as with the wrist, the elbow is a further representation of the human being's flexibility in understanding and action.

Shoulder. Taking the power and support of the main body of divine ideas, the shoulder transforms them into action and passes them along.

Leg. The legs are symbolic of our capacity to move forward into life.

Knee. Just as the elbow and wrist represent flexibility in the total arm function, so the knee and ankle are its instruments in the leg movement.

Ankle. The ankle further represents ease in determining the direction of our forward movement.

Foot. The foot is the classic symbol of understanding the meaning and purpose of life. "Put off thy shoes from off thy feet, for the place whereon thou standest is holy ground" (Ex. 3:5). As the leg moves us along the path of dealing with the ever-changing ideas and situations of life, the foot is the anchor which establishes us in the understanding that enables us to deal with them. Foot troubles are invariably the result of the faulty understanding which endeavors to find meaning and motivation solely from the material ground rather than the "holy ground" of Spirit.

Heel. The heel represents conviction and assurance in our understanding.

Toes and Toenails. The toes and toenails, of course, are to the foot what the fingers and fingernails are to the hand. They represent phases of our detailed dealing with ideas, understanding, movement and action.

ORGANS AND FUNCTIONS

Lungs. Inspiration is the word here: "to draw in by breathing." Since breath and life are virtually synonymous in spiritual symbolism, the significance of the lungs cannot be overstated. The actions of inspiration and expiration—of inhalation and exhalation—represent the coming and going of the "breath of life" or spirit. When we breathe, we are actually taking the Spirit—the Life of God—into our own bodies. The respiratory system is our lifeline from the Infinite. God infuses His Life into us when we breathe or when we meditatively think. The word *inspire* has the same meaning whether it is dealing with breath or spirit. The Hindu word *prana* and the Greek word *pneuma* both mean either "breath" or "spirit." It can easily be seen then that any congestion or disease of the lungs, such as pneumonia, is not primarily a physical condition at all, but a spiritual one. There can only be physical health when there is spiritual health.

Liver. The liver also has a vital function in the assimilative process of the individual's use and expression of Spirit, which is Life. The liver has to do with the *substance* of Spirit. After receiving this substance after the process of digestion of food, the liver works upon it to make it usable, utilize it, assimilates it into the blood stream, and carries on other complex functions of combustion, cleansing, purification and filtering. Just as with our other organs and functions, the liver is a physical organ, symbolic of a spiritual action. As its very name indicates, the liver is the organ of active life in the body.

Heart. The heart is the organ of love and joy which pumps the life stream (blood) through the body. It is closely aligned with our feeling nature—with our emotional structure. Always associated with love, the heart actually represents the inner consciousness of the individual—the subconscious mind, our subjective use of the One Creative Power. When the Bible says, "Keep thy heart with all diligence; for out of it are the issues of life" (Prov. 4:23), it is referring not to the physical heart, but to the inner life of the individual. The health of the beating heart is dependent on the health of the knowing heart.

Abdomen. The abdomen, containing the solar plexus, or soul-center, and the many inner organs, is symbolic of Soul, or Spirit individualized in man. It further represents intuition, or direct knowing.

Kidneys. As liquids and fluids represent various phases of Mind or Spirit, so the kidneys, with their filtering function, represent our capacity to cleanse and purify ourselves as we become whole (holy).

Generating organs. These represent the capacity to originate and project Life, based on the recognition that there is One Cause or Life which flows through all things. Our lives are our individual use of the One Life which flows through all things. The physical process of generation is merely the visible action of that which is constantly taking place in the invisible. Life is individualized in Spirit long before the body appears to house it.

Stomach. The stomach represents the capacity to receive and utilize ideas.

Bladder. The bladder represents the capacity to hold ideas before releasing them.

Bones. Forming the skeletal structure of the body, the bones are symbolic of the necessity of form and plan through which the amorphous ideas of Spirit flow into permanent expression.

Womb. The womb is symbolic of the creative center within the consciousness which gives life to individual ideas.

Bowels. The capacity to eliminate from our lives whatever has been used up, or cannot be used, is represented by the bowels. The fear and insecurity which cause us to hang onto useless things, habits, ideas, customs and procedures, along with greed and limitation, are the causes of constipation, colitis and other difficulties in this region.

Backbone. This is the central structural factor of our skeletal equipment. The spine connects everything and also provides protection for the trunk lines of communication between the brain and the rest of the body. The backbone is symbolic of man's idealistic nature—his uprightness.

Blood. The blood is symbolic of the circulation of Life and joy through our consciousness.

Veins and Arteries. These represent the channels through which Life and joy flow into expression.

Muscles. Muscles are symbolic of the force which is generated when the power of Spirit is transformed into action.

Touch. The sense of touch represents the spiritual capacity to recognize and select that which is good.

Glands. The glands are symbolic of the spiritual centers which establish and maintain order and balance in the distribution of the life forces throughout our being.

Solar plexus. This network of important ganglia makes this region the headquarters of the feeling nature just as the brain is the headquarters of the rational nature. The solar plexus is often called the brain of the soul.

Joints. These represent integration of the parts as the whole is maintained in unity.

These last two chapters have provided you with a new way of thinking about your body and your health. The approach may be different and perhaps somewhat puzzling at first, but a little study and thought about the principles of inner causation will give you a greater understanding and appreciation of yourself and what you really are. The health of the body is as dependent on the flow of good ideas, thoughts and feelings as it is on proper care, food, exercise and rest.

We shall depart slightly from the regular form of our Golden Bridge in this chapter so that we can complete the "Blessed be my ——— affirmations which were begun in Chapter 10.

DAILY THOUGHTS ABOUT HEALTH
From This Chapter

1. The body was made to function and it was made to last.
2. It is our physical misuse and our mental and emotional abuse that disturb our health.

3. Health is the result of greater understanding of and co-ordination between our inner and outer "selves."
4. When we let the cleansing power of Spirit heal our minds and hearts, we establish inner health, which in turn produces bodily health.
5. There can be physical health only when there is spiritual health.
6. The health of the body is as dependent on the flow of good ideas, thoughts and feelings, as it is upon proper care, food, exercise and rest.
7. Our lives are our individual use of the One Life.

From the Bible

1. I am the Lord that healeth thee.—*Exod. 15:26*
2. The Lord will take away from thee all sickness.—*Deut. 7:15*
3. The Lord is the strength of my life.—*Psalm 27:1*
4. I shall yet praise him, who is the health of my countenance, and my God.—*Psalm 42:11*
5. The tongue of the wise is health.—*Prov. 12:18*
6. A faithful ambassador is health.—*Prov. 13:17*
7. Then shall thy light break forth as the morning, and thine health shall spring forth speedily.—*Isa. 58:8*

From Great Thinkers Past and Present

1. Half the spiritual difficulties that men and women suffer arise from a morbid state of health.—*Henry Ward Beecher*
2. Without health life is not life; it is only a state of languor and suffering—an image of death.—*Rabelais*
3. Take care of your health; you have no right to neglect it, and thus become a burden to yourself, and perhaps to others.—*William Hall*
4. Health is the soul that animates all the enjoyments of life, which fade and are tasteless without it.—*Sir William Temple*
5. Never hurry; take plenty of exercise; always be cheerful, and take all the sleep you need, and you may expect to be well.—*James F. Clarke*
6. To become a thoroughly good man is the best prescription for keeping a sound mind in a sound body.—*Francis Bowen*
7. The ingredients of health and long life, are great temperance, open air, easy labor, and little care.—*Sir Philip Sidney*

GOLDEN BRIDGE TO YOUR HEALTH

Morning Projection

Blessed be my back which supports and strengthens me.

Blessed be my body which is the manifestation of God.

Blessed be my chest which reflects my consciousness of God.

Blessed be my hand with which I grasp God's ideas.

Blessed be my fingers with which I persistently handle details.

Blessed be my fingernails which help me to examine the small details of life.

Blessed be my thumbs which represent my capacity to compare and balance opposing forces.

Blessed be my wrists which give me the freedom to take hold of ideas no matter whence they come.

Blessed be my arms, the instruments through which I put God's ideas into action.

Blessed be my elbows which give me flexibility in thought and action.

Blessed be my shoulders which give me power and support.

Blessed be my legs which move me forward into life.

Blessed be my knees which enable me to move instantaneously and freely.

Blessed be my ankles which give me ease in determining my direction.

Blessed be my feet which stand upon God's "holy ground" of ideas.

Blessed be my heels which anchor me firmly in spiritual understanding.

Blessed be my toes which represent my power of concentration.

Blessed be my toenails which help me deal with details. And so it is.

Evening Retrospection

Blessed be my lungs through which I receive the spiritual breath of life.

Blessed be my liver with which I assimilate the substance of Spirit.

Blessed be my heart which pumps love and joy through my entire being.

Blessed be my abdomen, the house of my vital organs—the home of my soul.

Blessed be my kidneys through which I am cleansed and purified.

Blessed be my generating organs which represent my capacity to express life.

Blessed be my bladder which gives me the power to hold God's ideas before passing them on.

Blessed be my stomach through which I receive and utilize ideas.

Blessed be my bones which establish my permanent structure.

Blessed be my womb which is the creative center of life.

Blessed be my blood which is Life and joy circulating through my system.

Blessed be my blood vessels through which Life and joy freely flow.

Blessed be my muscles which express spiritual force and power.

Blessed be my touch with which I recognize and select good ideas.

Blessed be my glands which distribute the essence of Life through my system.

Blessed be my solar plexus, the brain of my soul.

Blessed be my joints which integrate and unify me. And so it is.

12 *𝒮*

TIME

All the Time There Is

AT the entrance to the Oakland Bay Bridge in San Francisco, a bus heads for Oakland. In Oakland, a car starts across the bridge for San Francisco. They proceed toward their destinations. For the bus, Oakland is in the future; San Francisco is in the past. For the car, San Francisco is in the future; Oakland is in the past. Several hundred feet above the bridge hovers a helicopter, suspended in space and time, quietly observing the movements of both the bus and the car. It is equally related to Oakland, San Francisco, and the moving vehicles. Past and future blend into the present. Divisions of time disappear.

As with the helicopter, each of us has the ability to erase the artificial distinctions of time. Measurement of time is a purely human invention. To animals, children, and all creatures who live completely, time is now. Time is being. Each moment represents a segment of eternity to be fully lived, because the moment that we are living right now is the one moment of eternity that we can do anything about. In a life lived fully, with a proper awareness of the here and now, the moments blend in a never-ending stream of constructive and joyous experience. It is in the enjoyment of the moment, free from bondage to the past and future, that we make the most of the gift of eternity—time.

"Where does the time go?" we exclaim, forgetting that time goes into everything we do. There is a time for everything; it is up to us to take time for the things which are important to us.

To everything there is a season, and a time to every purpose under the heaven.

A time to be born, and a time to die; a time to plant, and a time to pluck up that which is planted;

A time to kill, and a time to heal; a time to break down, and a time to build up;

A time to weep, and a time to laugh; a time to mourn, and a time to dance;

A time to cast away stones, and a time to gather stones together; a time to embrace, and a time to refrain from embracing;

A time to rend and a time to sew; a time to keep silence, and a time to speak;

A time to get, and a time to lose; a time to keep and a time to cast away;

A time to love, and a time to hate; a time of war, and a time of peace.

—*Ecclesiastes 3:1–8*

Everyone has an equal amount of time. It is how we use all the time there is that determines how well we are going to get along in life. We set up arbitrary divisions of time in units of seconds, minutes, hours, days, weeks, months and years. Time, itself, cannot be measured, and is most flexible. This fact is demonstrated by the famous statement of Albert Einstein: "When you sit with a nice girl for two hours, you think it is only a minute. But when you sit on a hot stove for a minute, you think it is two hours. That's relativity."

Of course, we need to be on time for appointments, and we need to schedule time for certain tasks. But we do not need to be pushed, pressured and hurried. Do not be a slave to time. Make time your servant. Life is a journey; slow down and enjoy the trip.

"Let us not hurry, gentlemen," a famous surgeon admonished his assistants. "We have no time to lose."

"Haste makes waste," says the old proverb.

"Forgive me for writing at such length," a great man wrote to a friend, "but I do not have time to be brief."

As precious as time is, and as jealous as we are of it, we paradoxically squander it in nonproductiveness and vain pursuits. Wasted time is wasted life. Time should be put to maximum advantage.

Ever since boyhood I have cherished the dream of writing books. However, I was well past forty before I had my first one published. Why? Because I had allowed myself to be hypnotized by the false idea that I had no time to write. Nearly everyone is hypnotized by the same false belief that he doesn't have time to do what he wants to do. Why not? Because we waste time convincing ourselves that we do not have time, until this error in belief becomes a fact in experience.

The secret is to *do* the thing which you decide is the most important for you to do. Just *do* it. Take the time, and *do* it. Once this important activity is scheduled, fit in everything else as you can. There will be plenty of time for everything you have to do, if you just plan for the most important one first. With your main avenue of expression open, you will discover all kinds of shortcuts and ways to use your time more efficiently. For instance, you can save time by making one task serve several purposes.

When I was writing my first book, *Your Thoughts Can Change Your Life,* I complained of my difficulty in finding time to Myron Boardman, President of the Trade Books Division of Prentice-Hall, Inc.

"Why don't you do as Norman Vincent Peale does?" he asked.

"I'd like to—in many ways," I laughed. "But just how do you mean?"

"Dr. Peale is a fairly busy man, wouldn't you say?"

"I certainly would."

"You would agree that his ministry, his counseling, his radio and TV broadcasts, his newspaper columns, writing his books, publishing *Guideposts,* administering the Foundation for Christian Living, not to mention traveling and speaking all over the world, take time?"

"Of course."

"Do you have a heavier schedule than Dr. Peale's?"

"No."

"Then why does he have enough time and you don't?"

"You've got me."

"Just think a moment. What have you done so far today?"

"Well, I wrote for a few hours this morning, then I did a radio broadcast, spoke at a luncheon, spent several hours in counseling, and this evening I'm teaching a class."

"Fine. Now what are you dealing with most of the time?"

"Thoughts . . . ideas . . . people . . ."

"Right. In every instance. You get ideas, you think them out, and you present them to people in various ways. Tell me, what happened to the ideas you used in this morning's radio broadcast?"

"Oh, I forgot about them so I could start thinking about my luncheon speech."

"Why did you forget them? Weren't they any good?"

"Of course. But I had to——."

Then I saw the point. Time-saving in my kind of work is simply a matter of making my ideas serve more than one purpose. Dr. Peale does it; I now do it; all busy and successful people do it. We make time work for us by "piggy-backing" ideas, so that several things are accomplished at once. You can do the same thing. Reorganize your thinking and planning and go to it! You have all the time you need. Just learn how to use it.

Another important lesson is to learn how to salvage time, how to use productively those leftover bits and pieces that get lost unless we use them. There is the time spent in routine tasks, waiting, and in coming and going. All of this is *thinking* time. Since constructive thought is the basis of any project, you can do the major part of any job by simply thinking correctly about it. Just *think*, wherever you are, and in whatever you are doing. Only a small part of our work uses our full capacity. Learn to use the part of your capacity that is left over. You can actually activate the inner mind and do a more complete job of thinking when something engages the periphery of your attention so that you can focus subjectively upon your major idea. For instance, Mrs. Curtis and I were at a movie the other night when some ideas began to stir in my subconscious. The picture was enjoyable but it wasn't taxing either my attention or my intellect, so I took out my ever-present note pad and started jotting down notes in the dark. By the time the movie was over, I'd had not only a good relaxing time, but I also had notes for a Sunday lecture, two radio broadcasts, and a chapter for this book.

Your conscious mind is concerned with temporal, time-measured matters; your subconscious is one with eternity, where there is all time, but actually no time. They are both available to us at all times. Infinity is being expressed at this moment. There is no restriction in time. It is an overflowing Source. Drink deeply from the unmeasured, pour it judiciously and efficiently into the measured, and get on with the business of living. Take time; it is yours.

TAKE TIME

1. *To live.* It is the secret of success.
2. *To think.* It is the source of power.
3. *To play.* It is the secret of perpetual youth.
4. *To read.* It is the foundation of knowledge and wisdom.

5. *To pray.* It is the greatest power on earth.
6. *To love and be loved.* It is a God-given privilege.
7. *To be friendly.* It is the road to happiness.
8. *To laugh.* It is the music of the soul.
9. *To give.* It is too short a day to be selfish.
10. *To work.* It is the price of success.
11. *To dream.* It hitches the soul to the stars.
12. *For God.* It is life's only lasting investment.
13. *For yourself.* You are a very important person.
14. *To loaf.* "I loaf and invite my soul" (Walt Whitman).
15. *To build.* "Build thee more stately mansions, O my soul" (Oliver Wendell Holmes).
16. *To enjoy.* Have a good time living.
17. *To appreciate beauty.* There is beauty everywhere.
18. *To rest.* Refill and renew from the fountain of life.
19. *To pay compliments.* You can catch more flies with honey than vinegar.
20. *To communicate.* Conversation stimulates the flow of ideas.
21. *To be thorough.* "Trifles make perfection, but perfection itself is no trifle" (Michelangelo).
22. *To explore.* There is more unknown than known.
23. *To seek.* "Seek and ye shall find" (Matt. 7:7).
24. *To care.* Everyone responds to loving attention.
25. *To plan.* First the idea, then the blueprint.
26. *To review.* Take inventory; see how you are doing.
27. *To exercise.* "Use it or lose it," says Nature.
28. *To eat.* Anything worth eating is worth eating well.
29. *To pay attention.* Power flows to the focus of attention.
30. *To hear.* The "still small voice" is speaking right now.
31. *To see.* There is more to be seen than we have ever seen.
32. *To travel.* See how the other 99 per cent live.
33. *To entertain.* Help others to have a good time.
34. *To have good manners.* Manners are the mark of a cultivated person.
35. *To see what the other fellow is doing.* You might learn something.

DAILY THOUGHTS ABOUT TIME
From This Chapter

1. Time is now. Time is being.
2. Each moment represents a segment of eternity to be lived fully.
3. Everyone has an equal amount of time. It is how we use ours that counts.

4. Do not be a slave to time; make time your servant.
5. Make maximum use of time by doing the thing you decide is most important for you to do.
6. Save time by making one task serve several purposes.
7. This moment is the one moment of eternity that we can do something about.

From the Bible

1. To every thing there is a season, and a time to every purpose under the heaven.—*Eccles. 3:1*
2. He changeth the times and the seasons.—*Dan. 2:21*
3. One day is with the Lord as a thousand years, and a thousand years as one day.—*II Pet. 3:8*
4. Take ye heed, watch and pray: for ye know not when the time is. —*Mark 13:33*
5. This is the day which the Lord hath made; we will rejoice and be glad in it.—*Psalm 118:24*
6. Sufficient unto the day is the evil thereof.—*Matt. 6:34*
7. Now is the accepted time; behold, now is the day of salvation.— *II Cor. 6:2*

From Great Thinkers Past and Present

1. As every thread of gold is valuable, so is every moment of time.— *John Mason*
2. Time is the chrysalis of eternity.—*Jean Paul*
3. To choose time is to save time.—*Francis Bacon*
4. The great rule of moral conduct is, next to God, to respect time.— *John Casper Lavater*
5. We always have time enough, if we will but use it aright.—*Goethe*
6. Each moment, as it passes, is the meeting place of two eternities. What I most value next to eternity, is time.—*Madame Swetchine*
7. There is not a single moment in life that we can afford to lose.— *Edward M. Goulburn*

GOLDEN BRIDGE TO TIME

Morning Projection

*Today I have a new gift of time. This entire day of golden mo-
ments and hours stretches promisingly before me. I have all the time
there is. I can do anything I want with my time. I plan my day. I
use my time wisely and well. I do good things with my time. Time
is my servant. I am the master of time. I fill my time with noble
thoughts and ideas. I project them into worthy deeds.*

*I live in the here and the now. I make the most of each moment.
Eternity is expressed at this moment. All the aeons of time past serve
me as I make the most of this moment. The perfect pattern of unfolding time insures a happy and abundant future as I make the most
of my present time.*

*I have a good time at all times today and always. I take time to en-
joy myself and to give love and encouragement to others. I am never
hurried or pressured. I live in a timeless, spaceless universe where all
things unfold in their proper time. I live in eternity. I move forward
into infinity. I give thanks for every second of eternal time; I live
them all—one at a time.* And so it is.

Evening Retrospection

*Serenely and quietly I pause in the midst of time and bring all
things to a point of rest. Time stands still tonight. I am unaware of
seconds, minutes or hours. I transcend restrictions and measurements
as I go straight to the center of life, penetrating into the mysteries of
time. I live in eternity. Past and future blend and meet in the present
tonight. They are all one, and I am free, free to roam the corridors
of time, free to be one with the Infinite Self.*

*I gather the moments of my day together. I go over and evaluate
them in the light of evolving time. I move backward as I return to my
moment of awakening on this day. Now I move forward from the
past to the present, reliving each moment and setting it right. My
time is in my hand. I correct the past. I enjoy the present. I project
the Golden Bridge of expectancy, enthusiasm and joyous anticipation into the future of my eternal life.*

*As I am alive now, I know I live forever. As I lie down now to
present dreams, I am rocked in the cradle of eternity. I drift into the
infinite. My soul journeys to distant spheres. I am one with the
magnificence of time.* And so it is.

13

POSSESSIONS
"What Doth It Profit a Man...?"

RICHARD GREY was a modern-day Croesus. Everything he touched turned to gold. Small in physical stature, but mighty in mind and ingenious in method, he became a business tycoon at the very outset of his career. A millionaire before he was thirty, he went on piling up more money and possessions until he himself had no idea what he was really worth.

Now, nearing seventy, he was master of very nearly all he surveyed, but he confided to me that he would trade it all for the happiness which had eluded him throughout his life.

"Look at this pile of rock." He gestured toward the 28-room Victorian monstrosity in which he lived atop one of Hollywood's highest hills. "My wife and I are lost in this ruin. Why, we need a loudspeaker to talk to each other across the dining-room table. An electric cart takes me from one room to the other, and I go upstairs to bed in an elevator. Imagine that!—an elevator in your own house! But do you think that makes me sleep any better when I get there? No! I haven't had a good night's sleep in years. To tell you the truth, Mamie and I were happier when we were living in our first cabin which I built with my own hands up there in the Colorado mountains more than forty years ago. Boy, those were the days ———"

He glanced nervously at his watch, fumbled for a handful of pills in his vest pocket, and washed them down with a highball. He called the butler for another, lighted a cigar which seemed a foot long, and settled back with a scowl on his face.

"I'll tell you what I want," he went on. "I want to give some money— I mean real money—to set up a monument to Mamie and me. I don't know how much longer I have—the doctor says my heart is shot, and goodness knows what this thing is in my stomach, but it's killing me."

"That's very generous of you, Mister Grey," I ventured.

"Generous, hell! I'm not giving my money away. I told you I want to set up a monument to myself—something that will make people remember me after I'm gone."

"What did you have in mind?"

"That's what I want to talk to you about. I've looked into everything —schools, scholarships, foundations, churches, hospitals—everything. I've talked to more crackpots and daydreamers than I ever knew existed, and that's saying something, but I haven't seen anything yet that interests me. Somebody told me about you and your work. I thought maybe you had some ideas that might be built up into a monument."

"Well . . . I have ideas and plans, of course, but I had hardly thought of them in this light," I said.

"Then start thinking!" Mr. Grey exploded. "Work out a plan and then call me. I'll expect to hear from you."

I was dismissed. What could I say to a man whose "gift" had as many strings on it as this one did? What could I say to a man who wasn't really interested in giving at all—just interested in buying a monument to his own memory? For most people, the work and accomplishments of a lifetime are their monument, but Richard Grey took little pride in the land and commodity speculations, the mining-stock promotions, and the borderline deals with which he had built his fortune. His life had been spent in a variety of pursuits, all motivated by a desire to possess and accumulate material things. Now, with an uneasy conscience, and with guilt and fear nipping at his heels, he was in company with the many, past and present, who have discovered—sometimes too late—that "a man's life consisteth not in the things which he possesseth" (Luke 12:15).

I thought of the well-known motion picture star who had taken her own life at the very peak of her fame and fortune. I thought of the multimillionaire in his hilltop mansion, with two swimming pools, but who never went swimming; with four expensive automobiles in his garage, but who took a taxi whenever he wanted to go anywhere, because he was too nervous to drive. I thought of the wealthy widow, adrift in an alcoholic haze as she wandered aimlessly through the gardens and across the acres of manicured lawns of her palatial estate. I thought of the influential banker and financier whose greed and cruelty had twisted his body and dried up his circulation until he was a mere shell of the vital and intelligent man who had driven his way to the top. I thought of the brilliant writer and minister who had promised hope and inspiration for millions for years, but who lost his way in a labyrinth of profit and possessions until he faded from view, his empty words no longer of any value to himself or to others—the light snuffed out because he was too busy to keep oil in the lamp and the wick trimmed.

"What doth it profit a man, if he shall gain the whole world, and lose his own soul?" (Mark 8:36). What is this strange malady that seems to afflict those who become too preoccupied with the things and the ways of the world?

Why did Jesus advise, "Lay not up for yourselves treasures upon earth, where moth and rust doth corrupt, and where thieves break through and steal" (Matt. 6:19)?

Is it necessary for a person to lose health, friends, faculties—even his own soul—just because he becomes rich in worldly possessions? Is it really easier for a camel to go through the eye of a needle, than for a rich man to enter into the kingdom of God? Are possessions, riches, money, power and influence evil? If so, why are they so eagerly sought after and why is so much importance placed on them, not only in today's world, but throughout man's history, and in the Bible itself?

My soul wrestled with these questions as I pondered what to do about Richard Grey's offer to finance my work, if I would turn it into a monument to him. Goodness knows, our church could use the money. I had just outlined a Fifty-Year Plan to our Board of Trustees, a plan that included regular world-wide television presentations of the Science of Mind, and the use of motion pictures, radio, records and study courses to bring this affirmative religious philosophy to people everywhere, including those on distant planets, before the fifty years were out. Of course, the plan included buildings and various functional organizational facilities, but the concept soared far beyond the dimension of local organization, buildings and real estate. My work is to teach people the nobility of their own souls and inspire them to rise above the material externals of life. My plan actually says, "Let's use every means available to bring this constructive teaching to people everywhere. If we do our job, God will provide whatever is needed."

"It looks like a lot of money is needed. I know that much," one Board member observed. "I'll tell you what—you bring in the money, and we'll help you spend it." The meeting adjourned on this note, and I was left alone with my dream, but I was confident that I was on the right track.

Now here was Richard Grey's money, if I would consent to make my work a monument to a man instead of an idea. I won't deny I was tempted to go along with him many times in our discussions during the months that followed. But I was adamant from the start: *My plan was for the purpose of spreading constructive ideas that would help people help themselves.*

"To hell with people!" Mr. Grey exclaimed. "I'm not interested in people; I'm interested in a monument to me and Mamie. Now, unless you can give me some ideas for that, I'm not interested."

Richard Grey is still looking for his monument. Even though we didn't get together on his terms, everything worked out for the best, because my plan continues to unfold, and along with his search for a suitable outer monument, Richard Grey has become an eager student of the Science of Mind, and is learning something of what Jesus meant when He gave the great requirement for eternal life to the rich young man: "If thou wilt be perfect, go and sell that thou hast, and give to the poor, and thou shalt have treasure in heaven: and come and follow me" (Matt. 19:21).

This passage has been troublesome to many people simply because they have missed the underlying meaning: *that you are impoverished when you think that the meaning and purpose of life is to be found only in outer possessions.* Give up this false belief and find the true "treasure in heaven." Realize that you must "seek . . . first the kingdom of God and his righteousness; and all these things shall be added unto you" (Matt. 6:33).

In other words, put first things first. All "things" and possessions are the product of our own inner consciousness, which is the real life of man. The outer things are tools and conveniences to help us with the real business of life—self-expression. The better job we do of making our own personal "self" an expression of the One Self, the more happy, healthy and successful we will be. Possessions as an end in themselves hinder us more than they help us.

Possessions are neither good nor bad, but they can be either, depending upon how we use them. By themselves, they have no power over us, but they will usurp it if we allow it. The secret is to "seek first the kingdom." Live from this center of inner balance and understanding, give thanks for, joyously use—and share—the abundance which is ours.

DAILY THOUGHTS ABOUT POSSESSIONS
From This Chapter

1. We are impoverished when we think that the meaning and purpose of life is to be found only in outer possessions.
2. Our possessions are the product of our own inner consciousness.
3. Possessions as an end in themselves hinder us more than they help us.
4. Possessions are neither good nor bad, but they can be either, depending on how we use them.
5. The better the job we do of making our own personal "self" an expression of the One Self, the more happy, healthy, and successful we will be.
6. There is much more to life than just accumulating possessions.
7. Give thanks for the many wonderful things you have. Use them but don't let them use you.

From the Bible

1. The Lord your God hath given you this land to possess it.—*Deut. 3:18*
2. So are the ways of every one that is greedy of gain; which taketh away the life of the owners thereof.—*Prov. 1:19*
3. The upright shall have good things in possession.—*Prov. 28:10*
4. Wealth gotten by vanity shall be diminished.—*Prov. 13:11*
5. A good name is rather to be chosen than great riches, and loving favour rather than silver and gold.—*Prov. 22:1*
6. I have coveted no man's silver, or gold, or apparel.—*Acts 20:33*
7. We brought nothing into this world, and it is certain we can carry nothing out.—*I Tim. 6:7*

From Great Thinkers Past and Present

1. No possessions are good but by the good use we make of them . . .
   —*Sir William Temple*

2. Man should not consider his outward possessions as his own, but as common to all, so as to share them without hesitation when others are in need.—*Saint Thomas Aquinas*

3. In life, as in chess, one's own pawns block one's way.—*Charles Buxton*

4. Possession, why more tasteless than pursuit? Why is a wish far dearer than a crown? That wish accomplished, why the grave of bliss? Because, in the great future buried deep, beyond our plans lies all that man with ardor should pursue.—*Owen D. Young*

5. In all worldly things that a man pursues with the greatest eagerness and intention of mind, he finds not half the pleasure in the actual possession of them as he proposed to himself in the expectation.—*Robert South*

6. When shall we learn that he who multiplieth possessions, multiplieth troubles, and that the one single use of things which we call our own, is that they may be his who hath need of them?—*Thomas Hughes*

7. It is preoccupation with possession, more than anything else, that prevents men from living freely and nobly.—*William Russell*

GOLDEN BRIDGE
TO POSSESSIONS

Morning Projection

I am grateful for the many wonderful things which I possess. I joyously use the many conveniences that make life easier and more efficient. While I have many things, I know that I do not really own any of them. I am steward over them. They are mine to use and take care of. I am interested in having things only insofar as they are helpful and enjoyable. I have no pride of possession. I know that I always have whatever I need whenever I need it, so there is no need to accumulate possessions. "The Father knows what things I have need of before I ask."

I own my possessions; they do not own me. I came into this world without possessions, and I will go out with none, but in this interval between I give thanks for the privilege of using and enjoying the things of this world. During my lifetime I possess many things, but I am never possessed by them.

God indwells every one of my possessions. I use them wisely and joyously. I bless every great and good thing in this world. I accept them, I use them, I release them. And so it is.

✐

Evening Retrospection

As I dwell in the realm of pure spirit, I release all the things of the world. I am free from use and possession. I release myself from worldly responsibilities and ties. I reside in the consciousness of peace and ease.

As I go back over my day, I give thanks for all the things which have made my life easier today. I am grateful for the material possessions which I have used and enjoyed. I am thankful for all the things which are in my possession. I endeavor to be a good steward. But tonight I am not interested in laying up for myself "treasures on earth." My business tonight is to "lay up treasures in heaven." This I now do.

I praise God from whom all blessings flow. The stately mansions which my soul builds during tonight's sleep become the cause of more wonderful things than I have ever known. I am now free from the things of this world. I possess and am possessed by the things of the Inner Kingdom. I am at peace. And so it is.

14 ✍

MONEY
How To Have Financial Security

SOMEONE said, "I don't want too much money—just a little more than enough." Most of us probably feel pretty much the same way. And why not? We should have money—as much as we need to provide the good things of life. There is no virtue in being poor. You can do a lot more good when you're rich.

Of course, we have to use our money wisely, and we need to understand what money is. We'll discuss the former point a little later, but right now let's get our minds clear about the definition of money. As such, money is neither good nor bad. It just *is*. Money is to be used. It is a medium of exchange. Money represents delayed service—something you can hold in order to use for desired purposes when you want to. Money represents the potential of desired possession or experience. Money is power, of course, and so is a good mind, a solid talent, a good idea. Money is the tangible form of our ability. Money is a convenience. Think of it as such, and use it accordingly.

In order to get all the money you need, it is necessary to free yourself from all superstition about it. So let's continue to clear our minds. Are you one of those people who has thoughtlessly said, "Money is the root of all evil?" It just isn't true. What is taught in the Bible is that, "The *love* of money is the root of all evil." (I Tim. 6:10). Thus, you can expect trouble when you love money for its own sake—if you are more interested in hoarding it than in putting it to a worthwhile use. You'll never have any problem about money as long as you look at it as

100

something to be spent—to be used by turning it into something valuable. We're not interested in being misers like old Silas Marner or Uriah Heep, those poor twisted psychopaths who didn't know what to do with their money when they got it, so they just sat there enjoying the feel and smell and taste of the coins themselves. But, you and I are not like that. In fact, most of us seldom see very much actual money—just the few dollars we use for daily spending. Our current supply is indicated by our bank balance and by the numbers on the checks that flow in and out of it, and by the worth of our investments, properties and possessions. Our potential supply is indicated by the feeling of richness which we have within ourselves.

This means that your money is the product of your state of mind. How you think and feel about money determines not only how much you have, but how much value it will have for you. Actually, it isn't only what you think and feel about money; it is what you think and feel about everything in life that determines the level of your financial security. Life's riches are measured not so much by the actual amount of money you have as by the content of your consciousness—your inner feeling of well-being, peace and security.

Consider how your state of mind has a direct bearing upon the state of your finances. The understanding of this cause-and-effect relationship is your key to continuous prosperity. Jesus, who was a very practical man, gave us some priceless instruction about prosperity. He said, "Seek ye first the kingdom . . . and all these things shall be added unto you" (Matt. 6:33). Of course, He was talking about the kingdom within you—the kingdom of your own mind.

Are you rich inside? Are you free from worry, fear, inferiority, greed, selfishness and anxiety? You'd better be, because those states of mind will make a pauper out of anybody, no matter how hard he may work to make money. Money isn't produced by hard work; it is produced out of our inner states of thought and feeling—our consciousness. Of course, hard work may be necessary as a follow-up to our ideas, plans and ambitions, but hard work by itself won't produce money. The world is full of people who are breaking their backs digging ditches or lifting, pulling and pushing at something or another who don't have a dime—and won't, until they learn the truth about money: *Money does not come from outside; it comes from inside.*

Redirect your thinking about money and the result will be a

consciousness of prosperity. Know that you can be what you want to be, do what you want to do, have what you want to have, and go where you want to go—*If* you do within yourself what is necessary to make these things possible. Build affirmative and constructive states of mind which give you a sense of inner security and make it possible for you to enjoy continuous prosperity. Learn how to increase your income. Become firmly convinced that from the kingdom within you comes a steady flow of thoughts, feelings and ideas which produce all the money you need now, or will ever need. This makes you richer than you have ever been before.

As you continue, and then repeat this lesson, you will turn into a regular mint, coining all of the money you can ever use. And what is more, you will know how to use your money wisely. You will spend it for worthwhile things. You will support worthy causes. You will share with those who can benefit from your sharing. You will be a good steward. You will be a good and faithful servant. You will be rich. You will feel right about money. You will have a sense of unlimited abundance. You will love all of the good that you can do with your money. Therefore, you will always have all the money you need.

You are now filled with the prosperity idea. Now let's go to work to strengthen this idea of inner prosperity, so that you can turn your inner feelings of prosperity into tangible, spendable money.

There are two basic things for you to do:

(1) Think prosperity.

(2) Build your feeling of prosperity.

As you develop positive attitudes in thought and feeling, you will climb the ladder of success and prosperity. There is no limit to the extent of your achievement, if you apply these principles faithfully. Remember, wealth comes from your state of mind—from nothing else. There is a Creative Power within you which drives toward your goals. Go to work on it, by disciplining your thought and feeling about prosperity.

Think prosperity. Eliminate all limiting thoughts from your mind now and forever. Say to yourself: "I am a prosperous person. I know that I can do anything I believe I can. I recognize no lack. I see only abundance. I see good everywhere. My thoughts are constantly on expansion and growth. I choose continuous financial security, and my mind is constantly upon peace, power, prosperity and plenty."

Remember, "Act as though you were and you will be." Think of yourself as a prosperous person and act accordingly.

Relate yourself to the rich things around you, so that your mind becomes accustomed to things of good quality and value.

Get used to good things. Wear clothes of quality material. It is better to buy one fine suit than three or four cheap ones. Spend intelligently, but never stint on yourself. Nothing is too good for you, remember that. Think well of yourself. You are a wonderful person. The riches of the kingdom are yours. All you have to do is lay claim to them, and this process starts within your mind. You have unlimited potential. Nothing can block you. Nothing can hold you back. Think seriously about this point and you will conclude that it is true. *You* are the master of your fate, the captain of your soul. *You* determine the level of your own prosperity and achievement. *You* create your own circumstances. It is you who provide your own riches from the unlimited account in the infinite bank of universal supply. As Jesus said, "All things that the father hath are mine . . ." (John 16:15). "It is your Father's good pleasure to give you the kingdom" (Luke 12:32). The message is clear. Think about those promises. Let your mind grasp them. They are true. *Think prosperity!*

Build your feeling of prosperity. Feeling is the secret. It is possible to *feel* rich without having a dime in your pocket. Of course it's easier when your wallet is full of nice crisp bills, but the money you have is the effect of your feeling—your conviction of prosperity—rather than the cause of it. The feeling must come first. If you actually feel rich, if you have a deep inner conviction that you will always have all that you need, it will be so.

Build your consciousness of financial security by working on your inner feelings. First of all, get rid of any negative feelings that may be blocking you. Fear, anxiety, concern, worry and tension must go. You may ask, "I know that, but how can I get rid of my worry and anxiety when they are caused by my financial problems?" Here's the answer: You can—if you want to, and if you will apply yourself. Dissolve your poor inner thoughts and feelings, and plant some constructive and creative ones. If you feel prosperous and secure inside, there is nothing that can keep you from becoming so. Remember, your thoughts and feelings come first. Results always follow. What you are depends pretty much upon how you feel.

How do you feel right now? This is where *you* must start. Our job is to get you to feel the way you want to feel—prosperous and secure. Even though the wolf may be knocking at your door, you must look him right in the teeth and convince yourself that within you is the controlling power to produce whatever you need and want in life. There is nothing that can keep it from you. You, alone, are responsible for the amount of good that flows into your experience. It is how you feel inside that determines what you experience outside.

Feel prosperous. The clarity of your thought and the intensity of your feeling of prosperity will produce unlimited abundance in your life. The Creative Power within you produces the flow of money in your life according to the level of your consciousness.

DAILY THOUGHTS ABOUT MONEY

From This Chapter

1. Money is the outer appearance of our inner sense of peace, prosperity and abundance.
2. God is the source of all things, including money.
3. We should have as much money as we need to provide the good things of life.
4. Money represents the potential of desired possession or experience.
5. Money is to be spent—to be turned into something valuable or worthwhile.
6. Love the good that you can do with your money, and you will always have all you need.
7. Money does not come from outside; it comes from inside.

From the Bible

1. Come, buy wine and milk without money and without price.—*Isa. 55:1*
2. Wherefore do ye spend money for that which is not bread?—*Isa. 55:2*
3. Silver and gold have I none; but such as I have give I thee.—*Acts 3:6*
4. The love of money is the root of all evil.—*I Tim. 6:10*
5. Where your treasure is, there will your heart be also.—*Matt. 6:21*
6. Lay not up for yourselves treasures upon earth . . . But lay up for yourselves treasures in heaven.—*Matt. 6:19, 20*
7. Ye cannot serve God and mammon.—*Matt. 6:24*

From Great Thinkers Past and Present

1. Put not your trust in money, but put your money in trust.—*Oliver Wendell Holmes*
2. It's good to have money and the things that money can buy, but it's good too, to check up once in a while and make sure that you haven't lost the things that money can't buy.—*George Horace Lorimer*
3. Money is a good servant, but a poor master.—*Dominique Bouhours*
4. A wise man should have money in his head, not in his heart.—*Jonathan Swift*
5. Money is the life blood of the nation.—*Jonathan Swift*
6. Money has little value to its possessor unless it also has value to others.—*Leland Stanford*
7. The use of money is all the advantage there is in having it.—*Benjamin Franklin*

GOLDEN BRIDGE
TO PROSPERITY

Morning Projection

The riches of the kingdom are mine today. Freely I give, freely I receive. I experience an abundance of all good things. The Infinite Law of Abundance flows through me. I am the channel of love and blessing through which all good things are expressed. God is the Source of my supply. I have an inner consciousness of peace and plenty. Good flows into my experience because I am good. I keep it that way.

I am a good steward. I have full use of all the riches of the universe. I am truly blessed. I give thanks for the never-ending supply that flows into my life from the One Source. I give thanks for my inner feelings of peace and prosperity. I give thanks for the outer abundance in my world.

I have all the money I need. I use my money wisely and well. I receive it gratefully, I increase it, I bless it, and I pass it along. I earn prodigiously, I spend wisely, I give freely and abundantly. I am in the main stream of life. I know that God is the source of my supply. And so it is.

Evening Retrospection

I place my entire store of worldly goods in God's hands tonight. I release them all into the Infinite. I refill from the foundation of abundance and plenty.

I give thanks for the riches which have flowed through my experience today. I am grateful for the money I have earned, and for the money which I have spent. I bless every cent that I have had the privilege of putting into circulation throughout my life. This tremendous stream of riches is flowing on its way, gaining in size and momentum, and doing good for everyone. Every cent I spend is releasing God into action in my world.

Tonight I tithe my time and my attention as I center my attention on the inner issues of life. I am aligned with the forces of eternity. I am enriched by my contact with Spirit. I am filled with abundant action of the Creative Law. I am God-filled. The riches of the kingdom are mine. I am filled to overflowing. And so it is.

15 🖋

PLAY
Life Is a Ball

KENNETH WALKER had worked hard for his success. He was the very image of the "self-made man." A poor farm boy, he rose above his background and environment by sheer tenacity of will. He didn't know exactly where he was going; he didn't really care as long as he could escape the drudgery and poverty of farm life.

Education was his first goal. He wasn't particularly bright, but he stuck to it and worked hard, often studying by a coal-oil lamp late into the night. Farm chores occupied the early morning hours, and evenings after school, so there was little time for play or sports. Saturdays and school vacations were occupied with farm work. There was very little fun in Kenneth's life. "All work and no play makes Jack a dull boy," fitted him perfectly.

He plodded along through the years, dogged and persistent, with a seemingly unlimited capacity for hard work. He worked his way through college. Then he started at the bottom and worked—literally—his way up to the presidency of his company. It took years of grueling overtime toil, but Kenneth kept stoically on the job.

He passed up the company picnics, office parties and even the coffee-break bull sessions, just as he had skipped the dances and football games in college, just as he had missed the games and pranks of boyhood.

"You never do anything but work!" his care-worn wife exclaimed despairingly. "Can't we do something together as a family? The children and I never see you. We need you, Kenneth. Let's try to have some fun together."

Kenneth tried, but after a few futile attempts at family fun, he slipped back into his old habit of continuous work. His children grew up without knowing him, and his wife and he remained virtual strangers, except for being parents of a family.

"We'll have some fun one of these days," Kenneth Walker used to say to placate his wife. "Just a few more years and we'll retire. Then we'll have a lot of time to play." He actually believed this. But, as the years sped on, he came to dread the specter of retirement and unlimited leisure time. To blot out the thought of it, he worked harder than ever, even though he had long since reached the top and was his own boss.

He need not have worried. Kenneth Walker dropped dead at his desk of a heart attack two months before he was to have retired. His epitaph could well have read: "He worked hard all his life. He never learned how to play."

A modern tragedy? Of course. One of many.

Rod Bellamy was another. They used to say laughingly, "Why Rod is just like any other average American boy with a million dollars in his own name." Rod was born with the proverbial silver spoon in his mouth. There was no drudgery in this young man's life as he grew up. There was no need to work and no incentive to study, so his youth became a constant round of pleasure and diversion. Rod was brought up in the tradition of the wealthy leisure class. He excelled in all the games, sports and diversions available to those with unlimited leisure time. He was a star athlete in prep school and college, a dashing figure on the dance floor, at the fraternity parties and behind the wheel of his sports car. He knew all about wine, women and song. He was living it up. He knew how to have "fun."

Following his graduation from college in June, 1929, Rod went to "work" for the Wall Street brokerage firm which handled his family's investments. Although his duties were nebulous, the job gave him a base of operations and didn't interfere with his playboy activities.

"Sure I get around and go to a lot of parties," he rationalized. "Why not? I meet a lot of people that way. It's good for business."

And so it was, until that particular business came to an abrupt halt in the stock market crash in the autumn of 1929. Rod lost his personal fortune, and most of the family fortune as well.

Forced to work now in earnest in order to earn a living, Rod Bellamy drifted in and out of many jobs—and barrooms—during the next few years. He worked hard when he worked, and he continued to play hard. Alcohol was his constant companion.

"What's wrong with a few drinks once in a while?" he asked his third wife. "What's wrong with having a little fun?"

Rod knew how to have fun all right; he knew how to play. Work had become a necessary evil, but he never lost his ability to have a good time, even though he occasionally had to work at it pretty strenuously.

World War II provided a welcome diversion. He enlisted immediately, obtaining a commission through the influence of old friends in high places. Assigned to detached service as a special liaison officer dealing with VIP's, Rod was in charge of entertaining them. Who could do it better? Everyone had a good time, including Rod.

He tried a variety of jobs after the war, but they were all boring after the excitement of the "Big Show." It was a little harder to have a good time now, but alcohol always helped. At one point he did settle down and started to enjoy success in a small business he started, but the old habits were too strong. He just neglected it too much. When he finally went bankrupt and his fourth wife left him, he let nothing interfere with his drinking. Rod Bellamy died in an alcoholic sanitarium in his early fifties. His epitaph could well have read, "He played hard all his life. He never learned how to work."

One man didn't play enough—the other played too much. Both missed the boat. It is obvious that the proper balance lies somewhere between these two extremes. Play, amusement, fun, constructive use of leisure time—all are essential to human health and balance. It may be necessary for us to earn our living by the sweat of our brow, but it is equally necessary that we learn to enjoy life if that living is to mean anything. Man cannot live without joy and fun, and he can't have fun unless he learns how to play. The brighter side of life may be even more important than the serious side.

The idea of "diversion" is inherent in the concept of "play." It is essential that we learn how to turn our attention to matters that have no real importance or significance except that we want to do them and have fun doing them. The scope of such activities is limitless, ranging from mountain climbing and big-game hunting to crocheting and

Scrabble. "Play" is anything you do for fun. It may actually be more intensive and strenuous than your daily work, but if it is fun for you, then you are playing. The only thing that is actually ruled out is your daily occupation of work, because one of the essentials of play is "abstinence or freedom from work."

You may say, "But I get more fun out of my work than anything else!" Fine! You should. Have fun working, but have fun doing other things, too. When our attention is held steady upon one thing for too long, a lag develops, and we go stale. This is part of the Law of Reversed Effort, which says simply that if we try too hard the power works against us instead of for us. Play is a form of release which relieves tension and channels creative energy so it works constructively. Play is a means of refilling. In play, we utilize aspects of ourselves that are neglected in everyday activities.

Play, to be worth anything, must be a joyous expression of life. The arts, hobbies of all kinds, sports of all varieties—both spectator and participating—travel, and the pursuit of the simple pleasures which nature offers—all offer a great field of play. Choose your form of play and have fun doing it. Play is an important part of life.

An old proverb says, "God does not subtract from men's lives the time spent fishing." This might well be given a modern paraphrase: "God *adds* to men's lives the time spent in constructive play."

DAILY THOUGHTS ABOUT PLAY
From This Chapter

1. Play is an important part of life—essential to human health and balance.
2. It is essential to strike a constructive balance between too much play and not enough.
3. Man cannot live without joy and fun, and he can't have fun unless he learns how to play.
4. Learn to turn your attention to matters that have no real importance or significance except that you want to do them and have fun doing them.
5. Play is anything you do for fun.
6. Play is a form of release which relieves tension.
7. Play, to be worth anything, must be a joyous expression of life.

From the Bible

1. At Thy right hand there are pleasures for evermore.—*Psalm 16:11*
2. Surely goodness and mercy shall follow me all the days of my life. —*Psalm 23:6*
3. Her ways are ways of pleasantness, and all her paths are peace.— *Prov. 3:17*
4. There is nothing better for a man, than that he should eat and drink, and that he should make his soul enjoy good in his labour.—*Eccles. 2:24*
5. Go thy way, eat thy bread with joy, and drink thy wine with a merry heart; for God now accepteth thy works.—*Eccles. 9:7*
6. Therefore did my heart rejoice, and my tongue was glad.—*Acts 2:26*
7. The fruit of the Spirit is . . . joy.—*Gal. 5:22*

From Great Thinkers Past and Present

1. Pleasure must first have the warrant that it is without sin; then the measure, that it is without excess.—*Henry Gardiner Adams*
2. Enjoy present pleasures in such a way as not to injure future ones. —*Seneca*
3. A man that knows how to mix pleasures with business, is never entirely possessed by them; he either quits or resumes them at his will; and in the use he makes of them he rather finds a relaxation of mind than a dangerous charm that might corrupt him.—*Charles de Saint-Evremond*
4. Choose such pleasures as recreate much and cost little.—*Richard Fuller*
5. The sweetest pleasures are those which do not exhaust hope. *Peter Gaston de Levis*
6. I look upon it as an equal injustice to loathe natural pleasures as to be too much in love with them.—*Montaigne*
7. Though a taste of pleasure may quicken the relish of life, an unrestrained indulgence leads to inevitable destruction.—*Robert Dodsley*

GOLDEN BRIDGE TO PLAY

Morning Projection

I awaken with joy and go forward into this day to have fun. I expect to have a good time in everything I do. I have a grand time living. Life is a joyous game and I play it to the hilt. I work well and I play well. Both are important to my health and balance. I have fun working and I have fun playing. I do not neglect one for the other. I wisely utilize the Creative Energy within me in constructive work. I refill and renew with constructive play.

I laugh, I sing, I exultantly proclaim the joy of living. I express my happiness in all that I do. My spirit is renewed as I learn to appreciate the lighter side of things. I know how to let go and let God. I find fun in simple pleasure. I utilize the wonders and beauties of Nature in my play. The muses of inspiration and beauty motivate me to play artistically and creatively. I abstain from drudgery and heaviness. I am free. I am constructively amused and diverted. I know how to play. I have fun all day long. And so it is.

Evening Retrospection

As I reflectively enter the quiet of my own inner consciousness, I give thanks for the joy of this day. The laughing, dancing beauty of life is reflected into my entire being. I have had fun today. I have done all things in the proper time and in the proper way. The spirit of refreshing enjoyment has blessed everything I have done. I have balanced work with play. I am constantly refilled from the inner Source.

As I prepare for sleep, I am ready for rest, but I am not tired. I release the work and the play of the world. I invite my soul and follow it into the green pastures of the Spirit. As I embark upon the joyous adventure of this night, I am free and easy in heart and mind. I eagerly anticipate my nighttime travels into the realm of the Infinite.

I am grateful for the spirit and action of play which have blessed my day. I am now receptive to the cosmic play of Spirit as it circulates through me, re-creating me and making me whole. And so it is.

16 ✍

RESPONSIBILITY
"To Thine Own Self Be True..."

ABRAHAM LINCOLN once said, "As I would not be a slave, so I would not be a master; this expresses my idea of democracy." We all know how he stood out against all opposition and worked unceasingly, during his term as President of the United States, to make this ideal a reality for all people. He felt it was his responsibility to do this. Responsibility, of course, must first start within the individual. The man who feels inferior is likely to behave as a petty tyrant, lording it over the weak and subordinate. He presses the advantage at every opportunity. We are all familiar with these minor-league Napoleons. They are more to be pitied than feared—and actually, they need our help.

It is by correcting our misconception of personal favor and prestige that we can be of greatest help to our neighbors. Only then, can we best help the unbalanced individuals who seek to dominate others. Arrogance is always unpleasant and annoying in human relationships. But it has explosive elements when it is the weapon of those in high positions of power. The glory-seeking egotist and the power-mad politician never last, but they can play havoc in the lives of everyone.

We are familiar with those who have abused positions of trust in our own country, and some misguided representatives of the people who are still in that category today. The memories of a Hitler and a Mussolini are not quickly erased from the minds of men. Unfortunately, our world is not yet free from the threat of others who covet the same measure of controlling power.

113

Responsibility is first a matter of our own personal development, and second, a factor in our attitudes toward and relationships with other people. We must develop a way of life based upon integrity, in which the rights of the individual are recognized and protected. At the same time, we share our freedom with others for the good of all. The person who knows himself truly to be free will not try to put others in bondage. The free, well-integrated, inwardly confident individual will inevitably be a leader and therefore will have the power of molding the destinies of other men. But he will exercise his leadership in the spirit of true democracy, knowing and adhering to the principle that what is good for one is good for all.

We can all share in this principle whether we are leaders or not, by not permitting encroachments on our individual rights. Spiritual democracy decrees that all men are equal in the sight of the Creative Power, and that we all have equal potential, even though some are more highly developed in certain respects than others. Such development accents the Law of Growth in operation. It provides no basis for the assertion of superiority on the part of individuals.

This elimination of the slave-master category is really the restatement of the Golden Rule, the foundation stone of fair play. This, in turn, is the basis of American democracy, which has moved from ideal to reality. We keep the principle alive and growing when we say with Lincoln, "As I would not be a slave, so I would not be a master; this expresses my idea of democracy." Living by these principles is a matter of personal responsibility.

What are the limits of personal responsibility? Jesus tells the story of a "certain man" who recognized none:

> And Jesus answering said, A certain man went down from Jerusalem to Jericho, and fell among thieves, which stripped him of his raiment, and wounded him, and departed, leaving him half dead.
>
> And by chance there came down a certain priest that way: and when he saw him, he passed by on the other side.
>
> And likewise a Levite, when he was at the place came and looked on him, and passed by on the other side.
>
> But a certain Samaritan, as he journeyed, came where he was: and when he saw him, he had compassion on him.
>
> And went to him, and bound up his wounds, pouring in oil and wine,

and set him on his own beast, and brought him to an inn, and took care of him.

And on the morrow when he departed, he took out two pence, and gave them to the host, and said unto him, Take care of him; and whatsoever thou spendest more, when I come again, I will repay thee.

Which now of these three, thinkest thou, was neighbour unto him that fell among the thieves?

And he said, He that shewed mercy on him. Then said Jesus unto him. Go, and do thou likewise.

—Luke 10:30–37

The "good Samaritan" was a "good neighbor," feeling that it was his responsibility to live by the Golden Rule, "Whatsoever ye would that men should do to you, do ye even so to them" (Matt. 7:12). This is the world's clearest definition of our responsibility to others. We cannot really live without assuming it. We can be responsible to others only insofar as we have a basis of inner integrity and responsibility to ourselves: Shakespeare gives us the standard for personal responsibility:

> "This above all: to thine own self be true
> And it must follow, as the night the day,
> Thou canst not then be false to any man."

—Hamlet I, iii

Rotary International, the great service club with more than half a million members in over eleven thousand Rotary clubs, uses a "Four-Way Test,"[1] by one of its ex-presidents, Herbert J. Taylor, as a guide to responsibility in making personal and business decisions. These famous "24 words" ask four basic questions:

1. Is it the *truth?*
2. Is it *fair* to all concerned?
3. Will it build *goodwill* and *better friendships?*
4. Will it be *beneficial* to all concerned?

These four check-points cannot help but make us more responsible in making decisions.

[1] Copyright 1946, Rotary International. Used by permission.

FIVE BASIC QUALITIES OF RESPONSIBILITY

1. *Honesty* comes first. Honesty is the keystone which holds everything else together. Without it, nothing good can be accomplished. With honesty and sincerity we have the basis for sustained effort and responsibility.

2. *Integrity*. We must each establish an inner basis of integrity, from which we will not deviate. Integrity is the essence both of character and individual responsibility. It is unqualified goodness, strength and love. Our integrity embodies those principles which are important to us. Integrity is the structure of the soul.

3. *Dependability* is the heart of responsibility. To be at the place agreed upon, at the time agreed, ready, willing and able to deliver the goods—this is dependability. Perhaps more than anything else the world needs people who are dependable. Dependability is the mark of a mature, responsible individual.

4. *Consistency* is the quality of steady, sustained, behavior. Except for necessary adjustments and adaptations, the consistent person maintains his highest possible level of character and performance. Even in the face of discouragement, he sticks to the task at hand until he succeeds. You can depend upon a consistent person because he is responsible.

5. *Stability*. The stable person is one who *acts* from his inner center of honesty, integrity, dependability, and consistency instead of reacting to the vicissitudes and confusions around him. The stable person is not easily upset. His mind is in control of his emotions. He knows what he is doing and why. He is responsible.

DAILY THOUGHTS ABOUT RESPONSIBILITY
From This Chapter

1. Responsibility is first a matter of personal development, and second, a factor in our attitudes toward and relationships with other people.
2. There are no limits to personal responsibility.
3. The Golden Rule gives the clearest definition of our responsibility to others.
4. We can be responsible to others only insofar as we have a basis of inner integrity and responsibility to ourselves.

5. Resolve, strength, courage and persistence are parts of responsibility.
6. Personal responsibility depends upon the development of the qualities of honesty, integrity, dependability, consistency, and stability.
7. Be true to yourself and you can't be false to others.

From the Bible

1. Thou shalt do that which is right and good in the sight of the Lord: that it may be well with thee.—*Deut. 6:18*
2. Withhold not good from them to whom it is due.—*Prov. 3:27*
3. Take fast hold of instruction; let her not go: keep her; for she is thy life.—*Prov. 4:13*
4. Let us hear the conclusion of the whole matter: Fear God, and keep his commandments: for this is the whole duty of man.—*Eccles. 12:13*
5. We have done that which was our duty to do.—*Luke 17:10*
6. Render therefore to all their dues: tribute to whom tribute is due; custom to whom custom; fear to whom fear; honour to whom honour. —*Rom. 13:7*
7. So then every one of us shall give account of himself to God.—*Rom. 14:12*

From Great Thinkers Past and Present

1. The most important thought I ever had was that of my individual responsibility to God.—*Daniel Webster*
2. No matter how lofty you are in your department, the responsibility for what your lowliest assistant is doing is yours.—*Bessie R. James and Mary Waterstreet* ("Adlai's Almanac")
3. Responsibility educates.—*Wendell Phillips*
4. Every human being has a work to carry on within, duties to perform abroad, influences to exert, which are peculiarly his, and which no conscience but his own can teach.—*William Ellery Channing*
5. Much misconstruction and bitterness are spared to him who thinks naturally upon what he owes to others rather than what he ought to expect from them.—*Madame Guizot*
6. Responsibility walks hand in hand with capacity and power.—*Josiah Gilbert Holland*
7. Responsibility is measured, not by the amount of injury resulting from wrong action, but by the distinctness with which conscience has the opportunity of distinguishing between the right and the wrong.—*Frederick W. Robertson*

GOLDEN BRIDGE
TO RESPONSIBILITY

Morning Projection

I have a definite responsibility to make the most of myself in every way. I am responsible for the great gifts which have been intrusted to me. I am responsible to God in whom I live and move and have my being. It is my responsibility to let my light so shine that men may see my good works and glorify my Father in heaven. I fulfill my responsibility to my Creator when I live life fully and abundantly, and when I love my neighbor as myself.

It is my responsibility to express my highest and best at all times. It is my responsibility to live so that every moment of my life can be taken as an example for all people to follow. It is my responsibility to be perfect even as my Father in heaven is perfect. There are no limits to my personal responsibility.

As I go forward into this day, I am aware of my responsibility to God, to Life, to myself and my world, and to other people. I have strength, courage and persistence as I go about my daily tasks. I have deep inner integrity. I am honest, dependable, consistent and stable. I am true to myself. This is my responsibility. And so it is.

Evening Retrospection

As I unwind from this day's activities, I review each moment to cleanse it and set it right before it is entered in the record books of eternal time. This day is my responsibility. It was my privilege to use it in whatever way I chose. It is my responsibility to correct it in whatever way I can.

It is my responsibility to forgive myself and others—so I forgive. It is my responsibility to live by the Law of Love—so I love. It is my responsibility to keep my heart with diligence—so I am alert. It is my responsibility to keep my heart untroubled and unafraid—so I have enduring faith. It is my responsibility to praise God from whom all blessings flow—so I worship the Lord. It is my responsibility to listen to the still small voice—so I am aware. It is my responsibility to know that I and my Father are one—so I pray. It is my responsibility to refill my vessel from the bottomless well of the Infinite Source—so I sleep. It is my responsibility to take instruction from the Masters of Wisdom—so I listen and dream. It is my responsibility to be one with God—and so I am. And so it is.

17 ✍

EDUCATION

Toward Becoming a Whole Person

"How early should I begin to educate my child?" a mother asked a famous educator.

"When will your child be born?" he inquired.

"He's already five years old," the mother answered.

"Well, don't waste any more time," the educator admonished. "Start now! You've already wasted the five best years!"

Education is the business of a lifetime. It is impossible to start too soon or continue too late. Education is life itself, a life process whereby we grow into an awareness and expression of our true self. An educated person is a "whole person."

In everything, there is more than meets the eye, things are not always what they seem to be, and we are more than we believe we are. A vast continent of undiscovered cause lies behind every effect. In the complexity of human nature, the undiscovered area is the greater portion. We must explore and develop the unknown if we are to realize our true potential—if we are to be educated. •

"This is what the Indian knows," scoffed the white man, as he drew a small circle on the ground. "And this is what the white man knows," he boasted, as he circumscribed the small circle with a much larger one.

Stolidly the Indian contemplated the two circles for a few minutes. "This is what the Indian knows," he said, pointing to the small circle, "and this is what the white man knows," indicating the larger circle. "And here"—he walked in a great circle around the other two with his arm outstretched toward the horizon—"here is where the Indian and the white man know nothing."

And so it must ever be. There are always new frontiers of knowledge. We must be careful not to draw our circles too tight. In our forward march toward wholeness, we must continue to learn and grow. The creative process is endless. There is no limit to what we can and will become. "Beloved, now are we the sons of God; and it doth not yet appear what we shall be" (I John 3:2).

"Who made you, sonny?" the minister inquired of the small boy. "I don't know, sir," he replied. "I ain't finished yet."

We make ourselves. "As a man thinketh in his heart, so is he," says one of the Proverbs. "Man is the sum total of all his experiences," is the teaching of our psychology. "You are what you eat," says the dietitian. "Act as though you are, and you will be," directs the behaviorist.

Thought, feeling, study, worship, action, nourishment, conditioning, and imagination all contribute to the whole picture. Every facet of our being and our experience is important. We can effectively relate ourselves to the whole only insofar as we recognize ourselves as a whole being, the total of which is greater than the sum of all its parts.

Man's spiritual nature is the plus factor which accounts for what seems a mathematical inconsistency. But Spirit manifests itself in a variety of ways. Spiritual knowing is the basis of effective living and it consists in bringing every phase of our thought, action, and experience into focus with the indwelling perfection.

We are spiritual beings, using mind, inhabiting a body, and living in the world. We can be whole only when we live in a manner that maintains perfect balance on each level of life experience. These levels are inextricably interrelated. All things flow from Spirit, therefore, all things are spiritual. It is not God and man; it is God *as* man. Our bodies, our environment, and our minds must all be taken care of if we are to experience wholeness (health).

We all recognize the importance of regular treatment or prayer, but we must also recognize that God can work for us only by working through us. Prayer itself is not enough. We must follow through. In prayer we establish and strengthen the concepts of perfection, wholeness, health, balance, and right action. But prayer can never be answered unless we assist its unfolding in every way possible. We are sometimes puzzled by our failure to demonstrate a desired good. People often lose faith in treatment when they don't get immediate results. This comes from a failure to see the whole picture, and a failure to do on every level what needs to be done to assist the prayer.

We must keep our minds open to scientific, social, and other changes around us. Remember, all things are part of the whole. Everything we say, think, feel, and do is part of our prayer. Let us not limit ourselves in concept. God is all-in-all, and He works through all things. An educated person realizes that we all need each other, and that every field of endeavor is necessary to complete the whole picture.

Devotion is no substitute for study. Mouthings about love are meaningless unless we love our fellow human beings. A treatment for purity doesn't mean much unless we also use soap when we bathe. A spoken affirmation is ridiculous unless we put it into practice. Meditation means nothing unless it is followed by action. A treatment is nonsense unless we apply ourselves to doing whatever is necessary to help it work. Illness, problems and troubles will never be healed unless we apply our whole being to eliminating the causes which brought them about.

If we are to achieve the goal of being a whole person, we must mature. Education is "the process of growing up"—of effectively expressing the "whole person." "Wisdom is the principal thing: therefore get wisdom: and with all thy getting get understanding" (Prov. 4:7).

When we are really educated we will be wise, because we will have learned to:

1. Understand ourselves.
2. Understand others.
3. Understand our world.
4. Understand life.
5. Understand God.

Education is the journey toward understanding.

Knowledge, wisdom and understanding are progressive steps in education. They come through the following channels:

1. Study and Investigation.
2. Observation and Thought.
3. Experience and Action.

4. Inspiration and Intuition.
5. Acceptance and Participation.

An educated person is one who:

1. Strives to become a whole person.
2. Identifies himself with others.
3. Disciplines his mind.
4. Can do anything within reason.
5. Knows who he is.
6. Knows where he is going.
7. Has an appreciation of the past.
8. Has a working knowledge of today's world.
9. Respects the rights of other people.
10. Supports worthy causes.
11. Assumes responsibility.
12. Is public-spirited.
13. Is loving, kind and compassionate.
14. Knows the meaning of friendship.
15. Is honest and trustworthy.
16. Is motivated by idealism.
17. Is dedicated to noble purpose.
18. Gives of himself freely and intelligently in service for the good of others.
19. Finds happiness.
20. Maintains health.
21. Is strong and courageous.
22. Is refined and cultured.
23. Is prepared and trained to make a living.
24. Has a basis and practice of true appreciation.
25. Understands and uses his imagination.
26. Has vision and insight.
27. Establishes and maintains perspective.
28. Has sound judgment and discrimination.
29. Exercises a solid sense of values.
30. Thinks clearly.
31. Has balanced emotions.
32. Has joy in living.
33. Lives by the law of love.
34. Has a strong faith.
35. Has confidence in himself.

36. Has an appreciation of art, literature and music.
37. Studies Nature.
38. Strives toward perfection.
39. Continues to grow.
40. Loves and worships God.

DAILY THOUGHTS ABOUT EDUCATION
From This Chapter

1. Education is the business of a lifetime.
2. Education is the process whereby we grow into an awareness and expression of our true self.
3. An educated person is a "whole person."
4. Education is the journey toward understanding.
5. An educated person knows who he is and where he is going.
6. An educated person has vision and insight.
7. Education is life itself.

From the Bible

1. Thou shalt teach them diligently unto they children.—*Deut. 6:7*
2. Train up a child in the way he should go: and when he is old, he will not depart from it.—*Prov. 22:6*
3. Go ye therefore, and teach all nations.—*Matt. 28:19*
4. Jesus increased in wisdom and stature, and in favor with God and man.—*Luke 2:52*
5. Wisdom is the principal thing; therefore get wisdom.—*Prov. 4:7*
6. Whoso loveth instruction loveth knowledge.—*Prov. 12:1*
7. Study to be quiet, and to do your own business, and to work with your own hands.—*I Thess. 4:11*

From Great Thinkers Past and Present

1. The first thing education teaches you is to walk alone.—*Trader Horn*
2. There are obviously two educations. One should teach us how to make a living and the other how to live.—*James Truslow Adams*
3. The aim of education should be to teach us rather how to think, than what to think—rather to improve our minds, so as to enable us to think for ourselves, than to load the memory with the thoughts of other men.—*James Beattie*

4. Education does not mean teaching people to know what they do not know; it means teaching them to behave as they do not behave.— *John Ruskin*

5. Character development is the great, if not the sole, aim of education.— *William James*

6. A man cannot leave a better legacy to the world than a well-educated family.—*Thomas Scott*

7. States should spend money and effort on this great all-underlying matter of spiritual education as they have hitherto spent them on beating and destroying each other.—*John Galsworthy*

GOLDEN BRIDGE TO EDUCATION

Morning Projection

Knowledge, wisdom and understanding go before me preparing the way for this day of noble endeavor. I go about my Father's business today—the business of learning and growing. Each day I know more and more. Each day I become more and more. There is no limit to what there is to be known. There is no limit to what I can become. Knowing these things is a step in my education.

I study and observe until I know. Then I put what I know into action. I know who I am and where I am going. I know what I am doing at all times. I am an educated person. Purposeful right action is established in my life. I leave nothing to chance. I know, I understand, then I do.

I see the larger scope of things. I have vision and insight. I draw upon Divine inspiration. I use my intuition. Direct knowing expands the boundaries of my education. I am one with the Source of all knowledge. I open my mind to the influx of new ideas. I participate in the magnificence of life. I give thanks for the scope and completeness of my education. And so it is.

Evening Retrospection

As I review this day of creative action, I take stock of what I know and what I do not know. I affirm those qualities which make me an educated person:

I am a whole person—body, mind and spirit.

My mind is disciplined.

I understand myself and others.

I know who I am and where I am going.

I appreciate the past, I bless the present, and I look forward to the future.

I make my way in this world with ease, order and efficiency.

I am inspired and enlightened from above.

I eagerly accept responsibility and joyously work in service to God and man.

I am loving, kind and compassionate.

I am motivated by unswerving idealism.

I am dedicated to noble purpose.

I maintain myself in vital health.
I live happily and joyously.
I appreciate the finer things of life.
I contemplate the facts of life from the highest point of view.
I see all things in their proper perspective.
I think clearly and feel deeply.
Love is the law of my life.
Faith is the structure of my life.
Nature is my teacher.
Life is my expression.
Growth is my action and dedication.
In God I live and move and have my being.

And so it is.

18 🖋

PROBLEMS

A New Way to Solve Old Problems

OUR only interest in problems, illness and difficulties is getting rid of them. In this chapter we are going to learn how to do this through scientific prayer treatment.

Treatment is a very practical way to meet any problem. Treatment is the first step in meeting any situation. Treatment is affirmative prayer. In treatment we turn away from the negative, violent, destructive outer appearances toward inner spiritual realization. Treatment is the process of identifying oneself with that which is whole and perfect. As we learn scientific prayer treatment, we are perfecting a new way to solve old problems.

PRAYER THERAPY

There is nothing new under the sun; the principles of therapeutic prayer are as old as man himself. The witch doctor with his dance and incantations, mantrams, and prayers opened a contact with a Higher Power. As the patient started to believe in this Power, he stopped giving power to his pain and fear, and he was transformed by the renewing of his mind.

Dr. Patrick Doyle, a well-known Canadian physician stated in *The Philosophy of Pain:* "If in treating disease, a doctor were forced to choose between the use of drugs only, or of prayer only, he would, if he were wise, choose prayer. The value of 99 per cent of drugs is

127

questionable, to say the least; but a state of true prayer in the sickroom never fails to improve the patient's condition."[1]

Now this is not meant to detract from the medical profession. Through science and medicine, man has done his best to solve human problems at the level of his understanding. But man is ever seeking new ways to solve problems, and he may not yet have investigated the most profitable areas. There is more to this business of problem-solving than meets the eye. To solve the old problems of curing diseases, getting along with people, making money, or stopping wars we must stop trying to solve the problem on the level of the problem. This obviously does not work. Remove the cause and the problem will disappear. We must be changed inside before we can be changed outside. Paul said, "Be ye transformed by the renewing of your mind" (Rom. 12:2). In scientific prayer treatment we endeavor to remove the cause of problems at the mental and emotional levels.

DISSOLVING FEAR

Fear is the one basic negative emotion. It can cause any number of unhappy outer consequences. Fear is behind many cases of so-called heart trouble and other organic and functional difficulties. As fear congeals the feeling of a person, it imbalances the functioning of his vital organs. It dumps adrenalin into his system and speeds up the bodily processes, but since they are unable to move freely, a destructive congestion develops within the person.

No one wants to be afraid. How do we probe our deep-seated fears and rid ourselves of them through scientific prayer treatment? Of what has the person been afraid? One man was afraid of parental disapproval. He was afraid of rejection and failure. This developed an inner drive that had no place to go because there wasn't anything definite in his mind but a fear, so only negative conditions could result.

As his mind was clouded with thoughts of fear and rejection, it naturally followed that over the years this was reflected into his body, and he became congested on every level. We corrected it by removing the inner cause, not with pills, medicines or drugs, but through corrective prayer.[2]

[1] See "A Doctor Discovered Prayer," by Alexander Lake, *Science of Mind* magazine, June, 1960.

[2] For further case histories and instruction on techniques of prayer treatment, see my books, *Your Thoughts Can Change Your Life* and *Human Problems and How To Solve Them* (Englewood Cliffs, N.J.: Prentice-Hall, Inc., 1961, 1962).

SCIENTIFIC PRAYER

Scientific prayer is not the old-fashioned kind of prayer where we beg, beseech, and ask. Such a prayer, usually filled with guilt, fear, and rejection, has no healing power at all. It doesn't matter what the problem or condition is. A person who implores, "Oh God, help me; do this for me!" gets nowhere. This type of prayer is filled with negativity, and only serves to reaffirm the condition.

To pray effectively, we must identify ourselves with a Power greater than ourselves. We must know that there is that within us which is whole and perfect. Do you believe it? Do you really believe that there is Something in you that is Whole, Perfect—that is All-Intelligent, that knows all things? There is.

INFINITE INTELLIGENCE

How do we know? Let's go back not so many years to the time when you were but a human embryo. You did not yet possess conscious volition. A great Law of Creativity was in action, and an Intelligence knew how to take the nourishment from your mother's bloodstream and fashion it into bone, flesh, skin and hair, a brain, organs, nerves and blood vessels. There was something there in the very first cell that was in direct contact with, and had never been separated from, the great Wholeness and Oneness that knows and does all things.

We have never been separated from it. It is always there; it is the basic reality. It is the Source of all things, and constant awareness of it is the new way—and also the oldest—to solve the problems that have always been with us. Jesus said, "Ye have the poor with you always" (Mark 14:7). . . . "In the World ye shall have tribulation: but be of good cheer. I have overcome the world" (John 16:33.) Jesus healed by knowing that that which was within him was greater than that which was in the world of conditions and symptoms.

APPEARANCES ARE MISLEADING

Do you know that you will never have a problem that you don't already know how to solve? We are never confronted with problems or situations that we are not capable of answering and meeting. We must realize that there is that within us which knows the answer to all things. More and more of us are beginning to realize this great truth. We are starting to do something about our problems just as the farmer did who for fifty years ploughed around a big rock in his field. Finally, tired of being plagued by this obstruction, he decided to take positive action. He pried it loose with no effort at all, because it was only about a foot deep. It looked much more formidable than it really was, since the farmer had been judging solely by the size of its outer appearance. He thought he couldn't move it, and he couldn't just because he hadn't tried.

But we can move—that is, remove—the blocks from consciousness if we start with Jesus' injunction, "Judge not according to the appearance, but judge righteous judgment" (John 7:24). Most of our problems are not as deep and destructive as they appear to be, if we give them the right kind of attention, if we are honest with ourselves, if we learn a few simple techniques, couple them with spiritual truths, and put them into practice every day.

PURPOSE OF LIFE

There is something we can do about our problems, if we apply ourselves intelligently to the situation at hand. The purpose of life is to find God—to find the nature of truth, goodness and beauty within ourselves. Our problems arise when we get separated from our purpose. When we lose our spiritual way, we develop psychological problems and outer symptoms. Our false beliefs and negative attitudes must be corrected sometime. Our so-called problems and symptoms are reminders that this must be done. Scientific prayer treatment is a new way, and we feel the best way to solve the oldest of man's problems— how to find himself.

DAILY THOUGHTS ABOUT SOLVING PROBLEMS
From This Chapter

1. Problems arise when we get separated from ourselves.
2. Solve problems by turning away from the negative, violent, destructive outer appearances, and turning toward inner spiritual realization.
3. We solve our problems in direct ratio to our understanding.
4. The real problem is a false belief. The outer expression is the symptom.

5. Remove the cause and the problem will disappear.
6. Do not try to solve a problem on the level of the problem. Identify yourself with the solution.
7. You will never have a problem that you don't already know how to solve.

From the Bible

1. Many are the afflictions of the righteous: but the Lord delivereth him out of them all.—*Psalm 34:19*
2. God is our refuge and strength, a very present help in trouble.—*Psalm 46:1*
3. Thou shalt not be afraid for the terror by night; nor for the arrow that flieth by day.—*Psalm 91:5*
4. Fret not.—*Psalm 37:1*
5. I will be with him in trouble; I will deliver him, and honour him.—*Psalm 91:15*
6. Let not your heart be troubled: ye believe in God, believe also in me.—*John 14:1*
7. We are troubled on every side, yet not distressed.—*II Cor. 4:8*

From Great Thinkers Past and Present

1. What is difficulty?—Only a word indicating the degree of strength requisite for accomplishing particular objects.—*Samuel Warren*
2. It cannot be too often repeated that it is not helps, but obstacles, not facilities, but difficulties that make men.—*William Mathews*
3. Difficulties strengthen the mind, as labor does the body.—*Seneca*
4. If all men were to bring their miseries together in one place, most would be glad to take each his own home again rather than take a portion out of the common stock.—*Solon*
5. Troubles are often the tools by which God fashions us for better things.—*Henry Ward Beecher*
6. Men's happiness springs mainly from moderate troubles, which afford the mind a healthful stimulus, and are followed by a reaction which produces a cheerful flow of spirits.—*Edward Wigglesworth*
7. I have had many troubles in my life, but the worst of them never came.—*James A. Garfield*

GOLDEN BRIDGE
TO SOLVING PROBLEMS

Morning Projection

I give thanks for this day and the opportunity to live and learn and grow. I give thanks for my good; I also give thanks for the situations that do not seem so good. I know that it is through solving problems that I grow. I develop mental, emotional and spiritual muscle as I triumph over the difficulties that sometimes arise to block my path. Today I recognize no obstructions. I see only opportunities. I know that each problem provides for me priceless opportunity for instruction, correction and growth. Where I am wrong, I set myself right. I am eager to improve myself. I learn from everything. My mind is ever alert to new ways of doing things. I find the way to solve all problems, heal all illnesses, and clear up all difficulties today. I think only in terms of answers and solutions.

I draw nigh unto the Source of inspiration, healing and guidance, and it draws nigh unto me. I am not alone. There is that within me which is greater and stronger than anything which can arise in the world. I go forward into this day eager, alert and strong. I am capable of handling anything and everything that comes my way. And so it is.

Evening Retrospection

Quietly now, I release the concerns of this day. I let all problems go completely. They are no part of me. They are neither person, place nor thing. They have no power. They did not happen. They are gone. My mind is free for the important business of communication with God within me. I receive guidance, inspiration and strength from this Inner Source.

Carefully and thoroughly, I retrace my steps of this day, setting everything in order. Nothing has power over me. I have power over myself. I have power to heal. I have power to learn. I have power to grow. The Inner Power is working through me right now, accomplishing all of these things.

My mind, my heart, my body, and my world are in perfect order. I am quiet, calm and peaceful. As the silence of night envelops me, I am one with the Infinite Healing Presence. I am attuned to the Inner Reality. I am immersed in total experience. I am one with God. I flow with Life. I experience all wonderful things. I express my true self. I live. I know. I love. I am. And so it is.

19 ✍

LOVE

"...Makes the World Go Round"

LOVE has been talked about many times. It is probably the most ancient of spiritual themes. As we talk about love, let's have love in our hearts. This is the only way we can have any conviction of what love is. Think of any part of God—understanding, benevolent goodness, creative power, completeness, a loving compassionate nature, a higher self, a guiding intelligence of life, inspiration. What is it that we are defining over and over again? We are defining the nature of love.

"God is love" (I John 4:8, 16). This definition clearly indicates that to know God we must first know the meaning of love. The primary lesson of life is to learn to love: to be kind, to be fair, to be just, to be compassionate, to be sympathetic, in every kind of situation, no matter what the reasons seem to be for being otherwise. Jesus lived love. Love is the basic teaching of Christianity.

Does love really exist? Consider the following definitions:

1. Love is the desire of Life to express Itself.
2. Love is the attraction of good to good.
3. "Love is the Soul flowing through us." (Emerson)
4. "Love makes the world go 'round."
5. "Love is the fulfilling of the Law." (Rom. 13:10)
6. Love is the language of the heart.
7. Love is the means by which we identify ourselves with another person, desiring that which is best for him, in any situation whatever it may be, even though we may come off second best in that situation.

133

8. Love is dedication to purpose.
9. Love is that state of mind which will not allow anything counter to it to intrude upon human consciousness.
10. Love is abundance of personality and individuality.
11. Love is the language of the soul.
12. Love is affirmative relationship to an idea.

If we have love, we don't need anything else. By the same token, it doesn't matter what else we have; if we do not have love, it isn't enough. We may be the smartest person in the world, the best artist, the best professional man, the best speaker, the best musician; all will be of no avail unless we have love. Unless the soloist sings from a heart of love he might as well not sing. Unless the orator speaks from a heart of love, his message is empty. Unless the prayer pours freely from a love-filled heart, it does more harm than good. Unless we identify ourselves with this Supreme Good, we remain in isolation.

We must learn to love here and now. Live today—in the market place, on the street, in the home, at the place of business. Live today! Love today! Release past glories and past mistakes. Love today the power that God has given you. Love today the talent entrusted to your stewardship. Love today the people around you. Love today the ideas that come into your mind today. If we know how to love, everything else will come to us.

Those of us who have been blessed in life to understand the true reality and experience of the words, "I love you," whether we hear or say them, and have experienced the blessing of married happiness, know what it means to be truly in love with the person of whom we are a part. This experience transcends all other human experience. Yet it is but a brief and wonderful glimmer of the state of marriage which the soul within us can always find with the Master Soul within the great Creative Intelligence of Life which is God. The power of love brings us home to a state of Oneness with all of Life and all of Being.

Love is not something that comes to fruition by chance. Love is realized inside, emanates from us, and attracts to it whatever it needs for fulfillment. When we find ourselves separated from love, the answer must be to go back deep, deep within. Search your heart; examine your motives. What have you worked upon? What thoughts have you harbored? What have you constructed? What temple have you sculptured out of the marble of the stuff of life? When love is the guiding influence in your life, your life will be full and abundant.

Ask yourself these four questions:

1. Do you love yourself?
2. Do you love what you are doing?
3. Do you love your environment?
4. Do you love other people?

Do you love yourself? Most people, unfortunately, do not. They center their interest upon themselves, they selfishly defend their opinions, they fight for their private interests to the last ditch; but, do they like themselves? All too often the answer is no. If we do not have self-esteem or self-love, how can we expect others to respect and love us? What do we do about it? Naturally we do not announce, "I do not like myself," but there is something to the observation, "What you are speaks so loudly I cannot hear what you say."

Our dislike for self is reflected in unmannerly conduct toward others. Criticism, overperfectionism, unreasonable demands push other people out of the circle of friendship, and betray our inner conflict, congestion, and tension. What can we do to reinstate our self-respect? Look honestly within and determine to construct there the kind of person you would like to become. Get the image clear and you will experience it. Go within, search for and find the person you can truly love. If you can see him and experience him, that is what you are. You don't have to do anything about it on the outside. People are beautiful, healthy, successful, and well-liked because they accept themselves in these terms. Learn to love yourself.

Do you love what you are doing? If you don't, nothing can come of it. We must love what we are doing because the purpose, expression, love and activity of a well-directed goal in life is the secret of love. Indeed, this is co-operation with the Great Love. If you love what you are doing, it will be successful and will come to fulfillment. If you despise your job, home, community, or anything else, each will be a total loss. Learn to love. Only in that way will a pattern be set up within you for larger experience.

Many people find themselves engaged in a job they literally despise. Working hours are a living hell—dull, annoying and meaningless. Bored and frustrated, they still wonder why they develop varicose veins, flat feet, stomach trouble, and heart difficulties. Why do they? It is because the reaction which does not express love starves one from the very thing that is necessary to sustain and keep life going. Where love of vocation does not exist, take the initiative and build an inner pattern of something you can love. You don't have to do a solitary thing about the outer picture. If you have accepted something that you love in your heart, that thing will appear in your life; it cannot help it. Love is what happens when feeling and thought come together. If you love the thing you think about, a marriage is consummated in your own soul, and love is expressed in your life. This is Law. Do what you love and you will love what you do.

Do you love other people? If not, what must you do? You must go inside yourself to become the sort of person that you can love. When you become that kind of person, people will appear in your life who will express love for you. You, in turn, will be drawn to them and feel the urge to express love. You will love others if you first love yourself.

Do you love your environment and your surroundings? Do you like the home in which you live? Do you like the sanctuary in which you worship? Do you like the car you drive? If you take the love of that which you consider important into your heart, you will find it fulfilling itself in your life. The important thing is to be careful where you place your affections: "Neither cast ye your pearls before swine . . ." Jesus said (Matt. 7:6). The thing that you love, you will experience. If you do not want to experience it, do not become too fond of it. We do not have to compromise or settle for half measures. Our environment is an expression of our inner consciousness. Our world is a projection of our love.

DAILY THOUGHTS ABOUT LOVE
From This Chapter

1. The primary lesson of life is to learn to love.
2. Love is unity and wholeness.
3. Love is the Supreme Good.
4. If we have love we don't need anything else. If we don't have love, nothing else will be enough.
5. Love draws all things to it.

6. Love dissolves fear and guilt.
7. Our world is the expression of our love.

From the Bible

1. Hatred stirreth up strifes: but love covereth all sins.—*Prov. 10:12*
2. Better is a dinner of herbs where love is, than a stalled ox and hatred therewith.—*Prov. 15:17*
3. Many waters cannot quench love, neither can the floods drown it.—*Song of Solomon 8:7*
4. By this shall all men know that ye are my disciples, if ye have love one to another.—*John 13:35*
5. Thou shalt love thy neighbour as thyself.—*Rom. 13:9*
6. God hath not given us the spirit of fear; but of power, and of love.—*II Tim. 1:7*
7. There is no fear in love; but perfect love casteth out fear.—*I John 4:18*

From Great Thinkers Past and Present

1. It is a beautiful necessity of our nature to love something.—*Douglas Jerrold*
2. The greatest pleasure of life is love.—*Sir William Temple*
3. Love gives itself; it is not bought.—*Henry Wadsworth Longfellow*
4. All true love is grounded on esteem.—*George Villiers Buckingham*
5. We are shaped and fashioned by what we love.—*Goethe*
6. Love is never lost. If not reciprocated it will flow back and soften and purify the heart.—*Washington Irving*
7. I have enjoyed the happiness of the world; I have lived and loved.—*Schiller*

GOLDEN BRIDGE TO LOVE

Morning Projection

I greet this day with love in my heart. Love flows from me as I go forward into my day's activities. I am in love with life. I love God. I love the whole human race. I love myself and the opportunity I have to express love and beauty in all that I do. Today I live, I love, I learn, I grow. I am related affirmatively to everything. I am a loving person.

Love prepares the way for harmonious and purposeful experience today. Love is the lodestone of my life. I develop that perfect love which casts out all fear. Love lifts me. Love dissolves all negative thoughts and attitudes from my life. I am made whole through love. Love is the great healer. I experience the therapy of love at all times.

Love vitalizes me as it circulates through my entire being and into my world. Love is the Golden Bridge across which I travel this day and throughout my life. Love is God in action through his creation. This love flows through me now. And so it is.

Evening Retrospection

The soothing serenity of love relaxes and refreshes me as I review my day. I examine every aspect of this day in the soft light of love. Did love lead the way in every thought and decision? I see that it does. Were all of my plans established in love? I see that they are. Is love my prevailing emotional attitude at all times? I earnestly desire that it be so. Does love describe my relations with everyone and everything? This is my avowed intention. Do my thoughts, feelings, words and deeds express love at all times and in every way? I determine that they shall.

The healing power of love flows from the heart of the Infinite into my heart, and suffuses itself through my consciousness, my body, and through my world throughout this night. Love indwells my entire being throughout this night and always. Love permeates me. Love makes me one with God. And so it is.

FAITH

"The Substance of Things Hoped for..."

THE widowed mother had toiled long and hard to earn the money to send her only son through the long years of college and medical school, and to support him through the low-earning years of internship and specialized study. Finally the proud day arrived when the fledgling physician hung out his shingle and set forth on his own.

Proud and fulfilled, the mother glowed with the inner security and satisfaction of a job well done.

"What did you say your son was doing now?" an interested neighbor inquired.

"What's he doing?" replied the mother. "Why, he's practicing medicine!"

"Practicing indeed!" scoffed the neighbor. "With all his study and experience, you'd think he could soon stop practicing and actually start to do it!"

The neighbor's analysis may leave something to be desired semantically, but from a practical point of view her remarks make sense. The time comes when we finally have to stop experimenting with faith, and actually live by it. There is a considerable difference. Prayer, treatment, and meditation are the "Big Three" of the inner life, but there comes the time when we must stop praying as an end in itself, and actually start doing.

The story is told of the rock-and-dirt farmer who had taken over the little run-down hillside farm and developed it to a high point of order, productivity, and beauty. One day he was proudly showing his acres to his minister, who had come to call.

"You and the Lord have done a fine job here," said the parson approvingly.

"Well, now thanks, Reverend, that's generous of you to say," returned the farmer. "But you should have seen the place when the Lord was running it alone."

There is a great deal more to practicing faith than just leaving everything up to God. Indeed, we must "render . . . to God the things that are God's," but we must precede this by learning to "render to Caesar the things that are Caesar's" (Mark 12:17)—our own personal, human responsibilities. If we would really practice faith, we must first set our individual houses in order. An examination of our fundamental beliefs in spiritual values is of primary importance in learning to order our minds and control our emotions. Thoughts and feelings are the tools of faith. We accept a thing and have faith in it when we both think and feel right about it. When we reach this point in specific treatment or prayer—or in the larger prayer which is life itself—then we no longer need to think about that particular thing any more. We accept it, and it becomes part of us.

For instance, we never question the working of the law of gravity. It always works, so we don't need to think about it. The same thing is true of other natural laws, whether we understand them or not. We have faith that snapping a switch will turn on the lights. We sit comfortably in our homes with no concern about the roof falling in. It has always remained aloft, and we have faith that it will continue to do so. We assume that the builder used the laws of construction which assure our security and protection.

The true practice of faith, of course, is premised upon the development of the ability to believe in the invisible laws of Spirit as readily as we now accept physical laws. Paul said it for all time: "Now faith is the substance of things hoped for, the evidence of things not seen" (Heb. 11:1), and ". . . things which are seen were not made of things which do appear" (Heb. 11:3). Jesus said very simply, "The wind bloweth where it listeth" (John 3:8).

All we actually need to do to practice faith is to develop our acceptance of the fact that there is a fundamental justice in the universe. The

Law is this spiritual fact in action, and all lesser laws are evidence of its operation. If we can once accept this basic premise, we will never again be hampered by weak faith. When our minds and souls agree upon the basic concept of Universal Justice, we can stop "practicing at" faith, and will then actually start to "practice" it.

When we accept an idea with faith, and release it into the natural Law of Mind, there is no way in the world to keep it from happening. An idea conceived in love (attention plus interest), and nourished by faith (expectancy and release), must come alive in our experience. The practice of faith merely demands that we stop interfering with the natural development of the embryonic idea during its normal gestation period. True practice of faith is giving oneself over completely to the dynamic of expectancy. When we act as if a thing were true, it becomes true to us.

Our faith must constantly be nourished by prayer, treatment, and meditation upon the Law of Universal Justice which decrees that when we practice faith we receive that which we have earned and need—which is invariably a greater demonstration than receiving merely what we have asked for. "Your Father knoweth what things ye have need of, before ye ask him" (Luke 13:30). "It is your Father's good pleasure to give you the kingdom" (Luke 12:32). The practice of faith inevitably leads one to the conclusion that it is impossible for Him to withhold.

The practice of faith is the process whereby we reach inner security. Our prayers, treatments, and meditations are techniques by which we practice faith by rehearsing our lives. The degree of our faith actually dictates the form of our inner spiritual work. Your life changes your meditation more than your meditation changes your life. The practice of faith does not require the endless affirmations and denials which are all too prevalent in purely mental treatment. Faith is a spiritual as well as a mental quality. Thoughts about faith must reach the feeling level and be transmuted into spiritual awareness.

The quiet acceptance of Divine Omnipresence and Universal Justice is the most effective practice of faith. As our thought and feelings turn upward and inward upon these great realities, we find that a warmth and radiance emanates from the kingdom within and transforms the entire outer picture of our lives. The process is very similar to the readying of a play for performance on the stage. Long, painstaking weeks are spent in rehearsal—in "practicing at" finding the meaning of the lines and the life of the characters. This is necessary preparation for the time when the play is ready to come to life, with lights, music, scenery, and costumes helping to translate into an outer picture before an audience that which has already been created within. When this is done, the rehearsals, or "practicing at," give way to the performance —the "practicing of" the art which has been perfected.

So it is with us. Our faith must be lived, performed, practiced in action, every moment of our lives. There comes a time when the period of prayer and treatment is seen as merely the preparation for the real event to follow—necessary, but incomplete without performance. The result of faith must be seen to be practical. The practice of faith brings us to the conclusion that the best prayers are lived—not learned.

DAILY THOUGHTS ABOUT FAITH
From This Chapter

1. There is more to faith than just leaving everything up to God.
2. Faith must be lived every moment of our lives.
3. Thoughts and feelings are the tools of faith.
4. True faith depends upon our ability to believe in the invisible laws of Spirit.
5. Faith is acceptance of the fact that there is a fundamental justice in the universe.
6. Faith must be constantly nourished by prayer.
7. Faith is a matter of recognizing and co-operating with the Infinite Intelligence.

From the Bible

1. According to your faith be it unto you.—Matt. 9:29
2. Now faith is the substance of things hoped for, the evidence of things not seen.—Heb. 11:1
3. Faith, if it hath not works, is dead.—James 2:17
4. The prayer of faith shall save the sick.—James 5:15
5. The just shall live by faith.—Rom. 1:17
6. By grace are ye saved through faith.—Eph. 2:8
7. Thy faith hath made thee whole.—Matt. 9:22

From Great Thinkers Past and Present

1. Faith affirms many things respecting which the senses are silent, but nothing which they deny.—It is superior to their testimony, but never opposed to it.—*Pascal*

2. Man is not naturally a cynic; he wants pitifully to believe, in himself, in his future, in his community and in the nation in which he is a part.—*Louis Bromfield*

3. Epochs of faith are epochs of fruitfulness; but epochs of unbelief, however glittering, are barren of all permanent good.—*Goethe*

4. In actual life every great enterprise begins with and takes its first forward step in faith.—*Schlegel*

5. Faith makes the discords of the present the harmonies of the future.—*Robert Collyer.*

6. As the flower is before the fruit, so is faith before good works.—*Richard Whately*

7. Faith is the pencil of the soul that pictures heavenly things.—*Thomas Burbridge*

GOLDEN BRIDGE TO FAITH

Morning Projection

Calmly, confidently and expectantly I arise from my bed and face my world. I know who I am, where I am going, and how to get there. With God all things are possible, and I am one with God. My strong faith dissolves all fear and uncertainty. Faith gives me strength and power. I never waver or turn back. Faith guides and sustains me.

I have faith in life, faith in other people, and faith in myself, because I have the faith of God. I never question or falter. I go forward purposefully, secure in my conviction of right and purpose as God has given me to see them. I am safe and secure in the everlasting arms. I follow the compass of faith. I can never go wrong as I believe in all that is fine and noble. This is the best day I have ever lived. Everything works out in perfect order and right action today. Faith flowing through me and from me makes it so. I believe it. I know it. I have faith that it is so. And so it is.

Evening Retrospection

As I dwell in the secret place of the most High, I abide under the shadow of the Almighty. I am in perfect peace, because my mind is in tune with the Infinite. Steadfast faith insures my safety and security.

As I review this day's activities, I have faith that unity of purpose and accomplishment is emerging from the multiplicity of my endeavors. I know that no good is ever lost. I have faith in the creative action of the Law. I release all outer concern as I place everything in God's hands.

As sleep invites me with the unseen forces of the inner world, I am sustained and soothed by an unfaltering trust. As my outer self is dormant throughout this night, I am cared for and protected by the loving action of life.

The Lord is my light and my salvation;
Whom shall I fear?
The Lord is the strength of my life;
Of whom shall I be afraid?

—Psalm 27:1

My faith makes me whole. And so it is.

21

BEAUTY

"... A Joy Forever"

A thing of beauty is a joy forever:
Its loveliness increases; it will never
Pass into nothingness; but still will keep
A bower of quiet for us, and a sleep
Full of sweet dreams, and health, and quiet breathing.

—*John Keats, "Endymion"*

We could not live without beauty. A life without beauty would be mere existence. Beauty is a way of life. The ability to see beauty in everything is the essence of constructive thinking and living. The awareness, appreciation and expression of beauty is the theme of this book as we explore the basic areas of human experience.

Beauty is so important to joyful living that this chapter, considerably longer than the others, may well be considered the major section of the book. Study it carefully and keep coming back to it so that the joy and understanding of beauty in every phase of life may become firmly entrenched in your soul.

SEVEN STEPS TO BEAUTY

There are seven steps in our individual experience of beauty:

1. Expectation
2. Perception
3. Reception
4. Appreciation

145

5. Absorption
6. Reflection
7. Expression

An attitude of expectancy opens the mind to the wonders around us everywhere. If we expect to find beauty, we will. If we expect ugliness, that will appear. The choice is ours.

Perception includes awareness. Just be aware of the beauty around you everywhere. Sharpen your senses and tune in on the wonders and beauties which abound in every facet of life.

It is one thing to see beauty and another to respond to it and imbibe it. Open your mind and heart, the portals of your soul, and receive the great feasts of beauty which God has provided for us.

Appreciation includes judgment and discrimination, of course. A trained eye can undoubtedly discern nuances and values, but true appreciation is merely joy in beholding and gratitude for the gift of beauty.

Drink deeply from the fountains of beauty and let your entire being absorb the harmonious vibrations of beauty. Store up pictures of beauty. Let the therapy of beauty transform your inner self.

Reflect upon the beauty which you have seen and it will reflect from you. We are like mirrors in that we receive what is shown to us, and reflect it through our own natures so that all may share in its beauty.

Express beauty in everything you think, feel, say and do. Pour love and dedication into your life and beauty will pour forth from you. Man is the projection of God's beauty in individual expression. You are beauty personified.

WHAT IS BEAUTY?

Beauty inspires us to be our highest and best. Beauty purifies and heals. Beauty ennobles us. Beauty units us with the Higher Self. Beauty is the expression which God wears.

> Beauty is truth, truth beauty,
>   that is all
> Ye know on earth, and all ye
>   need to know.

—John Keats, "Ode to a Grecian Urn"

In explaining or analyzing beauty too minutely, we run the danger of destroying its ephemeral essence. Beauty actually needs no explanation or justification. As Emerson said, "Beauty is its own excuse for being."

Beauty is that which delights us. This delight first starts with our senses, then extends through our intellectual and emotional processes into our subjective awareness and spiritual exaltation. True beauty activates in us the integrating action of total experience. We will now look at several channels through which beauty expresses:

I. Life

1. *Being.* There is great beauty in just being alive. To be the guardian of that particular ray of light with which we have been entrusted—our life—is the epitome of beauty. Life *is* beauty.

2. *Living.* The path of life is from being to becoming. It is what we do with our individual spark of light that counts. The dead still live, but a lot of living people are not alive. Living is the process of expressing beauty.

3. *Growing.* Every stage of growth is equally beautiful, from infancy to old age. Each phase of our growth reflects its own beauty. The process of growth, maturity and unfolding is beauty in action.

4. *Learning.* Great storehouses of knowledge, understanding and wisdom are available to us. It is beautiful to *know*. Learning is a beautiful experience. Beauty is expressed in the unfolding of the soul which comes to know itself.

5. *Expressing.* Beauty is enhanced in expression. One of the beauties of life is that everyone expresses individually, and therefore, differently, the beauty which he perceives in the inner nature of things.

6. *Sharing.* Beauty increases as we share it with others. The desire and the ability to share are among the most beautiful traits of human nature. We appreciate all beautiful things more when we share them with others.

7. *Loving.* Love is the expression of beauty. Love is the process by which the beauty in our soul meets the beauty in the soul of others. There is no beauty without love.

II. The Universe

1. *God* is the All-Good, the totality of all things—the essence of beauty. True beauty is the expression of Godliness. God is the most beautiful concept of which we are capable.

2. *Heaven* is the habitation of beauty. When every aspect of human aspiration and action are brought together, the kingdom of heaven —of beauty—is the result. Heaven is the expression of our beauty of consciousness.

3. *Spirit* is the essence of beauty. Spirit is the Mind of the universe in action through Creation. Since this One Mind knows only good, beauty can be the only result.

4. *Soul* is the creative action of the Divine Intelligence. Soul, as the expression of spiritual action, can only be beautiful. The soul of the universe *is* beauty.

5. *Law* is the system of universal principles upon which everything is based. It is mathematical in its certainty. It is the arbiter of justice and order. Its action insures beauty.

6. *Reality* is that which is—the Absolute. It cannot be compared since it is related only to itself. Reality is the one irreducible First Cause, the Source of all beauty.

7. *Truth* is Reality in expression. Mahatma Ghandi said, "Truth is God." Those things which are equal to the same thing are equal to each other. As God is the greatest beauty, Truth—His face—is beauty.

III. Self

1. *Body.* The body is the self in form and action. The mechanical principles of the body are perfect and beautiful. Body structure contains all the elements of beauty. The beauty of our consciousness is reflected in and through our bodies.

2. *Heart.* Feelings and responses come from our emotional nature— "the heart." There is nothing more beautiful than a heart filled with love. Beauty is expressed in all of our constructive feelings.

3. *Mind.* Reason has been called "heaven's greatest gift." Thought is its process. The human mind is the laboratory in which the instruments of beauty—reason, thought, logic, knowledge, wisdom,

understanding, and insight—are formulated and expressed. There could be no beauty without a mind to perceive it.

4. *Personality.* When the personality is the expression of the True Self it is undeniably beautiful. When it strays from this high standard, the personality must be brought back into line with its true purpose—to reflect inner beauty.

5. *Soul.* Our soul represents the development of God's Infinite Beauty within us up to this point. The growth of the soul is directly related to our ability to perceive and express beauty.

6. *Individuality.* The infinitude of Divine Beauty is emphasized when we realize that it has limitless variety. The beauty of our individuality is its uniqueness. Uniqueness is the expression of individual beauty.

7. *Worship* is the beautiful process through which all of the elements of the personal self are integrated into oneness. "Behold thou art made whole" (John 5:14), Jesus said. When we are whole we are beautiful, made in the image and likeness of God. Worship unifies and makes us so.

IV. NATURE

1. *Earth.* The earth, this celestial globe, is teeming with ineffable beauty. The land, plains, mountains, deserts, fields, hills, valleys and rocks and rills are all breathtakingly beautiful: ". . . this goodly frame, the earth, . . . this most excellent canopy, the air look you, this brave o'erhanging firmament, this majestical roof fretted with golden fire . . ." (Shakespeare, *Hamlet,* II, ii).

2. *Sky.* The bright blue of a cloudless sky is one of Nature's most beautiful and inspiring sights. Clouds, with their endless variety of shapes and sizes are beautiful to contemplate. When sun, clouds and sky collaborate on sunrises and sunsets, the beauty is truly "out of this world."

3. *Sun.* There is nothing more beautiful than light. The source of all our earthly light and energy is the sun. It is beautiful to see, it is beautiful to feel, and beautifully reassuring to know that it is there.

4. *Water.* One hundred and forty-three million square miles, or 70.8 per cent of the earth's surface is water—all beautiful and all providing myriad uses for man's utility and delight. The body of

man himself is largely constituted of water. We have within us an integral relationship with the sea, the lakes, the rivers and streams. And who has experienced anything more beautiful than the falling of the "gentle rain from heaven—upon the place beneath" (Shakespear, *Merchant of Venice*, IV, i)?

5. *Growing things.* Hope and life spring eternal. The Infinite is constantly appearing in new and beautiful forms. Among the most delightful of these are the trees, the flowers, the shrubs and vines, the grass and all inhabitants of the vegetable kingdom. The beauty of heaven may be glimpsed in the heart of a flower—or any place else if we know how to look for it.

6. *Animals, birds and fish.* The full scope of size and shapes, and the entire spectrum of manner and temperament are demonstrated by our friends in these three categories. No matter what the species, the beauty is always there, whether it be the snarling ferocity of a hungry wolf or the docile devotion of a cocker spaniel; the raucousness of a honking crane or the lilting song of a meadow lark; the savage horror of a crocodile or the flashing grace of a rainbow trout. All are beautiful.

7. *Space.* Eternal and infinite, space is around us everywhere, extending limitlessly in all directions. Air, atmosphere and wind are all beautiful in their way. The moon, the planets, and the stars are on beautiful journeys through space just as we are. Take a look into space. It is beautiful.

V. People

1. *Friendship* is loving, harmonious relationship between individuals or groups. It has many degrees and intensities, but true friendship is always constructive and always beautiful. Friends bring out the best in each other.

2. *Children* embody the joy and beauty of God himself. Jesus said, ". . . for of such is the kingdom of Heaven" (Matt. 19:14). We see the beauty of heaven in and through the eyes of a child. Is there anything more fascinating or beautiful than children at play?

> Backward, turn backward, O Time, in
> your flight,
> Make me a child again just for tonight!
> —*Elizabeth Akers Allen*

3. *Romance.* "The way of a man with a maid" (Prov. 30:19), is one of the most wonderful and beautiful of all of life's experiences. Romantic love can and should be the most beautiful of human relationships. Romance is the uniting in beauty of a man and woman who love each other.

4. *Family.* The family provides the cradle, the nursery, the school, and the laboratory of beauty. There is nothing more beautiful than the experience of living and sharing with those with whom we are related by family—and by love.

5. *Goodness.* Perhaps the most beautiful thing about people is their innate goodness. People are essentially good, even though mistakes and false opinions may often obscure the beauty of the underlying goodness. It is a beautiful experience to keep contact with this goodness.

6. *Love* is the most beautiful of human relationships. A person who loves the true self within him is invariably beautiful. When we feel true love for others we are literally transformed by the beauty of it. As we love God, the beauty of the Infinite shines from our faces and sings from our hearts.

7. *Brotherhood.* "He's not heavy—he's my brother," the famous slogan on the Community Chest poster picturing one small boy carrying another nearly as large, eloquently expresses the beauty of brotherhood. To live, worship and work with our brothers and sisters of all nationalities, colors and creeds is a great part of the beauty of life.

VI. Art

A true work of art must be beautiful. It must have balance, grace, harmony and order. It must express truth and reveal the Spirit within. It must do something beautiful to the one who expresses it and the one who appreciates it. Let us consider beauty in the so-called Seven Lively Arts:

1. *Music* is the voice of the spheres, and perhaps the most perfect medium for expressing beauty—both intimate and abstract. Life without beautiful music would be unthinkable. It is the means by which inexpressible beauty is expressed.

2. *Painting.* The interpretation of the beauty of life by acuity of eye, interpretation of consciousness, and skill of hand has provided

some of the world's greatest objects of beauty. "Beauty is in the eye of the beholder." The artist who knows this filters it through his consciousness, and presents it for all to see.

3. *Sculpture.* "What a beautiful statue you have sculpted," a friend observed to a great artist. "I didn't sculpt it," he replied. "I just removed the stone that didn't belong there." The sculptor releases from stone the beauty of the "imprisoned splendor." All artists are the servants of beauty.

4. *Literature.* The teller of tales weaves the beauty of legends, customs, insights, aspirations, ideals, hopes, dreams and adventures into a permanent form of communication so that the beauty of all ages and all peoples may be eternally shared. The poet is one of the great custodians of beauty.

5. *Dance* is the expression of the beauty of the human body in graceful action. The dancer uses his body to express the beauty of God and life. Dancing is the process of revealing the beauty of Spirit through the rhythmic grace of the body.

6. *Theatre.* "The purpose of playing—was and is to hold, as 'twere, the mirror up to nature; to show virtue her own feature, scorn her own image, and the very age and body of the time its form and presence" (Shakespeare, *Hamlet*, III, ii). In presenting and interpreting life, the theatre is one of the great channels for the expression of beauty.

7. *Architecture* is the means by which the "stately mansions" of the soul are projected into form for all to enjoy and use. Beauty in functional buildings is evidence of beauty in the consciousness of the people. The presence of such beauty is inspiring and ennobling.

VII. ACTION

1. *Movement.* From the molecular activity of the single cell, to the orbiting complex of the heavenly bodies, the universe is in a state of rhythmical movement. The beauty of life is expressed through movement.

2. *Words.* "In the beginning was the Word, and the Word was with God, and the Word was God" (John 1:1). Human words express the beauty of the One Word—the Divine Idea—the First Cause of all expression. There is nothing more beautiful than the words of one's native language spoken correctly.

3. *Deeds.* "I will recompense them according to their deeds . . ." (Jer. 25:14). We do what it is our nature to do; a noble character fathers noble deeds; beauty begets beauty. A person's life becomes a masterpiece of beauty as he acts in accordance with high principles of love and service. Worthy deeds reveal the beauty of the heart.

4. *Work* is the means by which we make our lives useful. There is great beauty in useful function. No matter what the job, if it is done well, it is an expression of beauty. Our attitude toward our work determines the beauty of the completed job.

5. *Skill.* Training and skill enable the dedicated workman to express the beauty within him. It is our personal responsibility to develop the full potential of our skill. The skillful performer in any field is both an object and an expression of beauty.

6. *Craftsmanship* is the result of dedicated workmanship and developed and practiced skill. Skilled craftsmanship produces results that reveal beauty in function and use. The crafts as well as the arts express the beauty of the artisans and artists.

7. *Relationship* is another channel for the expression of beauty—how we relate to ourselves, to God, to other people, to the world in which we live. The secret of experiencing beauty is to both express and receive love and beauty in every relationship.

VIII. Home

1. *Peace.* The essence of spiritual unfolding is to realize that there is available to us a beauty which is greater than the beauty of the world. It is expressed as peace. Jesus said, "Peace I give unto you, not as the world giveth, give I unto you" (John 14:27). The home is a haven of peace—beauty.

2. *Love* provides the climate in which beauty flourishes. Love is the most beautiful ingredient of the home. There can only be beauty in expression if there is first love in inception.

3. *Charm* is beauty expressed in highly personal and individual ways. Charm is the handmaiden of beauty. Beauty without charm is not beauty. Charm without beauty cannot exist. Charm brings beauty to the home, and beauty brings charm.

4. *"Order* is Heaven's first law." Heaven is a place of beauty and order. Order in the home enhances the beauty of the home. There can be no beauty without order. Order, by its very nature, is both an at-

tribute of, and an inspiration for the expression of further beauty.

5. *Functionalism.* One of the great beauties of most modern homes is their functional and practical nature. Space is organized and utilized, and everything is arranged for efficiency and ease of operation. Nature operates functionally, efficiently and beautifully. Usefulness adds to beauty.

6. *Comfort.* How we look forward to the comfort of our homes at the end of a busy day! The fireplace and the easy chair are items of comfort, but they are also symbols of beauty. Another aspect of beauty is the security we feel in the comfortable and familiar surroundings of our own homes.

7. *Hospitality* is another of the aspects of love and therefore of beauty. Hospitality is the extension of warmth and love toward others in a beautiful and friendly way. The true beauty of the home is hospitality. True hospitality makes everyone feel beautiful.

IX. Environment (*Where You Are*)

1. *Places* are beautiful in accordance with their nature. Everything has its own consciousness. We love to travel and soak up the beauty and exotic atmosphere of faraway places, but we are happiest when we realize that the most beautiful place in the world is the place where we are right now.

2. *Distances.* Since distance is the space between things, a certain unity is implied. This is in itself beautiful. Through a powerful microscope the distances between the neutrons and protons of the atom are easily discernible. Through a powerful telescope, the seemingly great distances of outer space disappear. Is distance real, or is it all an illusion? Dwell upon these ideas and beauty will fill your soul.

3. *Surroundings.* Our consciousness extends all around us. Our surroundings are the projections of the atmosphere of our own minds and hearts. We can make them as beautiful as we choose. There is beauty in the principle of this cause-and-effect relationship.

4. *Living quarters.* It is vitally important to be surrounded by beauty where we live. First, because our homes give us an opportunity to express our inner beauty. Second, because when we consciously surround ourselves with beauty, it feeds our souls and helps to make

us more beautiful. Thus, a beautiful circle is established which has no end.

5. *Place of business.* Which places do we most enjoy patronizing? The most attractive, of course. We like to trade at the most beautiful stores and dine at the most beautiful restaurants. Most businesses, industries and professions now recognize the importance of beauty in the places where their business is conducted. Banks and even factories often have the most beautiful buildings in the community.

6. *City.* The city can be, and is to many, a source of great beauty and inspiration. As we plan our cities and eliminate the slums and blight areas, as we build more beautiful buildings and lay out more spacious and beautiful residential areas, streets and parks, our cities may well be enduring monuments of beauty in both design and consciousness.

7. *Nation*

> Breathes there the man, with soul so
> dead,
> Who never to himself hath said,
> This is my own, my native land!
> —*Sir Walter Scott, "Lay of the Last Minstrel"*

The land in which we dwell is beautiful. The concepts of freedom, initiative, individuality, efficiency, purpose, energy and ingenuity which characterize the citizens of the United States of America are enduringly beautiful. It is the personal responsibility of each of us to make our land beautiful and keep it so.

X. THINGS

1. *Possessions* are not the most important things in life, but they are wonderful to have. We appreciate the beauty of our possessions more by owning them instead of letting them own us. Possessions are to be cared for and used intelligently. There is beauty in ownership.

2. *Personal objects* reflect the consciousness of the person to whom they belong. Inanimate possessions become more beautiful when they are in contact with beauty. A pearl takes on the luster of the beautiful woman who wears it. Diamonds pick up the sparkle in

the eyes of the one who wears them. Personal objects reflect personal beauty.

3. *Apparel.* Clothes may not completely make the man—or woman —but they can certainly add to our attractiveness. There is sheer beauty in well-fitted gowns or a well-tailored suit. The proper hat can emphasize the unnoticed beauty in an otherwise plain face. Beauty is the only word to describe the color and texture of many fabrics.

4. *Money* is generally misunderstood, sometimes vilified, often misused—but *always* sought-after. The concept of money as crystallized service is a beautiful one. The tinkle of silver is a beautiful sound, and the flash of a bill is even more so. But, of course, money is not to be sought for itself alone, but as a means to the end of giving and receiving increased service and effectiveness. That is the beauty of money.

5. *Automobiles* are very nearly worshiped by most Americans. But here again, in addition to the undeniable beauty of design, color, speed and harnessed power, the primary purpose of the automobile is functional. The great beauty of the automobile is that there are such beautiful contrivances in which to ride. And who does not feel more beautiful when riding in a beautiful car?

6. *Tools* are literally extensions of our own hands, abilities and powers. Their beauty is primarily functional. From the knife, fork and spoon, to the hammer, the broom, the pitchfork, the power lathe, the plow, the tractor, our tools express us. They are beautiful. Let us learn to use them beautifully.

7. *Furniture.* Beauty of design and craftsmanship is expressed in the furniture of our homes. Beauty in furniture includes both the decorative and functional aspects. The principles of harmony, color, balance, and design are all part of the beauty of our furniture. Our homes, as well as we ourselves, are beautified by the beauty of our furniture.

Conclusion

There is beauty everywhere. Isn't it a beautiful life? "If you get simple beauty and naught else, you get about the best thing God invents" (Robert Browning, "Fra Lippo Lippi").

DAILY THOUGHTS ABOUT BEAUTY
From This Chapter

1. Beauty is a way of life.
2. The ability to see beauty everywhere is the essence of constructive thinking and living.
3. Open your mind and heart and receive the great feasts of beauty which God has provided for us.
4. Let the things of beauty transform you.
5. Man is the projection of God's beauty in individual expression.
6. Beauty inspires us to our highest and best.
7. Beauty unites us with the Higher Self.

From the Bible

1. Let the beauty of the Lord our God be upon us.—*Psalm 90:17*
2. He hath made everything beautiful in his time.—*Eccles. 3:11*
3. Consider the lilies of the field, how they grow; they toil not, neither do they spin: And yet I say unto you, that even Solomon in all his glory was not arrayed like one of these.—*Matt. 6:28, 29*
4. Whatsoever things are lovely . . . think on these things.—*Phil. 4:8*
5. By the grace of God I am what I am.—*I Cor. 15:10*
6. Let your speech be always with grace.—*Col. 4:6*
7. The morning stars sang together, and all the sons of God shouted for joy.—*Job 33:7*

From Great Thinkers Past and Present

1. The beauty seen, is partly in him who sees it.—*Christian N. Bovee*
2. Beauty is but the sensible image of the Infinite.—*George Bancroft*
3. Beauty is the mark God sets on virtue.—*Ralph W. Emerson*
4. The soul, by an instinct stronger than reason, ever associates beauty with truth.—*Henry T. Tuckerman*
5. Beauty, unaccompanied by virtue, is as a flower without perfume.—*from the French*
6. I pray thee, O God, that I may be beautiful within.—*Socrates*
7. The best part of beauty is that which no picture can express.—*Sir Francis Bacon*

GOLDEN BRIDGE TO BEAUTY

Morning Projection

It's a beautiful day, a beautiful world, a beautiful life. I revel in the beauty which is all around me. I thrill to the wonderful things there are to see and do. Life is truly a wonderful experience!

I drink deeply from the fountain of beauty today. I am filled with the essence of infinity. I breathe in the fragrance of the Divine. I savor the flavor of exciting experience. I sing the song of the spheres. All is ineffably beautiful.

Today I think beautiful thoughts, feel beautiful emotions, say beautiful words, perform beautiful deeds and accomplish beautiful things. Beauty pours into this day as I identify myself with the idea of beauty. I am surrounded by an aura of beauty. Beauty radiates from me.

I expect beauty. I perceive beauty. I receive beauty. I appreciate beauty. I absorb beauty. I reflect beauty. I express beauty.

I am a beautiful person. And so it is.

Evening Retrospection

As the day has been beautiful, the night is even more so. Stillness and darkness are the channels through which the inner beauty shines. In silence I commune with beauty. Through the outer darkness I see the light of beauty.

Softly and tenderly the angels of beauty surround me. The beauty of being is almost unbearable. I am open to the Infinite. I perceive God directly. The universe is my home. My personal self is imbued with the beauty of the one Self. I am one with the great Laws of Nature. They are beautiful and true.

The beautiful things of this world have delighted me all through this day. I joyously review my beautiful experiences with other people. I relive the beautiful experiences which I have known. I remember the beauty which has surrounded me at all times.

I now release myself into the most beautiful of all experiences—the unconsciousness and the superconsciousness of sleep. I sleep beautifully. I dream beautiful dreams. I am one with all beauty, now and forever. And so it is.

22

SLEEP

"To Sleep, Perchance To Dream..."

. . . the innocent sleep,
Sleep that knits up the ravell'd sleeve of care,
The death of each day's life, sore labour's bath,
Balm of hurt minds, great nature's second course,
Chief nourisher in life's feast.

—Shakespeare, "Macbeth," II, ii

WHAT IS SLEEP?

Even though we spend approximately one third of our time in sleep, we know very little about the "great gift of sleep." We do know that living things, including plants and flowers, sleep. Periodically, all life subsides from objective activity into a state of rest and repose. In deep sleep this withdrawal into the subjective is so complete that we actually cease to live in the outer world, and are transported to the inner side of life.

The therapeutic value of sleep for the human body is well known. Equally important is the beneficial effect of sleep upon the psychic and spiritual life—the consciousness of the individual. By directing your mind affirmatively and expectantly, you can solve problems, break bad habits, remove limitations, improve your health, and expand your horizons of knowledge, wisdom and understanding—all while you are asleep.

As the body becomes inert during sleep, so does the conscious mind.

Objectivity is suspended, and the subjective side of life takes over. Even though we are unconscious, the subconscious remains active, life is sustained, autonomic functions continue, and the psychic side (the inner self, the consciousness) of the person becomes even more active than during the waking state. Freed from the external pressures and activities of the outside world, the soul (self) can proceed uninterruptedly about its business of growth and unfolding.

HOW TO GET THE MOST OUT OF YOUR SLEEP

For some who have difficulty in sleeping, the question may be somewhat simpler: "How do I *get* to sleep?" The requirements are simple: a relaxed body and a mind freed of cares. Prepare for sleep by relaxing both the mind and the body. This is the first step. Much has been written about physical relaxation. Somewhat less has been said about the importance of controlling the conscious mind so that we can turn it off and on, and decide what it is to think about at any given moment. Here we suggest techniques for the development of this ability to control our own minds, and to give us something worthwhile to think about when they are turned on.

Our immediate interest is to learn how to release the action of the conscious mind from troublesome matters so that it can formulate constructive suggestions for the subconscious to work upon during sleep. The principle is simple: *The suggestions you give yourself before going to sleep persist throughout the night.* The thoughts and attitudes you take to bed are the ones you awaken with—amplified by the creative action of the subconscious during sleep. If you retire to bed with problems, troubles and worries on your mind, not only will it be impossible for you to sleep well, but your difficulties will actually be amplified. The alternative is to *place the mind upon the solution rather than the problem,* with strong suggestions and direction to the subconscious to produce the desired good for you. Enter the sleeping state with faith and positive conviction that your orders are being carried out, and that the good you desire is already an established fact in your experience. Remember, what you believe to be so, *is* so for you. The creative power within you takes care of the details.

Review the suggestions for the use of this book in the Introduction and the use of the Golden Bridge in Chapter One.

The affirmative thoughts and ideas in each chapter are excellent replacements for the all too common daily fare of negativity. Read a chapter of this book each day of each month throughout the year, and you will put its techniques and suggestions into practice.

Use these techniques of scientific prayer treatment for half an hour just before going to bed each night, and you will increase the restfulness and effectiveness of your sleep many times. Let the affirmations sink deep into your subconscious. Spend part of your presleep treatment period in dealing with the immediate affairs of your life. Dissolve all pressure, tension, worry and anxiety concerning them, and affirm strong statements of your desired good, your intention to achieve this good, and your conviction of completion concerning it.

As part of this half-hour period of personal treatment work, go back over your day in reverse order as you have been instructed in using the Golden Bridge technique. Complete your inner work by repeating the "Evening Retrospection" part of your Golden Bridge at the end of the chapter for that day. You will then be ready for sleep and pleasant dreams.

A WORD ABOUT DREAMS

The subconscious mind is one with the universal subjective mind which is the repository of natural knowledge and wisdom, the storehouse of memory of the human race, and the creative aspect of Nature. The individual is in the subjective mind and the subjective mind is in the individual. When the conscious mind is asleep, we are living completely in the subjective, a vast universe of many wonderful things. The suggestions which we give to this great creative mind before we go to sleep are acted upon throughout the night. Give it a problem to solve and it will have the answer for you in the morning. Declare with faith that you are growing along certain lines, and your soul will expand and develop during sleep. Affirm that you will dream "true" and that you will recall these dreams and profit from them when you awaken, and you will be opening up a vast new area of fun, significant investigation and personal growth.

Since we dream whether we are aware of it or not, and since dreaming is absolutely essential to our psychic health and balance, some understanding of dreams and dreaming is essential in constructive living. Since ancient times, dreams have played a significant part in man's destiny. The Bible is filled with the accounts of dreams, including those of Nebuchadnezzar, King of Babylon, Joseph and his interpretation of Pharaoh's dream of the seven fat cattle and seven lean ones, and that of Pilate's wife prior to Jesus' trial.

John Bunyan was inspired to write *Pilgrim's Progress* in 1675 by a dream which he had while in prison. Abraham Lincoln was deeply troubled by a dream the night before his assassination, in which he was adrift on a vast ocean in a boat without a rudder or oars. In reporting this dream to his Cabinet, he said that something unexpected would soon take place. President Franklin Delano Roosevelt dreamed of a terrible accident at the Washington, D.C., airport, and as a result declared that it was imperative that a new one be built with more adequate facilities.

Since each person's dreams arise from within his own consciousness, the interpretation of dreams has become a significant tool of modern psychotherapy. The great philosophers and physicians of all ages have recognized the significance of dreams. Plato felt that dreams were significant and should be interpreted. He saw the relationship of dreams to the external life of the individual, and said that there could be prophetic and telepathic dreams which gave the individual communications from the soul world. Aristotle's and Cicero's approach to the subject was similar to that of modern psychologists. Hippocrates, the father of medicine, and others, used dreams as the basis for richer insights in diagnosing their patients' illnesses.

There are many types of dreams: initiatory (visits from spirits, entities, etc.), prodomic (matters of physical health), archetypal (great symbolic significance), prophetic (forthcoming events), religious, creative, teacher-image, adversary-image, grotesque happenings, overpowering by circumstances, as well as death dreams, fear dreams, falling dreams, flying dreams, and dreams involved with natural phenomena such as floods, fires, storms and catastrophes.

The important thing to remember is that dreams arise from within the individual and are important to that individual, but they cannot be taken at face value. Seldom do they mean what the rational faculties think they mean. For instance, every character in your dreams represents some aspect of yourself, and not necessarily the person dreamed of. The same is true of events. A flood may be symbolic of the sea of problems and difficulties which is engulfing you. Dreams are part of the related pattern of the individual. They provide a key to helping us understand ourselves even though we may not understand the dream. Dreams bring us to the borderline of the subconscious. They have a message that could benefit us. Erich Fromm calls dreams "The Forgotten Language."[1]

In his invaluable booklet, *An Introduction to Dream Interpretation,* Manly Palmer Hall lists the two major functions of dreams:

1. Interpretation by the psychic nature of those occurrences which dominate the waking state.
2. The release of subjective matter (or psychic energy) into the conscious life of the individual.[2]

See your dreams as a means to help you live more constructively. Develop constructive thoughts, attitudes, feelings, and habits and everything else will fall into place.

DAILY THOUGHTS ABOUT SLEEP AND DREAMS

From This Chapter

1. Sleep has a therapeutic value for both the physical and the psychic life of the individual.
2. Sleep is a natural equalizer which enables us to maintain our balance so that we may live effectively and well.
3. Sleep restores our sense of values.
4. Occupying approximately one third of our time, sleep may well be the most important part of our lives.
5. The suggestions you give yourself before going to sleep persist throughout the night.
6. We dream whether we are aware of it or not, and dreaming is essential to our psychic health and balance.
7. Intelligent interpretation of our dreams helps us learn more about ourselves and thereby helps us live more constructively.

From the Bible

1. Rest in the Lord.—*Psalm 37:7*
2. Come unto me, all ye that labor and are heavy laden, and I will give you rest.—*Matt. 11:28*

[1] *The Forgotten Language,* by Erich Fromm (New York: Holt, Rinehart & Winston, Inc., 1951).
[2] Published by the Philosophical Research Society, 3341 Griffith Park Blvd., Los Angeles, 1955.

3. God speaketh . . . in slumberings upon the bed.—*Job* 33:14, 15
4. I will both lay me down in peace, and sleep.—*Psalm* 4:8
5. It is vain for you to rise up early, to sit up late, to eat the bread of sorrows: for so He giveth his beloved sleep.—*Psalm* 127:2
6. When thou liest down, thou shalt not be afraid.—*Prov.* 3:24
7. God hath given them the spirit of slumber.—*Rom.* 11:8

From Great Thinkers Past and Present

1. Our foster-nurse of nature is repose.—*Shakespeare*
2. Sleep, to the homeless thou art home; the friendless find in thee a friend.—*Ebenezer Elliott*
3. Sleep is pain's easiest salve, and doth fulfil all offices of death, except to kill.—*John Donne*
4. Tired nature's sweet restorer, balmy sleep; he, like the world, his ready visit pays where fortune smiles—the wretched he forsakes.—*Owen D. Young*
5. Put off thy cares with thy clothes; so shall thy rest strengthen thy labor; and so shall thy labor sweeten thy rest.—*Francis Quarles*
6. When tir'd with vain rotations of the day, sleep winds us up for the succeeding dawn.—*Owen D. Young*
7. When one turns over in bed it is time to turn out.—*Duke of Wellington*

GOLDEN BRIDGE TO SLEEP

Morning Projection

As I awaken refreshed from a night of restful, refilling sleep, I am ready to go forward into my day. Sleep has erased all wounds and cares. During sleep my mind and my body have been healed. I have drunk deeply from the wellsprings of eternity. I have traveled into the reaches of inner and outer space. I have communed with God. I have been rocked in the cradle of the deep. I have been reborn during sleep. I am a new and better person now.

Now that I am awake, I retain the memories of the night's glorious adventures in Spirit. I recall the dreams which come to instruct and purify me. They have brought me messages of great good. They have freed me from psychic overload. My dreams have given me depth and dimension. I give thanks for my dreams and my recollection of them. I am grateful for the lessons they bring. The healing which has come to me during sleep sustains and maintains me throughout this day. And so it is.

Evening Retrospection

Quietly now, I lie down to pleasant dreams. "The cares that infest the day, fold their tents like the Arabs and quietly steal away." I release all concern. I cease all effort. I relax my attention. I let go and let God take over. I slip easily into the subconscious, as I go off into deep and satisfying sleep.

Whatever inner experience I need this night comes to me during sleep. My mind and heart are open and receptive to all that is good. I co-operate with the cleansing flow which purifies, heals and rebuilds me. My subjective consciousness is refilled in the Halls of Learning. My soul is newly inspired in the inner Temples of Wisdom.

I make the very most of my night's sleep by taking full advantage of the great natural order of things. I actually live more fully and meaningfully during sleep. All interference is removed and God takes over. I grow and unfold during sleep. I spend this night in the king-dom of heaven. I give thanks for the deep sleep which makes this possible. And so it is.

23 ✒

PERSONALITY AND GOD
"... *In Our Image, After Our Likeness*..."

DURING one of his popular lectures on the nature of God and the universe and man's relationship to it, the late Don Blanding spoke in very practical, everyday terms. His purpose was to remove fear and superstition, and to establish our relationship to God on a personal and workable basis. This frontal approach to deity was a bit too much for certain members of the audience, just as it is today for many who have no real concept of what God is, and who let their beliefs be limited by doctrinal, theological and denominational boundaries.

After the lecture, one dignified gentleman, obviously offended by Blanding's remarks, chided, "My dear Blanding, I hope you're not a lost soul."

"Tell me, sir," Don returned, "do you believe that God is all-in-all?"

"Why, I most certainly do," the man replied.

"Then tell me," the poet queried. "Where would I go to get lost?"

In Psalm 139, we read, "Whither shall I go from Thy spirit? or whither shall I flee from Thy presence? If I ascend up into heaven, Thou art there; if I make my bed in hell, behold, Thou art there."

An ancient fable has the lords of creation meeting to discuss the problem of where to hide man's divinity so that he would not discover it too easily.

"Let us bury it at the center of the earth," suggested one of the masters.

"No," objected another. "He will one day harness the forces of nature and penetrate the very earth itself. We must look elsewhere."

"Let us submerge it at the bottom of the sea," another great one thought.

"No," it was decided. "Man is ingenious. He will one day explore the very floor of the ocean."

"Let us anchor man's divinity high in the sky," the third initiate directed.

"No," they all agreed. "Man has absolutely no limitations. Some day he will fly to the reaches of outer space."

"Then where shall we hide it?" they questioned.

Finally they all agreed, "Let us place man's divinity within his own heart. He'll never think to look for it there."

In the quantum theory, Albert Einstein shook the scientific foundations of his day by proving that, "Both matter and light sometimes appear as particles, sometimes as waves." This was a preliminary to his basic theory of relativity which has formed the basis for modern science that, "The material universe is a uniform and interrelated whole —a special aspect of a rational cosmos." Einstein and a legion of scientists since have discovered that there is something—call it an Intelligence—back of all things, and that there can be no real development, growth or accomplishment unless we work in co-operation with this basic Intelligence. We are interested in finding this God-Presence and Power within ourselves. We are not so much interested in explaining what God is, as we are in developing a feeling, an awareness, a consciousness of reality within ourselves.

It has been said that to name God is to limit him, and to define Him is to defile him. But we continue to try, because of our insatiable need to find this light in the darkness.

Jesus said, "Let your light so shine before men, that they may see your good works, and glorify your Father which is in heaven" (Matt. 5:16).

Now what is it that can be so variously described as "Father," "Light," "It," "Thing?" In his great poem "L'Envoi," Rudyard Kipling describes the Great One as "The Master of all Good Workmen," while Jesus refers to the Indwelling Power as "Father." What do *you feel* that God is? That is the starting point. A modern thinker has said, "God is that which gives you climax." To some this is money, or power, or fame, or sense of gratification, or any one or number of thousands of things. But this is the problem. We get into trouble whenever we try to make false gods greater than God.

There are certain basic, fundamental values in life. It isn't enough just to think about eating, sleeping, working, and solving problems; there must be some attention given to faith and spiritual matters. Dr. Carl Jung said that he had never seen a cure accomplished in anyone over thirty-five years of age that was not accomplished by reorientation of the religious sense. This indicates that a cure on the mental or emotional level can take place only when it is accompanied by spiritual realization on the part of the individual.

This thing called life is the action of the Thing called God. It is available to us every moment of our lives, and can be approached consciously. This is one of life's most important discoveries: *God can be experienced consciously.* By using treatment or scientific prayer as a means of ordering our lives, we find that when we discipline our individual minds to think in terms of the One Mind, the One Mind begins to think through us and produce larger patterns of Good. When we plant a seed in the ground, we have no control over it; we can only have faith that it will grow. When we plant a seed of faith in our minds, we do not need to watch it every day. We only need to water it with the flood of spiritual conviction, which will nourish it and bring it to flower.

We are playing for keeps as we start on the spiritual path. Each must decide now whether he wants to continue. There is no real accomplishment, gain or gratification possible unless God is our Senior Partner. You may never find Him completely, but once started on the quest there is no turning back. All else pales into insignificance compared to our life's work of finding God within ourselves. The desire to know, to understand, to become one with this great Beingness demands full time, attention and energy. The reward for finding Him will exceed your greatest expectation. It will transform your life, shine through your face, form your relationships, and determine the pattern of your activities. You see, *God is all there is.*

God means the "All-Good." Everything that is good is of God. Everything that is limited or evil is not of God, but a result of interference with God. As someone said, "You can take 'God' out of 'good,' but you cannot take 'good' out of 'God.' " Try as we will, it seems impossible to find a word that is as all-inclusive as the word "God." Don't be afraid of it. Use the word; make it mean something to you, savor it. Immerse yourself in its limitless expanse, and let your inner consciousness glory in the wonder of it. *Make God personal to you.* To love God is to become so identified with good that it becomes impossible to do, think or be other than good and to live in harmony with the great natural Law of life. Our objective in learning about God is that we may *become* better than we know ourselves to be. *When we become the embodiment of good, only good can come to us.*

We seek to develop mental and emotional attitudes that are consistently good—that is, constructive and affirmative. Every one is searching for God—greater good—in his life. As we embody affirmative ideas and constructive attitudes, we cannot help but accomplish our objective. As we let these ideas sink down into our subconscious, we are steadily advancing from where we are to where we want to be. In this book we are developing our inner power of recognition of good. As we make this a habit, the good automatically becomes a fact.

We must learn to turn our daily thoughts toward encouragement, enthusiasm, affirmation, joy and love. Let's learn to say, "I have faith. I believe in my own ability. I believe in life, and I intend to live it fully and well." This is a conscious approach to faith. Right living results when we expect the best.

Jesus said, "Do you believe? Then according to your faith be it unto you" (Matt. 9:29). In the little story about the ship and the wind and the waves, He said, "Why are ye fearful, O ye of little faith?" (Matt. 8:26) He prayed, and the turbulence of the sea and the wind died away, and there was peace and quiet. This is exactly what you and I must do every day of our lives. There is a way of prayer which recognizes the power that indwells all things, and therefore knows that this power indwells us. This is pure deductive reasoning: *If God is in all things, then he is in me.* Doesn't this make sense? It is impossible to conceive of a God who isn't in all things and all places.

Now we see that pure deductive reasoning used consciously helps to build our faith. If we believe in God, then we must believe in ourselves. We can't believe in God without believing in ourselves. If we don't believe in ourselves, we don't believe in God. It's that simple. Say each day: "I believe in That Which Is. I know that It is all of me, and everything I do is a part of It. God is what I am, what I do, and what I think."

Form the habit of seeing only good in everything and everybody so that you cannot see anything else. Look *through* the outer appearance to the truth within. Build your life around the worship of the good, the true and the beautiful. Spend time consciously disciplining your mind so that you express God—good—in every word and action. Become filled with the idea. Make your life a romance with all the noble and fine things which bear evidence of the great perfection which is the First Cause back of all things. Direct your mind in the upward path and start climbing. You will find God, and your whole life will be filled with meaning and richness.

DAILY THOUGHTS ABOUT PERSONALITY AND GOD

From This Chapter

1. Look for your divinity within your own heart.
2. There is an Intelligence back of all things, and there can be no real development, growth or accomplishment for us unless we work in co-operation with it.
3. We come closer to understanding God as we develop an awareness of the reality within ourselves.
4. Mankind has an insatiable need to find God.
5. We get into trouble whenever we try to make false gods greater than God.
6. There is no real accomplishment, gain or gratification possible without God as your Senior Partner.
7. *God is all there is.*

From the Bible

1. My righteousness I hold fast, and will not let it go.—*Job 27:6*
2. Let your light so shine before men, that they may see your good works, and glorify your Father which is in heaven.—*Matt. 6:16*
3. Brethren, let every man, wherein he is called, therein abide with God.—*I Cor. 7:24*
4. Wherefore take unto you the whole armor of God, that ye may be able to withstand in the evil day, and having done all, to stand.—*Eph. 6:13*
5. God hath not given us the spirit of fear; but of power, and of love, and of a sound mind.—*II Tim. 1:7*
6. Follow righteousness, faith, charity, peace, with them that call on the Lord out of a pure heart.—*II Tim. 2:22*

7. Honour all men. Love the brotherhood. Fear God. Honour the king.
—*I Pet. 2:17*

From Great Thinkers Past and Present

1. We know God easily, if we do not constrain ourselves to define him.
—*Joseph Joubert*
2. God is a circle whose center is everywhere, and its circumference nowhere.—*Empedocles*
3. If God did not exist it would be necessary to invent him.—*Voltaire*
4. God governs the world, and we have only to do our duty wisely, and leave the issue to him.—*John Gay*
5. There is a God in science, a God in history, and a God in conscience, and these three are one.—*Joseph Cook*
6. There is nothing on earth worth being known but God and our own souls.—*Gamaliel Bailey*
7. Live near to God, and so all things will appear to you little in comparison with eternal realities.—*Robert Murray McCheyne*

GOLDEN BRIDGE
TO GODLINESS

Morning Projection

That which is true of God is true of me. I am made in the image and likeness of God. I am in the small what God is in the large. I am the microcosm. God is the macrocosm. I am a point of light within the mind of God. I am a point of love within the heart of God. I am that I Am which God knows himself to be.

There is no place where God leaves off and I begin. God in man, as man, is man. There is only perfect God, perfect man, perfect Being. I am an expression of divine Wholeness. I have infinite possibility, I have limitless potentiality, I have innate divinity. Trailing clouds of glory I come, from God who is my home.

I live from the center of the God-self within me today and forever. I am here for the purpose of finding, developing and expressing the God within me. For this purpose I came into this world. Toward this end I devote my entire being. Nothing else matters. I live to express my oneness with God. And so it is.

Evening Retrospection

God has had his arm around me throughout this day, and I know He is never going to take it away. As I dwell in the secret place of the Most High, I abide in the shadow of the Almighty. I am never separated from God. He is my rock and my fortress, an ever-present help in time of trouble. I am safe in the everlasting arms.

I am safe and secure as I place myself in God's hands. I live completely with God during sleep. First Cause is the only cause in my life. My personality gives way to my individuality. I sit on the right-hand side of Him as the true self within hears the Voice proclaim, "This is my beloved son, in whom I am well pleased."

The wonders of the Kingdom are revealed to me as I journey easily and peacefully into the inner realm. Sleep takes me into my native habitat. Sleep removes all barriers and blockages which have separated me from God. I am One with Him now. And so it is.

24 ✍

PROSPERITY
The Law of Increase

LET'S examine the spiritual significance of the principle of tithing. Tithing has been practiced through the ages. Actually, it is the only sound basis for prosperity. We run into difficulty if we forget that God is the Source of all of our supply. The first fruits of life's increase belong to God. If we do not share our seed, our attention, our time, our service, and our money by supporting His work, we are actually being dishonest, because we are withholding that which belongs to someone else.

Tithing is based upon sound spiritual values. It is up to you to reach your own decision concerning it, and it is up to me to reach mine. Our purpose here is to deal with spiritual values and principles which can be shared and used by all of us for the best interests of everyone concerned. The principle of tithing is that of recognizing God as the one Source of all being. He is the owner of all things and we are the stewards. We must learn to be good stewards. To say that we cannot receive until we give, and we cannot give until we receive is not a paradox, but a basic principle of life.

A Sunday School tot asked, "If God created the Heavens and the earth, who created God?" The answer is simple: God created himself. We create ourselves out of what we are—out of what we know. We must start with a recognition of the source of all things. When we think of God as that Source, we immediately reorganize much of our thinking including our concepts of money and prosperity. A man naturally thinks that his job is the source of his supply. But it isn't.

The source of our supply is God; the job is merely the channel through which the supply comes.

There is a rhythm in the universe. Seasonal changes, the rising and setting of the sun, the lunar phases, the ebb and flow of the tides, the orbital movement of the planets; all bear evidence of the universal rhythm. When man is in harmony with this rhythm, things go well for him. When he is at odds with it, he seems to lose his energy and force. We can only live effectively by learning how to co-operate with the rhythm of life. The practice of tithing conforms to this purpose.

Throughout history, when people have tithed, their affairs have prospered, and they have reached a high level of moral, spiritual and cultural development. Tithing started when King Melchizedek explained to Abraham the nature of peace and righteousness. Abraham then decided to tithe of his substance to this King of Peace. Throughout the Old Testament, the prophets proclaimed that the Messiah who was to come would be "after the Order of Melchizedek." Tithing is a part of the recognition of the Fatherhood of God and the brotherhood of man.

Great teachers have never taught man to tithe so that he could receive; he was taught to tithe because this was the best thing to do. When we establish this rhythm in giving, and recognize God as the Source, we have a constant sense of belonging to something bigger and more abundant than we are individually. Tithing is a matter of giving of ourselves—our time, our resources—as an affirmation of our loyalty to, and our Oneness with That which is the Father of us all.

A tithe is one tenth. Considering all that God has given us, giving one tenth to Him seems like a reasonable arrangement, doesn't it? We would suggest that when you are ready to tithe, when you have reached the point in your thinking where you see it as the means of spiritual and material discipline by which you wish to live, that you do it for one reason only—because you are convinced that it is right. Our purpose here is to explain the spiritual basis for the tithe. To tithe, simply to profit in return, is to miss the entire spirit of it. This would do no one any good. Our motive must be pure. We return gifts to God out of our love for Him. We give back to God because we develop an understanding in ourselves that as we act toward the universe, the universe will act toward us.

What does tithing do? It establishes order in our affairs. Tithing is a form of prayer. Tithing is a material declaration of faith. We are told many times in the Bible that all things are done unto us according to our faith.

" 'Believe ye that I am able to do this?' Jesus asked.

"The followers replied, 'Yea, Lord.'

" 'According to your faith be it unto you,' " He declared (Matt. 9:29). And, their prayers were answered on the level of their own consciousness. If we are unhappy with anything that we find in our lives, we should stop blaming the externals—taxes, high prices, and conditions in general—and ask ourselves, "What am I doing to help? What am I giving? What am I sharing? Do I have a tenth of the faith that I profess?

If I give a tenth, or a tithe, isn't it logical to assume then that the other nine tenths which I retain are going to be multiplied and increased so that I will never miss my proportionate donation? One law of physics teaches that "nature abhors a vacuum." A natural law goes into action to fill the emptiness whenever any displacement occurs. What then must happen if we have one hundred dollars and give ten to a spiritual work? The Law decrees that we will never miss that ten dollars because the increase in our consciousness which comes from giving returns to us more than we give. The principle, of course, is that the ten dollars of the hundred isn't ours in the first place. It really isn't! We are merely stewards of that hundred dollars. Ten of it belongs to the Source. Straight spiritual thinking convinces us this is true.

The full potential of tithing is realized when we give one tenth of our attention, interest and substance to a spiritual work. A tithe of money is necessary material support, but a tithe of attention, time and services is the completion of this tithing. The tithe at the economic level is completed by our attention and interest. It is important that we replenish what we use.

Your decision to tithe to your church must be based upon a desire to bring Truth into the minds and hearts of all people. The purpose of a spiritual organization is to bring a Way of Life into people's awareness for the best interests of everybody concerned. Our dedication is to the teaching of Truth—that which *is* in its highest and best development. If spiritual organizations are adequately supported, most of our problems and troubles will be eliminated. Giving to a spiritual work is a prayer. It is doing the same thing for your world that you do for yourself when you go into the closet and close the door and pray. When you tithe to a spiritual work you are saying, "A tenth of my substance and my attention goes with my desire that man shall be helped through developing spiritual understanding, an awareness of the higher self, and a consciousness of God.

This automatically answers certain questions that we have about tithing. Someone says that he supports his mother, or his mother-in-law, his brother, or another relative, and that he cannot afford to tithe to his church. *Can he afford not to?* Everyone has economic responsibilities, but they do not take the place of tithing to a spiritual work. Tithing to a spiritual work means that a person is investing in the Spirit of God. When we give to charity we are doing a very necessary thing, but we are all too often prolonging a focus upon the condition instead of the solution. We should give to various charitable funds and drives, but this does not take the place of our spiritual tithe. Public and social institutions are necessary for the purpose of dealing with the outer conditions until such time as man grows enough spiritually so that the negative conditions do not exist. When we have an honest desire to aid the spiritual growth of mankind, we will tithe.

There is so much to be done in the world, so much to be accomplished that can only come about by spiritual means. It is futile to try to solve conditions and problems without paying attention to the causes that produce them. These causes are invariably within the individual, and conditions will not change until there is a change in the consciousness of the person. Helping people to make these changes within themselves should be the spiritual mission of every church. When you tithe to your church you are making it possible for spiritual teaching to be carried on for the benefit of yourself and of all people.

The principle of tithing should be used in all your thought and planning. Here is the way it works: You have a job to do. It's going to take you ten hours to do it. You have no business embarking on any part of that job until you have planned, prayed and thought about it for one hour. How many of us do that? How many of us give back to God that which is God's—the hour of attention and time? Mahatma Ghandi devoted the first three hours of each day to prayer and meditation. This was his tithe. There are at least thirty days in a month. An equivalent of three full days should be spent in prayer, treatment, thought, and enjoying things of beauty. This is tithing to ourselves, and the benefits will return a hundredfold. Can we do it? Let's try.

There are captains of industry in this country who have become what they are because they have tithed since they were children. They live by the principle of tithing, and find that it has many surprises in store for them. When you tithe you will be surprised by the amount of good you accomplish with the money which you give. You will be equally surprised to discover how much money there remains for your own use. Above all, you will be surprised at your own spiritual growth, and the inner joy you experience from the knowledge that you are a good steward. When you tithe your money, time and thought, you make it possible for the Infinite Mind to complete the circle of fulfillment within you.

DAILY THOUGHTS ABOUT PROSPERITY
THROUGH TITHING
From This Chapter

1. We cannot receive until we give, and we cannot give until we receive.
2. We can only live effectively by learning how to co-operate with the rhythm of life.
3. God is the supplier of all things; man is the steward who uses them.
4. When we establish rhythm in giving and recognize God as the Source of all things, we have a constant sense of being part of something bigger and more abundant than we are individually.
5. The full potential of tithing is realized when we give one tenth of our attention, interest and substance to spiritual work.
6. When we tithe our money and our thought we make it possible for the Infinite Mind to complete the circle of fulfillment within us.
7. Use the principle of tithing by spending one tenth of your time in prayer, thought and planning before starting any project.

From the Bible

1. And the tithe of all things brought they in abundantly.—II Chron. 31:5
2. Give, and it shall be given unto you; good measure, pressed down, and shaken together, and running over.—Luke 6:38
3. Freely ye have received, freely give.—Matt. 10:8

4. God loveth a cheerful giver.—*II Cor.* 9:7
5. Honor the Lord with thy substance, and the first fruits of all thine increase.—*Prov.* 3:9
6. Bring ye all the tithes into the storehouse. . . . *Mal.* 3:10
7. And blessed be the most high God. . . . And he gave him tithes of all.—*Gen.* 14:20

From Great Thinkers Past and Present

1. Those who tithe are always certain that they have God for a partner. —*John Murray*
2. The connection between tithing and prosperity is, after all, but a particular expression of the general law that what we are to the universe, that will the universe be to us.—*Emmet Fox*
3. Everyone should give as he receives; in fact, it is only through giving that he can receive.—*Charles Fillmore*
4. Give according to your means, or God will make your means according to your gift.—*John Hall*
5. He gives only the worthless gold who gives from a sense of duty.— *James Russell Lowell*
6. The only gift is a portion of thyself.—*Ralph Waldo Emerson*
7. There never was a person who did anything worth doing that did not receive more than he gave.—*Henry Ward Beecher*

GOLDEN BRIDGE
TO PROSPERITY

Morning Projection

I prosper in all that I do today. I pray clearly and affirmatively and all my prayers are answered. My prosperity is my answered prayer. I have what I need, I go where I want to go, I do what I want to do. I am a prosperous person in every way.

My mind is alert, alive and awake, attuned to Divine Intelligence, the one Source of all things. My good flows from this Source. God is the Source of my supply. I am the channel through which the riches of the kingdom abundantly flow. I have more than enough of everything. I use my abundance wisely and well, and I share it wisely and generously.

All limitation and lack are dissolved from my thought and feeling. I am filled with the consciousness of abundance and plenty. I express the authority of answered prayer. I am rich in all ways. God's prosperity is my prosperity now. And so it is.

Evening Retrospection

I free myself from the world and its busy ways as I immerse myself in the deep pools of spiritual reflection. I drink deeply from the nourishing fountains of the inner life. I am nourished by the food of thought. I am cleansed by the flow of Spirit. I am made whole by the action of the One Life.

My heart is filled to overflowing. I am deeply grateful for the gifts which life showers upon me. I am thankful for the great rewards which come to me. I never want for anything. God has provided for my every need. With praise and thanksgiving I accept the outpouring of His love. I am filled.

Inner peace is my most priceless possession. As I go off to sleep now, I travel the healing highway which leads directly into the heart of the Infinite. I spend this night in Abraham's bosom. I visit my heavenly home. I am one with all that is. And so it is.

25

SELF-DISCOVERY
AND SELF-EXPRESSION

The "Father's Business"

SELF-EXPRESSION is first of all a matter of self-discovery. One man when asked, "How did you find yourself this morning?" said, "I looked under the bed and there I was." We discover ourselves by looking within and finding that we have been there all the time. We don't have to travel around seeking knowledge and the material things of the world nearly as much as we must realize that any journey we take must inevitably lead us back to an awareness of self-development, self-growth, self-awareness, self-appreciation, self-improvement and self-realization. There is no limit to the number of things we can discover about ourselves.

We live in this wonderful "self," but we don't realize how wonderful it is that we are part of a larger and higher Self. We have a limiting tendency to think only in terms of jobs, names, conditions and problems. But, such thoughts have nothing to do with the higher Self. They are just something that the smaller self happens to be doing. Let us learn how to become aware of, understand and develop the true Self.

The smaller self is always guided and protected by the Inner Self which is one with God. The carpenter of Nazareth simply said, "He who hath seen me, hath seen the Father" (John 14:9), and then based his entire teaching upon the principle that That which is within us is greater than that which is in the world. Modern psychology has probed this Inner Power and added to self-understanding by revealing the marvelous properties of the subconscious mind. Successful, harmonious

180

living results when we learn to bring the outer experience into focus with the Inner Reality. Instead of condemning ourselves for our inadequacies and mistakes, we can turn weakness into strength, and faults into virtues by allowing the "Imprisoned Splendour" to come out and express itself. We are all beautiful, strong and virtuous inside. When we start to believe this, we see the appearance of it in our lives.

Self-discovery and self-expression are closely tied in with our relations with other people. We can never really judge or evaluate another person unless we put ourselves in his position and understand why he is the way he is and why he reacts the way he reacts. Even if we were to put ourselves completely in another person's position, we couldn't understand him adequately unless we traveled backward in consciousness with him to the time he was born, and saw the circumstances, the environment, the conditioning, and the forces which helped to build him.

Adequately to understand another person means to become one with him. And when we become one with this person, what do we find in him? We find ourselves. We do ourselves no service when we think of ourselves as apart from other people, or when we think of other people as being a threat to us, or in competition with us, or when we think of other people as different from us, because we are not different one from another. When we give others the freedom of expressing their purpose in life we are discovering ourselves in them, thereby gaining that which we free. When we learn to give, identify ourselves with others and understand them, we begin to make great strides toward self-discovery.

Man is a soul. This soul is immortal and lives eternally. We have always existed, we exist now, and will always exist. We cannot conceive the time when we did not live, and we cannot conceive of the time when we will not live. As Einstein pointed out for us, time moves in a curve, and eventually returns to the place where it started. We find that this same current works in the affairs of men. People are continually discovering more about things by discovering more about themselves.

Medicine, for instance, is coming around more and more to the point of view that mental and emotional attitudes are the most important factors in the diagnosis of illness. An understanding of the patient's thoughts, attitudes, and emotional factors is often more helpful in treating a case than prescriptions or surgery. A famous surgeon said recently that if he were just going into medicine he would take up biochemistry instead of surgery, because he definitely believes that surgery as a means of therapy is on the way out. The teachings of the first physician, Hippocrates, would never consider such a thing as surgery or forceful application of any external means to the human body. Hippocrates worked to develop the inner consciousness of the individual so that the illness, growth or malfunctioning would be starved out and disappear.

The ancient basic principle of "mind over matter" recognizes that there is a Law which produces what is thought into it. There is no separation between your body and your mind. You simply have a mind which at certain phases of its expression is a body. Mind seen is body; body is mind in form. What we eat provides the substance which the mind uses to build the body. The tangible form of body is of short duration, but the intangible which is our soul or consciousness—what we really are—goes on eternally. Can you doubt that? Our faith on this point has a great deal to do with discovering and expressing ourselves and, incidentally, with the experience of bodily health.

Self-discovery is a matter of getting on speaking terms with your own inner being—your soul. The soul is simply what you are. Talk to what you are, and if you don't like what you are, instruct it to become something better. If you like the direction it is going, give it free rein, go all the way with it, and co-operate with it by instructing it to "build more stately mansions."

We discover ourselves by paying unswerving attention to the inhabitants of our own consciousness. If you become discouraged today and say, "I can't seem to find my way," do not look at how far you have to go, but see how far you've already come, and you will find that there have been tremendous changes and tremendous growth. Life is kind when it removes the memory of pain from our minds, but it is kinder still when the experience remains there in consciousness as great growth, great tolerance, great beauty of soul, and great joy.

We can discover a great deal about ourselves by identifying ourselves with that which is best. We each have the choice, and within us is the equivalent of all things that present themselves to choice. Self-discovery must include a desire to grow and to be a part of the best that God has created.

Our goals may seem very distant at the moment, but remember how far you have come. Don't look to the millions of years we have to go, but look at the great distance we have come and know that here and now we have the tools for discovering and expressing ourselves. We don't have to be rich, we don't have to be handsome, we don't even have to be healthy to start with. All the tools that we need are here—now. And what are they?—an inquiring mind, a pliable point of view, a heart filled with love, an emotional content filled with peace, and a memory that serves to identify ourselves with the mother lode of all discovery: that *there is a strain within us which is common to all people, because it is an incarnation of the great Original Cause of all Being which some people call God, some call Principle, and some call Intelligence.*

There is a purpose behind all life, and it doesn't matter on what level it is—mineral, vegetable, animal or human—all is here for a purpose. This purpose is self-discovery and self-expression, because we are by nature basically self-centered. Enlightenment and growth come, not by abandoning our self-centeredness, but by expanding this center so that our awareness may extend into an ever-widening circumference. Inner knowing—or self-discovery—gives us an identification with all of life.

Whatever we are, we are possessed with a Higher Self, the Creative Intelligence, individualized and indwelling. We call it the Christ, and it is within all of us. Self expression is the process of letting our hearts beat with the Heart of the only Life there is, the great Creative Intelligence called God which is common to each and every one of us.

DAILY THOUGHTS ABOUT SELF-DISCOVERY AND SELF-EXPRESSION
From This Chapter

1. Self-expression is first of all a matter of self-discovery.
2. We discover ourselves by looking within ourselves and finding that we have been there all the time.
3. There is no limit to the things we can discover about ourselves.
4. Selfhood implies that we are part of a larger and higher Self, which is one with God.
5. Successful, harmonious living results when we learn to bring the outer experience into focus with the Inner Reality.

6. We can turn weakness into strength and faults into virtues by expressing the "Imprisoned Splendour" within us.
7. We are all beautiful, strong and virtuous inside. When we believe this, we see the appearance of it in our lives.

From the Bible

1. The desire accomplished is sweet to the soul.—*Prov. 13:19*
2. My meat is to do the will of Him that sent me, and to finish His work.—*John 4:34*
3. Even a child is known by his doings, whether his work be pure, and whether it be right.—*Prov. 20:11*
4. He is strong that executeth his word.—*Joel 2:11*
5. God . . . will render to every man according to his deeds.—*Rom. 2:5, 6*
6. A doer of the work . . . shall be blessed in his deed.—*James 1:25*
7. Now therefore perform the doing of it; that as there was a readiness to will, so there may be a performance also out of that which ye have.—*II Cor. 8:11*

From Great Thinkers Past and Present

1. Our deeds determine us, as much as we determine our deeds.— *George Eliot*
2. The flighty purpose never is o'er took, unless the deed go with it.— *Shakespeare*
3. Good actions ennoble us, and we are the sons of our own deeds.— *Cervantes*
4. No matter what a man's aims, or resolutions, or professions may be, it is by one's deeds that he is to be judged, both by God and man.— *Henry Ward Beecher*
5. Good deeds ring clear through heaven like a bell.—*Jean Paul*
6. A noble deed is a step toward God.—*J. G. Holland*
7. A life spent worthily should be measured by deeds, not years.— *Richard Brinsley Sheridan*

GOLDEN BRIDGE TO SELF-DISCOVERY AND SELF-EXPRESSION

Morning Projection

As I take inventory of who and what I am, I discover that I am a wonderful person and that I have a wonderful life to live. God dwells within me, and everything I think, feel and do is an expression of my awareness of this truth. I am God in action at the level of my comprehension. I have a long way to go, but I am encouraged and strengthened by realizing how far I have come. I move forward with great strides today.

The light which emanates from me is the light of Spirit shining through me. I express love and beauty in my world because they first live in my heart. I do great works because they are first born in my mind. I weave the tapestry of my life on the loom of Spirit, from the pattern of wholeness which Nature has established in my being.

Joyously I work outward from within. Today my world and my life are my expression of the kingdom of heaven in which my true Self dwells. And so it is.

Evening Retrospection

All through this day I have endeavored to express outwardly the wonders and beauty of the Inner Life. Now as I review my day I bring everything back into focus with the inner pattern which is God's idea of me. When I have been wrong, I admit it, and correct the situation in my mind. I correct all mistakes so that the creative action of the Law works only upon that which is true and good as I sleep.

My true mission in life is to discover God within my heart and to express him in all that I think, feel, say and do. I get my little self out of the way and express only the true Self at all times. I release all cares and concerns, and what I really am emerges and expresses itself.

The old things have passed away. The new life is in free, full flow through me now. The kingdom, the power and the glory express through my soul throughout this night and always. And so it is.

26 ✐

ATTITUDES AND HABITS
"Every Day in Every Way..."

A number of years ago, a French psychologist named Emile Coué had a considerable vogue in this country by teaching a form of affirmative mental suggestion based upon the statement, "Every day in every way I am getting better and better."

A high percentage of those who used Coué's optimistic and cheerful affirmation actually *did* get better—or thought they did—and this is actually the same thing, because what we think, we tend to become. At the same time, those who scoffed at the statement and the idea behind it, *didn't* get better, and many actually got worse, because derogatory and belittling attitudes are definitely unhealthy states of mind, and no personal good can ever come from them.

Affirmations help build healthy attitudes toward life when we want them to, and when we believe they do. A person could think about and repeat affirmations many times every day for the rest of his life and still be miserable—that is, unless he made up his mind that he *wanted* to get better, that he *wanted* to improve and grow. This is the secret of making anything work. One must desire it to work. One must respond with feeling to the idea implanted in the mind. When we think clearly and feel strongly about an idea, that idea has to happen; it can't do otherwise. Feeling releases the power of the great inner Law which accomplishes anything we desire—provided we *know* what we want.

It is my opinion that those who scoff at such an affirmation as: "Every day in every way I am getting better and better" don't want to

186

get better; they don't want to change, to grow, to become finer people. They want to stay the way they are and let others, the world, and God adjust themselves to the individual's false concept and adjustment to life.

What is it that makes a statement like Coué's work for us? Ideas become facts in our experience when we want them to, and when we believe they are going to. This is faith. Faith is the co-operation of the individual mind with the universal Law of Good.

The working principle is embodied in one word—Co-operation. There is a natural Law of Growth working through everyone of us. When we co-operate with it instead of resisting it, the Law's power is stepped up, and we achieve our true—limitless—potential. We can do and be anything we can conceive of and believe in. The only obstruction is self. A statement such as, "Every day in every way, I am getting better and better" helps us get ourselves out of the way, so that bigger things may come through.

There isn't anyone in the world who isn't interested in turning failure into success, illness into health, defeat into victory—and enjoying the best of all experiences. You are interested in these things. So am I. How do we accomplish this, except by thinking about what we want, and letting it happen? Pascal said, "Man is a thinker." When we think, we create. Good thinking creates good results. Negative or destructive thinking creates warped and unhappy situations and results. A little simple reasoning shows us that if we can think about what we want and achieve them in this way, then the way to avoid what we don't want is not to think about unhappiness, illness, lack or any other unpleasantness. Stay on the right side. We think things into existence.

Our attitudes and habits determine the pattern of our lives. They must be constantly maintained, disciplined, and controlled. "Keep thy heart with all diligence; for out of it are the issues of life" (Prov. 4:23).

Are you working too hard? Do you feel rested and refreshed, vital and full of pep, raring to go, and eager to take on life's problems and challenges? Or do you feel like a rubber band that has been stretched too long—dead, dumpy and out of shape? If this latter unsavory description fits you, pause for a moment; sit or lie down and do a little inventory-taking. Let's approach this business of living from a different point of view.

Learn to put a little less effort into things; stop trying so hard to make things happen. This may seem like strange advice, but there are occasions when matters should be left alone. Of course, this could be overdone, too, but we can learn a lot by endeavoring to understand the principle involved. The truth is that we have a great, inner Silent Partner which works for us and takes most of the load off our shoulders, if we only let it.

This business of living is for the purpose of learning from the great natural laws of the universe. Nature itself, and all living creatures except man co-operate with these laws, and therefore actually do a better job of living than we do. A tree doesn't know anything other than to be a tree. Your dog is unconcerned with everything except being himself, and in doing his best to please you, because he is a creature of love. Why then do you and I sweat and strain, when we would accomplish much more if we learned to "relax, let go and let God?"

There are many reasons why we struggle and suffer—reasons rooted in fear, insecurity, a false sense of values, and just plain not knowing— reasons too extensive to explore here. But, we can overcome them all by making a habit of approaching life joyously and expectantly, and with faith that perfect order and right action are taking place in all that we do.

When we look about our wonderful world we see man's tremendous achievements, evidences of his skill and ingenuity, a mammoth chart of growth and accomplishment. These things—great cities, beautiful homes, breath-taking bridges, awe-inspiring buildings, not to mention airplanes, automobiles, missiles and the wonders of modern scientific research—should inspire us to realize that they are only the evidence of the part of man's capacities that he has used, and that the best is yet to come.

It encourages and strengthens us as we review the accomplishments of great men of the past and present. We are all partners in all that has been done and will be done in the past, present and future. We are re-born within as we gaze upon the beauties of nature, thrilling to the brilliance of a sunset, tingling with the freshness of the dawn, and surging with power as we watch the roll of the ocean waves or ascend to the heights of lofty inspiration and fix our attention upon a distant snow-capped mountain peak. These reactions occur because we in-tuitively identify ourselves with the action of a Greater Hand which has wrought the wonders of nature.

Yes, the works of God are mighty, but the works of men—though lesser in scope—are great, and are evidence that God works through man and that we are vitally necessary in the great scheme of things to assist the great process of evolution.

Many times we are confronted with insurmountable tasks and situations. We doubt that we can make the grade. But a moment's pause and reflection suffices to remind us that others have passed this way before and have won. We find courage in their example, rediscover our own strength and wed our resources to the inner strength of life itself. These forces combine to work through us to accomplish the task.

The expectant mother resolutely and joyously co-operates with the scheme of things as she is delivered of her child. The miracle of birth has occurred billions of times and will continue. The necessary strength is always there. And men have felt that they couldn't face trouble, loss, illness and death—but these, too, are faced daily. There is no limit to man's experience and to his potential accomplishment. The Presence within us paints the picture, builds the building, and unlocks itself when we gaze into it—always becoming that which we know it to be.

DAILY THOUGHTS ABOUT ATTITUDES AND HABITS
From This Chapter

1. What we think, we tend to become.
2. Affirmations build healthy attitudes toward life when we want them to, and when we believe they will.
3. When we think clearly and feel strongly about an idea, that idea has to happen.
4. Faith is co-operation of the individual mind with the universal Law of Good.
5. The only thing that can get in the way of any of us is ourselves.
6. When we think, we create.
7. Attitudes and habits determine the pattern of our lives. They must be constantly maintained, disciplined and controlled.

From the Bible

1. Let us behave ourselves valiantly.—I Chron. 19:13
2. Depart from evil, and do good.—Psalm 34:14
3. I will behave myself wisely in a perfect way.—Psalm 101:2

4. Evil communications corrupt good manners.—*I Cor. 15:33*
5. Ask for the old paths, where is the good way, and walk therein. —*Jer. 6:16*
6. In the way of righteousness is life.—*Prov. 12:28*
7. Whatsoever ye do, do all to the glory of God.—*I Cor. 10:31*

From Great Thinkers Past and Present

1. How use doth breed a habit in a man.—*Shakespeare*
2. We first make our habits, and then our habits make us.—*John Dryden*
3. Habit is a cable. We weave a thread of it every day, and at last we cannot break it.—*Horace Mann*
4. Habit is either the best of servants, or the worst of masters.—*Nathaniel Emmons*
5. Habit is the deepest law of human nature.—*Thomas Carlyle*
6. The underlying cause of all weakness and unhappiness in man has always been, and still is, weak habit-of-thought.—*Horace Fletcher*
7. Habit, if not resisted, soon becomes necessity.—*Saint Augustine*

GOLDEN BRIDGE
TO ATTITUDES AND HABITS

Morning Projection

I don't know what is ahead for me today, but I know it can only be good. I maintain an attitude of positive expectancy. I anticipate all impending events with enthusiasm and expectation of good. I express only affirmative attitudes. I maintain positive states of mind. I have only constructive ideas. My thoughts are clear and wholesome. My emotions are controlled and balanced. My attitudes are spiritually oriented. My habits express my integration and unity in outer patterns of exemplary behavior.

I am free from all that is false and unworthy. I cleanse my life of everything that does not belong there. I examine my thoughts, feelings and attitudes carefully, and change them when necessary in order to express sustained and consistent good in my life. I am in control of all of my habits. I make sure that each one helps to express me at my highest and best at all times.

My constructive attitudes and habits are my tools of effective living throughout this day. And so it is.

Evening Retrospection

Still waters run deep. I take time to probe the heights and depths of my soul tonight. I am fearfully and wonderfully made. There is much more to me than meets the eye. I am part of the Larger Dimension. In God I live and move and have my being.

Everything unlike the nature of good is dissolved from my consciousness here and now. I express the perfect self that God knows me to be. I re-examine my attitudes and habits to be sure that this is so. I am alert and thorough in my scrutiny of my inner self. I am ruthless in weeding out all unwanted causative factors. I am diligent in my self-examination and uncompromising in my determination to change that which it is necessary to change. I embrace the disciplines of self-control and self-realization.

Quietly now, I release all concern. My attitudes and habits are in focus with the Real Self. I rest in the assurance that the creative power of the Law is healing me now. And so it is.

27 ✍

AIMS AND GOALS
The Art of Standing Tall

EVERY successful man is married to a constructive idea. This marriage unites the desire to do something worthwhile with the conviction that it can be done. The resulting power is usually sufficient to provide a life's work for an individual. When we choose this path and follow it with dedication, application, interest, and faith, our inner nature expands to the point where it is capable of meeting all difficulties and overcoming all obstacles. What is more, we will have fun doing it.

Accompanying a life lived with high purpose and noble ideals will be an abundance and satisfaction beyond our dreams, that never existed before we started creating them. Naturally, we will enjoy the fruits of our labors and so will everyone else. To the extent that our efforts benefit mankind, they express God; and to the extent that God is expressed, the individual also benefits. For those who find it, the rewards of the kingdom are great and include all things. This kingdom is right here, now, so we do not need to fear how we are going to fare, "for your Father knoweth what things ye have need of, before ye ask him" (Matt. 6:8).

Have you ever planted a seed? What happened? The seed grew, didn't it? Whatever seed we plant determines the kind of plant we can expect. If the ground is fertile, fresh and sweet and if the seed is good, then we get a good crop. So it is with your mind when you think clearly, when you have definite, strong, vital and good ideas. Place them in the creative soil of your mind and good crops will result. This is an automatic and almost mechanical action in nature. It works according to your conviction, and your belief. If you understand that

192

life cannot say "no" to you, then you get rid of all inferiority, doubt, and feelings of weakness and inadequacy.

The inner mind works to produce that which the outer mind selects for it. This inner mind cannot help but produce what you give it, any more than the earth can reject the seed or fail to contribute to its growth. We all have read the story of Aladdin and his wonderful lamp. The genie that appeared when the lamp was rubbed would do Aladdin's bidding and could accomplish the most difficult tasks at Aladdin's command. This is symbolic of the power within each of us. Call forth your genie; the giant within you. It will respond and work, because it can't do otherwise.

What do you want in your world? Most of our ambitions, desires and goals are centered around these major objectives: health, happiness, success, prosperity, freedom, and creative self-expression. All of our dreams and objectives focus somewhere along the line of these major classifications. Don't be afraid to choose. Be bold: be convinced that you can achieve what you want to achieve, that you can do what you want to do. As soon as you make up your mind, this creative power within you goes to work to give form, substance, shape and action to what you have chosen. Anyone who has ever gotten anywhere knows about this principle.

Here is the big secret: *The inner mind is amenable to suggestion; it must obey. It can only accept and do; it cannot reject.*

Here is another great secret: *Not only is the inner mind (the subconscious mind) amenable to suggestion, but it works better when you believe in it.* Your subconscious mind responds to mental concepts, to pictures, to strong feelings, to faith, to conviction, and to orders. But if you are fearful, uncertain, or disturbed, your subconscious mind will reproduce and multiply that confusion in your thought and feeling.

Your conscious mind is the control center. Thus, you can weed out this inner garden of the subconscious mind occasionally by getting rid of feelings of inferiority, guilt, hostility and fear. Just clean them up. You see, the thing that made us sick or troubled also has the power to heal us and get us out of trouble. There is something within us that is much more beautiful and wonderful than anything we've ever known about. It works. It has to work.

There is a great inner working of Nature that we must not overlook. Consider, for example, the growth potential of a tiny seed. Consider the regularity of the seasons. Consider the flight instinct of the homing pigeon. Some great Inner Intelligence is at work in all instances. Similarly, there is something within us that knows how to take care of many things we never even think about. Do you know how to digest your food? Do you know how to fill your lungs with air? Do you know how to establish, regulate and direct the metabolism of your body—the assimilation of foodstuff so that it builds muscles, bones and flesh? No, you don't know how consciously, but there is a wisdom within you that does know. There is a power within you that is working under the creative direction of Infinite Intelligence.

With our conscious minds we can make decisions and also give orders to this Inner Intelligence. It is as if we had all the wisdom, all the power, all the strength and all the knowledge that ever existed, available to be used whenever we want to use it, in whatever way we want to use it. All we have to do is to have ideas and clear thoughts, back them up with conviction and faith, put them deep down into the subconscious mind that is waiting to receive the orders, and let it happen.

Change your mind and your life will change. The genie will come when you rub your lamp. When we learn to think, when we wake up and live, when we formulate ideas, plans and goals, we are summoning our genie.

Your big job is to impress upon the inner mind that which you want to experience and let it produce it for you. It can't help but do so. It can't say no. It can't reject. It doesn't discriminate, choose, select, evaluate or judge. It only works according to the specifications of your thought, your choice, your will—that which you have decided upon. So, decide wisely and well. Let us do this right now with these positive treatments. They are orders to your subconscious mind. As you repeat these constructive ideas, you are building the inner structure of your aims and goals.

PERSONAL TREATMENT FOR GUIDANCE
AND DIRECTION

I know who I am, where I am going, and how to get there. I receive guidance and direction from the Infinite Mind within me. I get on course, and I stay there, moving steadily forward along the journey of life. I am never lost, never alone. God is my compass, my guide and my director. *And so it is.*

PERSONAL TREATMENT FOR SAFETY AND PROTECTION

I am safe. I am protected. God has had his arm around me for a long time, and he is never going to take it away. No evil can befall me, either from inside or outside. I am filled with good. I am surrounded with light. I am in tune with the Infinite. I am one with God. I am safe and secure. *And so it is.*

PERSONAL TREATMENT FOR ORDER AND RIGHT ACTION

Perfect order and right action are established in my life today. All that I do is ordered and purposeful. I am sure within myself and true in my actions. I am clear and definite in my mind. I have my feelings under control. I am specific in my intentions. I do the best possible job of being myself. The pattern of purposeful accomplishment unfolds in my experience. *And so it is.*

PERSONAL TREATMENT FOR BALANCE AND HARMONY

I am serenely poised on the delicate scales of life. I maintain balance in all that I think, feel, say and do. I experience harmony in my private life, in my relations with other people, and in my world of experience. I am a mature and balanced individual. I express the perfect symmetry and unity of the well-lived life. I endeavor to be a good example at all times and in all ways. *And so it is.*

DAILY THOUGHTS ABOUT AIMS AND GOALS
From This Chapter

1. We get out of life exactly what we put into it.
2. Having worthy goals and purposes in life helps both others and ourselves.
3. There has never been a successful man who has not been married to a constructive idea.
4. Constructive aims unite the desire to do something worthwhile with the conviction that it can be done.
5. When we choose a worthy goal and follow it with dedication, appli-

cation, interest and faith, our inner nature expands to the point where it is capable of meeting all difficulties and overcoming all obstacles.

6. Constructive attitudes and efforts produce abundance and satisfaction which cannot exist until we start creating them.
7. To the extent that our efforts benefit mankind, they express God; to the extent that God is expressed, the individual also benefits.

From the Bible

1. Ponder the path of thy feet, and let all thy ways be established. —*Prov. 4:26*
2. Turn not to the right hand nor to the left: remove thy foot from evil. —*Prov. 4:27*
3. A man's heart deviseth his way: but the Lord directeth his steps. —*Prov. 16:9*
4. Every man that striveth for the mastery is temperate in all things. —*I Cor. 9:25*
5. Covet earnestly the best gifts.—*I Cor. 12:31*
6. This one thing I do, forgetting those things which are behind, and reaching forth unto those things which are before, I press toward the mark for the prize. . . .—*Phil. 3:13, 14*
7. The path of the just is as the shining light, that shineth more and more unto the perfect day.—*Prov. 4:18*

From Great Thinkers Past and Present

1. High aims form high characters, and great objects bring out great minds.—*Tyron Edwards*
2. Have a purpose in life, and having it, throw into your work such strength of mind and muscle as God has given you.—*Thomas Carlyle*
3. Not failure, but low aim, is crime.—*James Russell Lowell*
4. Aim at the sun, and you may not reach it; but your arrow will fly far higher than if aimed at an object on a level with yourself.—*Joel Hawes*
5. Dream manfully and nobly, and thy dreams shall be prophets.—*Bulwer Lytton*
6. In great attempts it is glorious even to fail.—*Longinus*
7. High aims and lofty purposes are the wings of the soul aiding it to mount to heaven.—*Samuel Spring*
8. Providence has nothing good or high in store for one who does not resolutely aim at something high or good.—A purpose is the eternal condition of success.—*Theodore T. Munger*

GOLDEN BRIDGE
TO ACHIEVEMENT

Morning Projection

I set my sights high today. Nothing is too wonderful to happen. Nothing is too good to be true. I hitch my wagon to a star, and away I go! Heaven is my destination, and I experience it in everything I do. The sky is the limit. Nothing can hamper or limit me. The free, full flow of life is surging through me now, sweeping me along to the top.

Those things which I want are chosen from the standard of that which is for the greatest good of the greatest number. I always endeavor to do that which is for the best interests of everyone concerned. As I am clear, definite and specific in my thought; as I am filled with love, faith and dedication; as I act from purity of motive and efficiency of execution, my consciousness develops to the point where I know I can be anything I want to be and do everything I want to do.

"I can do all things through Christ which strengtheneth me" (Phil. 4:13). *"The Father that dwelleth in me, he doeth the works"* (John 14:10).

Evening Retrospection

The satisfaction of jobs well done and a day well spent in being about my Father's business gives me complete peace as this day ends. I have run the race to the swift. I have fought the good fight. I have done the best that I could at that moment. Now I align myself with God's healing forces so that my best can become better.

I forgive myself my failures by turning them into successes and achievements. I examine myself to find the ways in which I was wanting, and I correct them. I will never make the same mistake twice. I resolve to press steadily onward, fulfilling my purpose in life and living up to my full potential.

Having done the best that I could throughout this day, and having cleansed my heart and mind of everything less than my image and conviction of true achievement, I now stand. I let God take over. I let Him who knows how to do that which needs to be done, do it. In deep and fulfilling sleep, the creative power of life moves me upward on the path of life. And so it is.

28 ✍

RELIGION

Something to Live By

Two guests seated near the foot of the table at a fashionable dinner party were engaged in low-voiced but earnest conversation. Unable to hear the conversation, the host finally inquired, "I say, what are you fellows discussing?"

"We were talking about God," one of the guests replied.

"Oh, really now!" the host exclaimed. "Hardly the subject for a dinner party, now is it?"

Such is the trend of the times. Yet, we are not entirely to blame. Unable to find a satisfactory spiritual philosophy which he can understand and use, modern man has turned his attention where his understanding and his ability to achieve results are seemingly more effective —to science and its study of the phenomena of the world and the physical universe, with its focus on outer rather than inner space. But the emphasis will change and proper balance will be attained when we develop a spiritual philosophy that we can both believe in and live by. This starts with the necessity of a concept which removes all fear and superstition concerning God by recognizing It as an Intelligence and a Power—the one First Cause back of all things.

Unfortunately, the churches have only recently provided help in this direction. Dogmas and theologies which have grown out of ignorance, faulty and literal interpretation of the Bible, and human opinion without benefit of either insight or revelation, have obscured rather than enlightened. Emerson observed that in his day most ministers spoke from the pulpit as if God were dead. Fortunately, in order to survive, modern religion is forced to give people something they can use to meet the everyday problems of life. The ultimatum is clear and definite, "Deliver the goods or perish." This is a very healthy situation. The law of survival of the fittest is basic in Nature. No part of life is immune. The requirement applies to philosophies, teachers, books and churches. The religion which gives the greatest help will be the one which we will follow. Man's first basic need is to find God within himself. The problem never changes. Systems come and go, but each generation continues its quest for the answer.

Religion deals with intangibles about which more and more is being discovered. It must always remain fluid, adapting itself to the framework and language of each age. If the church remains rigid, this resistance causes a revolution, as has happened several times in the past. But, usually there is a process of evolution, such as we witness today, where the emphasis is placed upon the mind and the inner life of the individual. We are intuitively aware that we must develop the areas of inner space before our penetrations into outer space can have any purpose or meaning. Even in the countries where false ideologies have endeavored to stamp out the very idea of God, "truth springs eternal" and man continues his search for God. He does this to meet his most basic need—a sense of oneness with that which is greater than he is.

All roads lead to God. Some are more winding and tortuous than others; that's all. But we do all eventually get there. A wise and humorous teacher of mine used to say, "We're all hell-bent for heaven by way of evolution." Life is a journey. God (good) is our destination. The secret is to experience the good every step along the way, to live every moment from the point of our highest awareness—with the constant recognition of the presence of God. Brother Lawrence, the humble monk, called this "practicing the presence of God." His life became one of ineffable peace and inspiration as this was his constant guide. Whether peeling potatoes in the kitchen of the abbey, or serving his fellow monastics in a menial position, he saw God in everything, in every person, and in every situation. This made him a mature person, just as you and I will be when we realize that the mature individual is the one who relates himself affirmatively to life.

In looking around us, we see that we are relating ourselves affirmatively in many ways, but that our connection with other aspects of life is purely negative. Nearly everyone senses this within himself, but it is seldom that we know what to do about it. Answers have been sought in education, religion, psychiatry, governmental and social reforms, but none of these has ever furnished the full answer. It becomes more and more clear that the solution to our problems cannot be found by looking outside of ourselves. We must look within. The integrated individual is the one who has recognized the issues of life, and is making an honest effort to face and solve them by aligning himself with the infallible resources of his own higher nature.

The true nature of man, of course, is God—All Good. When we recognize the true axis of our potential and destiny, we can turn directly to the Source of our being—that area within ourselves where God and man are one. Many people are ready for this step in their thinking, but they seem unable to find the link which will connect them with what they seek. Psychiatry, with its scientific method of analyzing the hidden causes within the individual, may seem to be the answer, but by itself it offers no constructive help toward building the integration which is our goal. Man still must search.

Religion has long claimed dominion over the spiritual side of man, but the accomplishments of religion will not support its right to this claim. Superstition, ritual, dogma, theology, and rock-ribbed self-righteousness and inflexibility have made religion in the orthodox sense all but useless in being any practical help to us in our everyday lives. But despite orthodox religion's failure to grow and adapt itself to the demands and needs of modern man, man himself insists on having a religion which will work, and he is slowly evolving one through channels of understanding from within himself.

In the past few years, many seeking people have said, "Give me something which bridges the gap between psychiatry and religion, and I will go all the way with it." What they really mean is, "I believe in God, and I want to work with him, but I don't know how. Will you show me the way?" Man's interest in God actually begins and ends at the personal level. No idea can be grasped until it is understood and experienced within the individual. God is the Infinite Idea. He can be observed in outer forms and events, but he can only be experienced within the individual consciousness. Before we can get very far with religion of any kind, we must face the fact that God, the Universal Aspect of Life, is a highly personal matter. No one can experience life for us. No one can explain God to us. No one can express the love in us. And no one can define truth for us. The infinite defies restriction. There has never yet been a completely satisfactory practical approach to religion. A man's religion is what he himself knows about God. We can only know what we have personally experienced. Therefore, the true religion must really be a process of unfolding and development. The individual must be shown the way to become what he really is. Since man is evolving as an individual expression of the Infinite Idea, any religion which limits itself to set procedures and beliefs may do more harm than good.

The above is written with full recognition that this sad state of affairs results from ignorance and human frailty rather than from evil intent, but the situation exists nevertheless. Orthodox religion has not done its job, and it will not do it until its leaders view their work as an agency of life. Something is radically wrong with a teaching or philosophy which instills guilt in the individual, and tries to show him salvation through outer conformity rather than through inner spiritual development. It is probably true that the best of intentions lie behind these mistakes in teaching, but ineptitude and superstition have no place in modern religion. We must face reality. "Ignorance of the Law is no excuse."

Many ministers and spiritual leaders have recognized the situation and their responsibility toward it, and have started to break through the crusts of orthodoxy and religious bigotry. Recognizing that Christianity has never really been tried, several modern orthodox ministers have set about teaching it, only to meet with opposition at every turn. The new wine usually cracks the old bottles, and the great message has to be diluted before it will be drunk by the elders. Some of the modern orthodox teachers start with a clear conception of the process of individual spiritual development, but attempt the explanation in vague and meaningless orthodox terms, so that the student, having been fired with hope and expectancy, is left more confused than ever. He knows there is something that he needs to know, but no one seems to be able to tell him what it is.

This "something" we all want to know, of course, is how to reach God. What do we do? What do we say? How do we pray? There are answers to all of these questions. We must learn to find these answers within ourselves. When we reach the conviction that this faculty is available to each and every one of us, we will have taken a great step forward in the development of a practical, modern religion.

God is Infinite Intelligence. He works through us as a Law of Mind. As we realize that what we are determines what God is in us, we have found the religion that works.

DAILY THOUGHTS ABOUT RELIGION
From This Chapter

1. Man needs a spiritual philosophy he can both believe in and live by.
2. The purpose of religion is to teach us to live by teaching us to find God within ourselves.
3. Since it deals with the intangibles about which more and more is being discovered, religion must always remain fluid and adapt itself to each age.
4. When we are filled with love, gentleness and enthusiasm we are filled with God.
5. The mature person is one who relates himself affirmatively to life.
6. The integrated person recognizes the issues of life and makes an effort to face them and solve them by aligning himself with his own higher nature.
7. God can be observed in outer forms and events, but he can only be experienced within the individual consciousness.

From the Bible

1. According to your faith be it unto you.—*Matt. 9:29*
2. If thou canst believe, all things are possible to him that believeth. *Mark 9:23*
3. Lord, I believe: help thou mine unbelief.—*Mark 9:24*
4. Let us hold fast the profession of our faith without wavering.—*Heb. 10:23*
5. If any man among you seem to be religious, and bridleth not his tongue, but deceiveth his own heart, this man's religion is vain.—*James 1:27*
6. Pure religion and undefiled before God and the Father is this, To visit the fatherless and widows in their affliction, and to keep himself unspotted from the world.—*James 1:27*
7. Ye should earnestly contend for the faith which was once delivered unto the saints.—*Jude 1:3*

From Great Thinkers Past and Present

1. Religion is the sum of the expansive impulses of a being.—*Havelock Ellis*

2. Take away God and religion, and men live to no purpose, without proposing any worthy and considerable end of life to themselves.—*John Tillotson*

3. Science and religion no more contradict each other than light and electricity.—*William Hiram Foulkes*

4. True religion and virtue give a cheerful and happy turn to the mind; admit of all true pleasures, and even procure for us the highest.—*Joseph Addison*

5. No sciences are better attested than the religion of the Bible.—*Newton*

6. Men will wrangle for religion; write for it; fight for it; die for it; anything but live for it.—*Caleb C. Colton*

7. A man who puts aside his religion because he is going into society, is like one taking off his shoes because he is about to walk upon thorns.—*Richard Cecil*

GOLDEN BRIDGE TO RELIGION

Morning Projection

My religion is the set of beliefs that I live by. I believe in God, I believe in Life, I believe in myself, I believe in people. I believe in the process whereby the universal is constantly individualizing itself. I believe that I am an individual expression of the One Mind which is God.

The Infinite is personal to me because I believe that the Divine Presence is incarnated in me, and expresses itself through me as a creative Law of Love. I know that in reality I am perfect and that my life's work is to make this truth a fact in my experience. I know that my personal consciousness is the key to everything that happens in my world. As I align myself with the Life Force within me, the law of cause and effect orders and harmonizes my world.

Mine is a religion of healthy-mindedness. I am a whole being, an integrated wholeness of spirit, soul, mind, emotion, body and experience. This wholeness is my living expression of my personal religion. And so it is.

Evening Retrospection

I surrender my personality into the everlasting arms of Spirit. I travel upward and inward in consciousness away from the world around me as I encourage my soul to find its way into communion with the One.

My body is relaxed and receptive as I experience perfect circulation, perfect assimilation and perfect elimination. My mind is quiet and still as I focus it on the inner spaces of the cosmos. The wonders of the heavens become a living experience in my soul as I surrender it into the keeping of the higher self.

I am aligned with life. I am in tune with the Infinite. I orbit freely among the celestial spheres of the cosmos. I individualize Infinity. I am consciously aware of my divinity. All barriers and boundaries dissolve as I float serenely into the Light. I achieve total experience. The Higher Forces have their way with me. I sleep, but more than ever before—I am awake. And so it is.

29 ❧

PRAYER AND TREATMENT
"Teach Us to Pray"

Prayer is talking to God in language which we both can understand.

This is the only key we need. True prayer is talking things over with the Power which knows more about things than we do. Prayer is the highest power available to man, but we know too little about it to be able to practice it effectively. "We pray, but we pray amiss."

Who is there who hasn't prayed, or at least tried to? We all have. Someone has said that all difficulties of mankind come from the frustration of unanswered prayer. Can you conceive of a power which would answer your prayer and not mine, or who would answer prayers at one time and not another? I am very much afraid that all too many times we pray to something outside of ourselves, rather than praying to realize the Essence and Unity which indwells.

It is natural to pray. Prayer is the gateway to God—to guidance, strength, and greater understanding. Prayer is the means by which we become one with the Indwelling Source of everything there is. Prayer is a way of life. Emerson says, "Prayer is the contemplation of the facts of life from the highest point of view." St. Paul admonishes us to "pray without ceasing" (I Thess. 5:17). Prayer is a process of identification— a process of becoming one with that which is higher and better than we are.

Prayer serves the purpose of bringing about a psychological change in a person. Prayer advances us from where we are to where we want to be in mental and spiritual realization. Prayer is the process by which man changes himself to become more like his true higher self. A prayer is not a prayer unless a man undergoes a change within his own consciousness—within his own mind.

Prayer is the journey which the personality must take in order to become one with the Spirit. Every time we send this personality—the thinking mind—on up into the atmosphere of the Spirit we permanently change ourselves for the better.

The Master said, "Seek ye first the Kingdom . . . and all these things shall be added unto you" (Matt. 6:33). This kingdom is the goal of prayer. Prayer should be positive and affirmative, and we must give thanks for what we are about to receive before we pray for it. We don't really pray for anything; we pray to know our unity and identification with that thing. We do not pray to an outside power. We pray to an indwelling Presence because there is no separation. All is One.

Prayer is the nourisher of the soul, the teacher of the mind, and the guide to purposeful activity. Prayer is the means by which we receive our spiritual food, without which our lives become empty, meaningless, and filled with desperation and trouble. A life without prayer can never reach its full potential. A person who learns and uses prayer will obtain access to means for obtaining fulfillment and purpose. Prayer is active participation with Universal Headquarters. Prayer is a conference with the Head Man. *Prayer is talking to God in language which we both can understand.*

Prayers have been offered to gods and to God since man first developed a glimmering of spiritual awareness, but our prayers have still not grown beyond the blind instinct of hope which drives us to seek union with a greater power. Usually this hope is a "last-ditch" proposition, and we only try prayer when everything else has failed. Therefore, it is usually effective only in part, because we not only have little faith in prayer, but we have never really taken the time to learn how to pray effectively.

The time has come for us to take the mystery and superstition out of prayer. Prayer is both an art and a science, and as such, we can learn about it, and develop our powers of expression through prayer. It is an art because it is based upon universal principles of truth. It is a science because by learning definite techniques and procedures, and following them, we activate causes which bring about specific results. In the

Science of Mind, we teach a technique of scientific prayer called "treatment."[1]

Scientific prayer gives us the opportunity to treat ourselves to full and abundant living, to rewards, fulfillment, and appreciation of life greater than we have ever experienced. Knowing how to treat can well be the most important knowledge which we possesss. Knowledge of treatment can change our lives eternally for the better, if we learn and apply its principles. Treatment is a matter of synchronizing the individual mind with the Universal Mind. Many unpleasant situations of life will change, if we are willing to amend our patterns of thought and recondition them along lines of constructive thought. What happens to us is determined by the thoughts and attitudes which we occupy in our minds.

Our job in treating ourselves to life is to keep ever alive and burning brightly the fires of hope, of faith, of love and fulfillment within our own hearts. When we do that, we are developing an ability to choose what we want in our lives, and are conditioning and directing the subconscious mind to produce it for us. This takes constant and continuous practice in treatment. Treatment is first a matter of training the conscious mind how to choose what it wants. This is completely different from saying that prayer is just to be used to get what we want. Notice the difference. Treatment trains the conscious mind to choose what it wants. When the conscious mind is well trained, it can't possibly want anything that isn't good.

Treatment is a way of keeping our thought clear and keeping our attitudes toward life balanced. Treatment is a matter of using the conscious mind to select what we want in life, and in conditioning the subconscious mind to produce it for us. Treatment is a scientific, affirmative statement of truth, for the purpose of bringing about a change for the better. The conscious mind is always thinking about something. Our job in treatment is to train our conscious mind to think only along constructive lines. It is important that we control our conscious thinking, because in this way we establish dominion over our entire consciousness. Thoughts and beliefs held in our conscious mind are received by and impressed upon our subconscious mind—which is one with the Universal Subjective Mind, and works as Law

[1] See the author's *Human Problems and How To Solve Them*, Chapter 6.

to produce what is thought into it. This is the same law of cause and effect which produces the plant from the seed.

There is that which initiates and that which creates. The male principle acts, and the female reacts. The male selects and the female receives. Since God is the One Mind, and these two functions are operating in the Universal Mind as Spirit and Law, they are also present and active in your mind and mine. On the individual level, we call these twin aspects of the mind the conscious and the subconscious. God is both personal and impersonal. The Presence is personal; the Principle is impersonal—"a blind force, not knowing, only doing."

God (the ultimate Allness) has always been described as a Trinity—three aspects in One. A little thought shows us that this is completely true. As God is everything that is, then all things are contained therein. As the male and female aspects are naturally productive, the third aspect of the Trinity is the Son—or that which is born out of the interaction of the Father's and Mother's functions. In modern terms, the Trinity is described as Spirit, Mind, and Body. Spirit, the power that knows itself, is the First Cause. Mind, the universal creative Law as Principle, is the way Spirit works. And Body is that which is produced. Spirit acts; Mind reacts; and Body is acted upon. This process is taking place throughout nature, and therefore through us individually. A little thought about it will greatly increase our recognition of God and our capacity for accomplishment through prayer.

Everything in our experience springs from attitudes and concepts consciously or subconsciously held within our own minds. A thought in mind is the cause of what appears in our lives. Treatment, scientific prayer, is a matter of controlling these thoughts by affirming the reality of constructive and creative good until the subconscious accepts it. This takes some doing. There is no royal road to spiritual or material fulfillment. It all takes work.

Treatment is the key which opens the gates to our own magnificent inner potential. Instead of believing what the world says, let us believe what our inner realization has to tell us, and we will start to experience more perfect conditions in our lives.

It is up to us to re-educate ourselves intellectually and spiritually. "Spiritual" simply describes our higher and finer values. Each man must discover the reality of these values within himself. This can be done only by spending some time on it. Would we expect to have a beautiful home without spending some time in keeping it up? Would we expect to have lovely children without spending time training them? Would we expect to have a good business without putting time, money, effort, and prayer into it? Then how can we expect to have a beautiful life, healthy and happy, abundant and free, if we don't spend some time on it?

The way to spend this time is not in worry, in struggle, or in unhappiness, but in treatment—stating those things which we know intuitively to be true, so that the subconscious reaction may work as a Law to bring them about. Treatment is the first step in a way of life which teaches how to be perfect, even as our Father in heaven is perfect.

PERSONAL DAILY TREATMENT

"This is a personal treatment recognizing wholeness, order and right action taking place through my life and everything that I do. I am constantly working in co-operation with the forces of good that surround and indwell me.

"I am always in my right place, doing that which is necessary and right for me to do. I have the strength, interest and energy to discharge all my responsibilities and obligations effectively. A constant stream of Divine energy is flowing through me and I am refreshed by constructive activities. Every night I sleep in peace, with full sustained rest, and I awake in joy.

"I now institute harmony and right action in my life. I see the whole picture clearly. I establish it in my inner mind, and I let the Law of Creative Right Action take over. I release these things. I am free from concern. I know that the Law of Right Action is fulfilling my entire life pattern now. The power that created me and put me here motivates and activates me throughout this day. *And so it is.*"

PERSONAL TREATMENT FOR EMOTIONAL MATURITY

"Today I get my inner life in order. My feelings, emotions, urges and desires are all attuned to an inner pattern which is whole and perfect. 'Today I am a man [or woman].' I am adult. I am grown up. 'I put aside childish things.' I give thanks for my emotional maturity now. *And so it is."*

PERSONAL TREATMENT FOR INTELLECTUAL MATURITY

"My mind is my use of the One Mind—the Infinite Intelligence which is God. I align my thoughts and ideas with the Source of all knowledge, inspiration, understanding, and wisdom. I learn to organize my mind. I direct my brain constructively. I use my head. I think straight. I know what I am doing. *And so it is."*

PERSONAL TREATMENT FOR SPIRITUAL MATURITY

"The Spirit within me is whole, eternal, enduring—perfect. I am one with this Spirit. 'I and my Father are one. He that hath seen me hath seen the Father. I am in the Father, and the Father in me.' I know that the 'Father which is in heaven' is truly my Father—Divine Spirit flowing through, creating and re-creating me now. *And so it is."*

PERSONAL TREATMENT FOR WHOLENESS

"The wholeness of life indwells every cell of my being. I am one with God's perfect idea of what I am. All obstructions are cleared from my consciousness as I identify with the Infinite Healing Presence—the Mind and Life of God indwelling. I express my higher self at all times. I am an integrated person—complete in body, mind and spirit. I am whole now. I am healed. I give thanks that this is so. *And so it is."*

DAILY THOUGHTS ABOUT PRAYER
From This Chapter

1. Prayer is talking to God in language which we both can understand.
2. Prayer is the process of becoming one with God.
3. Prayer is for the purpose of bringing about a psychological change within the individual.
4. Prayer is a way of life.
5. Effective prayer must be positive and affirmative.

6. Prayer is the journey which the personality must take in order to become one with Spirit.
7. Prayer is both an art and a science.

From the Bible

1. Where two or three are gathered together in my name, there am I in the midst of them.—*Matt. 18:20*
2. Watch and pray, that ye enter not into temptation.—*Matt. 26:41*
3. Men ought always to pray, and not to faint.—*Luke 18:1*
4. I will pray with the spirit, and I will pray with the understanding also.—*I Cor. 14:15*
5. Pray without ceasing.—*I Thess. 5:17*
6. The Lord . . . heareth the prayer of the righteous.—*Prov. 15:29*
7. Therefore I say unto you, What things soever ye desire, when ye pray, believe that ye receive them, and ye shall have them.—*Mark 11:24*

From Great Thinkers Past and Present

1. Prayer is not overcoming God's reluctance; it is laying hold of His highest willingness.—*Richard C. Trench*
2. The prayer that begins with trustfulness, and passes on into waiting, will always end in thankfulness, triumph, and praise.—*Alexander Maclaren*
3. I know no blessing so small as to be reasonably expected without prayer, nor any so great but may be attained by it.—*Robert South*
4. A prayer in its simplest definition is merely a wish turned God-ward. —*Phillips Brooks*
5. Our prayers should be for blessings in general, for God knows best what is good for us.—*Socrates*
6. The fewer words the better prayer.—*Martin Luther*
7. Practice in life whatever you pray for, and God will give it to you more abundantly.—*Edward B. Pusey*

GOLDEN BRIDGE OF PRAYER

Morning Projection

Today I recognize my completeness and oneness with the Eternal Spirit of Life which flows through me. I am one with the Christ of my being. I can do all things through Christ which strengtheneth me. I am a native of eternity. I have always existed and I will always exist. I am completely at home in God's limitless universe. I know who I am and where I am going. I am a perfect child of a perfect Father and I dwell in the house of the Lord forever. My eye is single and my entire being is filled with light as I take my place in the secret place of the Most High. My constant companion is that Great Being which inhabits the lonely places and brings richness and fulfillment to the loving heart. I embrace the universe today. I clasp all of God's creatures to my heart and I let the teeming love from on high flow out through me making all things whole and new. I live because I love. Love fulfills my life today and I am one with Him. Thank you Father. And so it is.

Evening Retrospection

During my evening prayer I talk all things over with the Father. I and my Father are one, and I share all things with him. I pray without ceasing, constantly keeping my thoughts and feelings attuned to the indwelling perfection which is the pattern of my true being. My prayer expresses what I am. Through prayer I recognize and affirm the presence of God in my life.

In this sweet hour of prayer I wash this day clean of all negativity, failure and impurity. Through this prayer this day becomes what it should have been. Through prayer my life becomes that which it should be. In prayer I cleanse my heart of everything except the good, the true and the beautiful. Through prayer I build the inner pattern of that which I become.

> Our Father which art in heaven,
> Hallowed by thy name.
> Thy kingdom come.
> Thy will be done in earth,
> As it is in heaven.
> Give us this day our daily bread.
> And forgive us our trespasses,

As we forgive those who trespass against us.
And lead us not into temptation,
But deliver us from evil:
For thine is the kingdom,
And the power,
And the glory, for ever.
Amen.

And so it is.

30

AGE

Breaking the Age Barrier

Grow old along with me!
The best is yet to be,
The last of life, for which the first was made:
Our times are in his hand
Who saith, "A whole I planned,
Youth shows but half; trust God, see all, nor be afraid."

—*Robert Browning*, "Rabbi Ben Ezra"

As man has learned more about himself and the nature of the world and the universe in which he dwells, as science is constantly making significant discoveries about the human body and the food that we eat, as we are learning how to channel our thoughts, feelings and attitudes constructively, and as more and more people are breaking the age barrier, "old age" is mercifully becoming a thing of the past.

One modern researcher has observed that second childhood comes because the individual never outgrew his first. The consensus is that the best insurance against old age is intelligent, sensible, balanced, constructive living at every age—that there are no specific problems of age, only problems of living. Gerontology, the science of aging, holds that aging is a part of living and that we will overcome the fear of age and the problems usually associated with it when we believe with Browning that "the best is yet to be." Gerontologists point out that many attributes improve as age sets in. Speed may slow down, but endurance often improves. Judgment, wisdom and understanding increase—providing that there was intelligence in the earlier periods of life. There seems much to be said in favor of Browning's observation: "The last of life, for which the first was made."

The literal belief in the Biblical statement that "the days of our years are three-score years and ten" (Psalm 90:10), has kept mankind in the bondage of false belief in limited life expectancy for thousands of years. The Bible was never meant to be interpreted literally, and even if it were, a little intelligence would show us that they either measured time differently in those days, with Methuselah living nine hundred years and others nearly as long, or that the Bible speaks with a language of numerical symbolism which has nothing to do with time measurements as we know them. It hardly seems likely that since Moses lived to be one hundred and twenty with "his eye . . . not dim, nor his natural force abated" (Deut. 34:7), that the "three-score years and ten" in Moses' prayer refer to literal life expectancy. It is more logical to assume that in both instances the use of numbers have a symbolic meaning having to do with man's spiritual development.

Moses' life, for instance, was made up of three periods of forty years each spent in Egypt, Midian and wandering in the wilderness. Forty is used in the Bible to indicate a period of preparation for important work to follow. Each of the periods of Moses' life was preparation for the next. The Gospels relate that Jesus spent "forty days fasting" and "forty days in the wilderness" at several different periods, always preceding important and significant events in his ministry. In our own lives, the first forty years may well be thought of as preparation for the really important part of our lives. Victor Hugo said, "Forty is the old age of youth; fifty is the youth of old age." We have just prepared ourselves at forty and are just getting started at fifty.

Remember, the numbers are only symbolic of stages of development, and have nothing to do with chronological age. God does not deal in time, place or detail. Our life is God's life living itself through us. It is infinite and eternal, it had no beginning and will have no end. As for the "three-score years and ten," the numbered symbolism is most revealing. The total is seventy, an extension of seven, the most remarkable of all numbers, indicating the seven levels of man's nature, seven aspects of God, the seven days of creation (seven steps in the creative process), and other significant groupings of seven. Seven does not act, and is not acted upon. It is a complete number. Now, take this complete number, and multiply it by ten, which is merely an amplification of one, the number of God, or wholeness. In other words, the seventy "years" of man's life indicate that his life is God's life, and we live in him. We have lived many lifetimes and will live many more, and seventy will always be "the days of our years," because the business of life is to attain spiritual development or wholeness.

The seventy can be reached in several other ways: (1) Add thirty (the number of the Trinity—Spirit, Mind and Body) to forty (the number of preparation), and we find that the seventy "days of our years" represent maturity on these three levels of our make-up. (2) Now add up the "three-score years and ten"; they total seventy. A score is twenty—two multiplied by ten. Two is the number of man— the belief in good *and* evil, the belief in God *and* man. The "three-score" represents the stages in our development as we grow out of the false belief in duality on the three levels of Spirit, Mind and Body— the Trinity again. We reach seventy by adding ten—the activation of one, the number of God.

No matter how we approach it, we arrive at the conclusion that all roads lead to God, and that "the days of our years" are for the purpose of conducting "the Father's business." A person who dedicates his life to this purpose will not and cannot grow old. Age is a myth and a delusion. The phrase "old age" must be erased from our minds and from our vocabulary.

General Douglas MacArthur, Winston Churchill, Konrad Adenauer, Somerset Maugham, Samuel Goldwyn, former President Herbert Hoover, Carl Sandburg, and Henry Kaiser are but a few of the modern giants who have successfully broken the age barrier. They may have slowed down but they give no sign of stopping. Their contribution to our world continues to be constructive and inspiring. These famous people who have long since passed the "three-score years and ten" are making full use of "the last of life, for which the first was made." Earthly life, that is; they know that life itself goes on forever.

Our longevity is dependent upon the quality of the thoughts, feelings and attitudes which inhabit our minds. The body cannot and does not wear out. How could it? Its cells are completely renewed at frequent intervals. The fountain of youth is our own consciousness. Recognize this and you will be eternally young. Your body was made to last as long as you need it. Take good care of it; insist that it serve your purposes, and it will do so. The power of life flows from our minds as we discipline them to work in co-operation with the One Mind.

In a recent survey to determine the secret of their long life, a group of senior citizens past eighty were questioned. Some drank, some smoked, some worked and some loafed, some were married and some weren't, some went to church and some didn't, some followed special diets and some didn't, some exercised and others abhorred it—they were all different except in one respect: *every one of them had an intense interest and enjoyment in life.* They were *alive.*

"How do you account for your long life?" they asked one hearty oldster of a hundred and two.

"Well, I'll tell you, he replied. "When I wake up each morning, I'm confronted with two choices: one is to be miserable; the other to be happy. I always decide to be happy."

"How do you account for the fact that you have lived to nearly one hundred and haven't an enemy in the world?" another venerable one was asked.

"That's easy," he laughed. "I just outlived the so-and-so's!"

These two might well serve as examples for all of us. The key to our longevity and our happiness lies within our own minds and hearts.

The National Retired Teachers Association for the Advancement of Knowledge, Learning and Research in Retirement Education is one of many groups which is helping to remove the curse from retirement, compulsory or voluntary. Their philosophy is set forth in the masthead of their official publication, the *NRTA Journal:* "The NRTA is a non-profit organization, built upon the thesis that creative energy is ageless—that our years of experience, understanding and skill are reserves of energy and power that we must put to work to build richer, more interesting lives, to help in movements, crusades, that reach beyond the here and now, and to find, each of us, in such activity, content and faith and hope."

These fine senior citizens have retired "to" not "from" constructive activity, worthwhile purpose, and joyous living. With such examples we will soon be able to eliminate the curse of compulsory retirement. Premature retirement actually causes people to die. An authority recently stated that the current negative concepts of old age actually cause many persons to begin dying a year or two before they actually retire. These "negative concepts" of old age must be corrected. Since neither scientifically, physically, mentally, emotionally, spiritually, socially, economically, professionally—or any other way—is there such a thing as "old age," the current concept of compulsory retirement not only makes no sense whatever, but is destructive to the individual and society as a whole. The idea of an inactive retirement is a hangover from an earlier era of ignorance, fear, and limited thinking about age, life in general, and other negative views.

We have broken the sound barrier. We are breaking the space barrier. Let's break the age barrier and get on with this business of living.

> Winter is on my head, but eternal spring
> is in my heart; I breathe at this hour the
> fragrance of the lilacs, the violets, and
> the roses, as at twenty years ago. The nearer
> I approach to the end, the plainer I hear
> around me the immortal symphonies of the
> worlds which invite me.
>
> —*Victor Hugo*

DAILY THOUGHTS ABOUT AGE
From This Chapter

1. Second childhood indicates that the individual has never grown out of his first one.
2. There are no problems of aging, just those of living.
3. The best insurance against old age is intelligent, sensible, balanced constructive living at every age.
4. Judgment, wisdom and understanding improve with age, providing there was intelligence in the earlier periods of life.
5. Our life is God's life living itself through us. It is infinite and eternal; it had no beginning and will have no end.
6. Our longevity is dependent upon the quality of the thoughts, feelings and attitudes which inhabit our minds.
7. Age is a myth and a delusion. The phrase "old age" must be erased from our minds and from our vocabulary.

From the Bible

1. So the Lord blessed the latter end of Job more than his beginning.
   —*Job 42:12*
2. Mine age is as nothing before Thee.—*Psalm 39:5*
3. We spend our years as a tale that is told.—*Psalm 90:9*
4. So teach us to number our days, that we may apply our hearts unto wisdom.—*Psalm 90:12*
5. The hoary head is a crown of glory.—*Prov. 16:31*
6. They shall still bring forth fruit in old age.—*Prov. 92:14*
7. No man also having drunk old wine straightway desireth new: for he saith, The old is better.—*Luke 5:39*

From Great Thinkers Past and Present

1. You take all the experience and judgment of men over fifty out of the world and there wouldn't be enough left to run it.—*Henry Ford*
2. Some men are born old, and some never grow so.—*Tyron Edwards*
3. Let us respect gray hairs, especially our own.—*J. P. Senn*
4. No wise man ever wished to be younger.—*Jonathan Swift*
5. To be happy, we must be true to nature, and carry our age along with us.—*William Hazlitt*
6. Childhood itself is scarcely more lovely than a cheerful, kindly, sunshiny old age.—*L. M. Child*
7. A graceful and honorable old age is the childhood of immortality.—*Pindar*

GOLDEN BRIDGE
TO GOLDEN AGE

Morning Projection

*I am a new person as I greet this new day. My youth is restored.
Refreshed from the night's sleep, I am reborn into this day of glorious adventure. I embrace life as for the first time and I live it fully
now.*

*My chronological age is of no importance to me whatsoever. I am
a child of God, therefore I am eternally new. I am as young as time.
I am as old as eternity. I have no age. I am as spontaneous as this
moment. I live in the here and the now. I live each moment as it
appears, so I am always as young as the present. I cannot age because I am constantly being reborn.*

*My life develops in depth, not in time. No one has ever lived this
life before. I do my best to make it a masterpiece. The challenge of it
keeps me young. No one has ever lived this day before. The challenge of it makes me young. In all things I am as wide-eyed and
eager as a child. I am a child of the Infinite. I am eternally new.
And so it is.*

Evening Retrospection

*As I free myself from the toils and the cares of the day, the fresh
mantle of new life descends upon me and I am refilled from the
Spirit. I drink from the fountain of youth tonight. The water which
I drink is a well of water in me bubbling up into everlasting life.*

*My mind is renewed as I contemplate the great mysteries of being.
My soul is restored as I immerse in the healing tide of life. The
flow of Divine energy cleanses and purifies me, inside and out. The
Christ within me—the Higher Self, the Son of God—sits on the right
hand of the Father and expands vertically into new life.*

*Every atom of my being, every cell of my body is recharged and
now released into the great revivifying action of the subjective.
Sleep makes all things new. I sleep deeply—with the realization that
sleep erases all age and time and rebuilds me in the image of That
which is forever new. And so it is.*

31

ETERNAL LIFE
The Great Adventure

"Life is the soul's nursery—its training place for the destinies of eternity."

—*Thackeray*

As a young minister I was fortunate to have the counsel of Dr. Ernest Holmes, founder of the Church of Religious Science.

"What does the minister do at a funeral?" I asked him upon one occasion.

"Just one thing," he replied quietly. "He convinces the people who have come to bid farewell that there is no death."

There is no death.

Down through the corridors of time man has sought to convince himself that this is true. I am sure you believe it. I believe there is no death, although I have seen him pay his visit a thousand times—on hospital beds of suffering during the gray light of dawn, in the seat beside me as a friend took sudden leave, in tangled wreckage on the highway in the arms of a praying father as he held his injured child, on the clammy shore of a cold lake as the fisherman struggled in vain to force air into his drowned friend's lungs through mouth-to-mouth resuscitation.

I, too, have been shocked and numbed with grief at the passing of a loved one. I, too, have experienced the lonely realization that I would see a friend no more. I, too, have cried out, "Oh God! Why? Why did you have to take him? Why him?" when my boyhood pal did not return from the hospital because of a surgeon's careless mistake. I have

spent countless hours beside afflicted ones, praying for healing and re-
covery—only to lose in the end.

Or did we lose? Do we ever lose? Who is the ultimate victor?

In resisting so-called death, could it be that we are fighting an illusion—a false belief that has projected itself as fact, but has no basis of
reality? It would seem so. In conducting countless memorial services
for those who have gone on—friends and strangers alike—I have never
felt that I was in the presence of Death, even as I look upon the still
form lying in the casket. I seem to hear the voice of the departed one
saying,

> Faithful friends! It lies, I know,
> Pale and white and cold as snow;
> And ye say, "Abdellah's dead!"—
> Weeping at the feet and head.
>
> Yet I smile and whisper this,—
> "I am not the thing you kiss;
> Cease your tears, and let it lie;
> It was mine, it is not I."
>
> —*Sir Edwin Arnold*, "After
> Death in Arabia"

At such times, alone before the service, and then following a period
of silence just before speaking, I affirm, "There is no Death; there is
only Life, vital, surging, unfolding, expressive Life—Life Eternal, Life
abundant and everlasting. We are in the presence of Life. We are here
to observe the reality and continuity of Life."

As this realization comes to those gathered there, the sobs cease,
and the grief gives way to a quiet and solemn expectancy as family and
friends prepare for the final visit with the loved one. Then something
wonderful always happens. *The departed person conducts his own
service.* My function is merely to assist him in such a way as to convince those there that *there is no death*. You see, no one knows this
better than one who has had the experience. There is no greater authority on life than one who has died. He alone knows the truth about
the experience of life which he has lived.

> Our birth is but a sleep and a forgetting;
> The Soul that rises with us, our life's star,

Hath had elsewhere its setting
And cometh from afar;
Not in entire forgetfulness,
And not in utter nakedness,
But trailing clouds of glory do we come
From God, who is our home.

—*Wordsworth,* "Ode on Intimations of
Immortality"

He alone knows the truth about the experience through which he
has just passed:

Never the spirit was born;
  the spirit shall cease to be never;
Never was time it was not, End and Beginning are dreams!
Birthless and deathless and changeless remaineth
  the spirit forever;
Death hath not touched it at all, dead though
  the house of it seems!

Nay, but as one who layeth
His worn-out robes away,
And, taking new ones, sayeth,
  "These will I wear today!"
So putteth by the spirit
  Lightly its garb of flesh,
And passeth to inherit
  A residence afresh.

—*The Song Celestial*
The Bhagavad-Gita, translated from the
Sanskrit text by Sir Edwin Arnold.

The great Hindu poet, Rabindranath Tagore, once wrote to his
friend C. F. Andrews:

My mind must realize itself anew. Once I give form to my thought,
I must free myself from it. For the time being it seems to me that I
want absolute freedom to create new forms for new ideas. I am sure
physical death has the same meaning for us—the creative impulse of
our soul must have new forms for its realization. Death can continue
to dwell in the same sepulchre, but Life must increasingly outgrow

its dwelling-place otherwise the form gets the upper hand and becomes a prison. Man is immortal; therefore he must die endlessly. For life is a creative idea; it can only find itself in changing forms.[1]

The poets, mystics and idealistic philosophers of the ages have been unanimous in their affirmation of man's immortality.

Socrates is reported to have said:

You may bury me if you can catch me. . . . Do not call this poor body Socrates. When I have drunk the poison, I shall leave you, and go to the joys of the blessed. I would not have you sorrow at my hard lot, or say at the interment, 'Thus we lay out Socrates'; or, 'Thus we follow him to the grave, and bury him.' Be of good cheer: say that you are burying my body only.

—*Plato,* "Phaedo"

Then Socrates said, "I . . . pray to the gods that my journey hence may be prosperous. That is my prayer—be it so."

What is this "journey hence"? What is the nature of the undiscovered country from whose domain no traveler returns? Death represents the unknown. It "puzzles the will and makes us rather bear those ills we have than fly to others that we know not of" (Shakespeare, *Hamlet,* III, i). Why do we continue to fear death, even though all logic, reason, spiritual insight and scientific evidence shows it as nonexistent in itself—merely an incident along our pathway of eternal life?

Of all the wonders that I yet have heard,
It seems to me most strange that men should fear;
Seeing that death, a necessary end,
Will come when it will come.

—*Shakespeare,* "Julius Caesar," *II, i*

That which lives can never die. There is a great natural principle called the Law of the Conservation of Energy. Nothing is ever lost. Nothing can disappear in God's universe. It may be transformed into minerals, liquids and gases, but nothing in it can ever be destroyed. It is simply expressed differently. Water may be in the form of a block of ice, melted down into liquid, and then heated until it apparently

---

[1] Quoted in *The Imprisoned Splendour,* by Raynor C. Johnson (New York: Harper & Row, Publishers, 1955).

disappears, but it is not *lost*. The steam recondenses into water, and can then be frozen back into ice. Nothing is ever lost. A living man cannot die.

Try an experiment. Close your eyes and try to visualize nonexistence, nothingness, not-being. Can you do it? Of course not. We are *living beings*. We have an eternal soul—an ever-living, active consciousness which is the cause of constant expression. Our consciousness—the Self within us, God indwelling—is pure Spirit and lives forever. Its form and expression change as we are reincarnated through the cycle of many lives, but It—the Self within—never changes. Since it is impossible to think of or imagine not being, it is impossible for us not to be. Since we will always be, we must be something. By simple logic, and observance of the working of the natural law of cause and effect, this seems to me a conclusive proof of immortality.

Reincarnation goes hand in hand with immortality—deathlessness of the spirit. Since this spirit must always be something, doesn't it stand to reason that it will continue to express itself in a way that is consistent with its nature and needs? Since the physical body meets these requirements during this lifetime, and since few, if any, of us can learn all the potential and necessary lessons during this lifetime, the teaching of the wise ones of the ages has been that the soul incarnates, is re-embodied—re-enfleshed—again and again, and continues to return to a physical world in a physical body until all the lessons of "the cycle of necessity" are learned.

A belief in immortality is the single most important requirement for abundant living. All we need to do is to believe in life and live it fully. As we do a good job with the here and the now, the where, what, why, when and then will take care of themselves. Belief in immortality is inescapable. At the present time in the world, understanding of and belief in reincarnation is somewhat confused and controversial, but think about it, learn about it, weigh and consider. Let your consciousness unfold and the mysteries of the kingdom will be revealed unto you. It isn't what we *think* about something; it is what we come to *know*. That which is, *is*, no matter how we may argue the pros and cons. The Father knows what things we have need of before we ask him. We need life. We have it—eternally. We are immortal—now and forever.

DAILY THOUGHTS ABOUT ETERNAL LIFE
From This Chapter

1. Death is an illusion, a false belief that has projected itself as fact, but has no basis in reality.
2. Death is an experience within the larger scope of living.
3. Immortality is deathlessness of the spirit.
4. Reincarnation is continuous re-embodiment of the spirit in physical form.
5. The great idealistic thinkers of the ages have been unanimous in their affirmation of man's immortality.
6. Since we cannot conceive of nonexistence, we must always exist.
7. There is no death—only life eternal.

From the Bible

1. Yea, though I walk through the valley of the shadow of death, I will fear no evil: for Thou art with me.—*Psalm 23:4*
2. She is not dead, but sleepeth.—*Luke 8:52*
3. If a man keep My saying, he shall never see death.—*John 8:51*
4. There shall be no more death.—*Rev. 21:4*
5. God is not the God of the dead, but of the living.—*Matt. 22:32*
6. I give unto them eternal life.—*John 10:28*
7. He that soweth to the Spirit shall of the Spirit reap life everlasting.—*Gal. 6:8*

From Great Thinkers Past and Present

1. Death is not a foe, but an inevitable adventure.—*Sir Oliver Lodge*
2. It is impossible that anything so natural, so necessary, and so universal as death, should ever have been designed by Providence as an evil to mankind.—*Jonathan Swift*
3. Death is the golden key that opens the palace of eternity.—*John Milton*
4. Death is the crown of life. Were death denied, poor man would live in vain; to live would not be life; even fools would wish to die.—*Owen D. Young*
5. Be still prepared for death: and death or life shall thereby be the sweeter.—*Shakespeare*
6. He who should teach men to die, would, at the same time, teach them to live.—*Montaigne*
7. Is death the last sleep? No, it is the last and final awakening.—*Sir Walter Scott*

Surely goodness and mercy shall follow me
   all the days of my life:
And I will dwell in the house of the Lord
Forever. Amen.

And so it is.

GOLDEN BRIDGE
TO ETERNAL LIFE

Morning Projection

I live forever—one day at a time. Since life has no beginning or end, I live each moment fully, pouring my entire being into its glorious expression. I am unconcerned with the passing of days, years and lifetimes. I am not the slave of time. Time serves me throughout eternity. I have always lived, and I continue to do so—always.

I believe in the immortality, the continuity, and the eternality of my soul. I know that in my Father's house there are many mansions and that I will dwell in every one of them as the time comes. I am ready to move on into greater experience whenever I am ready for it.

I cannot stand still. I am continually growing into new expressions of the perfect pattern which God has instilled in me. God is life. God is Infinite. Life is eternal. Since I am one with God, I am one with life. I know I live forever. I give thanks that this is so. And so it is.

Evening Retrospection

I am a native of eternity. As I lie down to sleep I know my soul is in God's keeping. I have no concern—now or ever—because I know

> The Lord is my shepherd;
> I shall not want.
> He maketh me to lie down in green pastures:
> He leadeth me beside the still waters.
> He restoreth my soul.
> He leadeth me in the paths of righteousness
>   for His name's sake.
> Yea, though I walk through the valley
>   of the shadow of death,
> I will fear no evil:
> For thou art with me;
> Thy rod and thy staff they comfort me.
> Thou preparest a table before me
>   in the presence of mine enemies:
> Thou anointest my head with oil;
> My cup runneth over.

366 PERSONAL DAILY AFFIRMATIONS

1. I start this year right and keep it right every day.
2. I do my best to be my best at all times.
3. I enjoy every moment of my long life.
4. I am constantly growing and developing into my true potential.
5. I am a kind, gentle and loving person.
6. I get along with other people and they get along with me.
7. I anticipate all impending events with enthusiasm and expectation of good.
8. I am completely attuned to the Life Force within me.
9. I am aware that I am part of something that is greater than I.
10. I give thanks for the abundance that is mine.
11. I do good wherever I go.
12. I am a success in everything I undertake.
13. I express love toward everyone and in everything I do.
14. I know that nothing is too wonderful to happen; nothing is too good to be true.
15. I love God with all my heart, with all my mind, with all my strength, and with all my soul.
16. I love my neighbor as myself.
17. I love my work.
18. I love life and I love to live.
19. I know where I am going and how to get there.
20. I think and feel constructively at all times and in all situations.
21. I feel the full, free flow of life constantly circulating through me.

229

22. I quietly and calmly go about minding my own business.
23. I move steadily ahead toward my goal.
24. I experience only good in my life.
25. I am a cell within the great Mind, Soul and Body of God.
26. I help others in every possible way.
27. I am a whole person.
28. I give thanks for the abundance which is mine.
29. I am building more stately mansions in my soul.
30. I give my best to life and life gives its best to me.
31. I give thanks for a month of solid accomplishment and growth.

FEBRUARY

1. The power that created me and put me here motivates and activates me throughout this day.
2. When I am right on the inside, everything is right on the outside.
3. I praise God with my entire being.
4. I experience happiness in everything I do.
5. Inner strength flows through me at all times and in everything I do.
6. My mind is clear, alert and aware at all times.
7. I can do all things through the life power which strengthens me.
8. I build a larger mental equivalent today.
9. I am calm, cool and collected at all times.
10. I am in tune with life and life is in tune with me.
11. I am constantly growing in maturity and spiritual understanding.
12. The healing flow of love motivates my life today and every day.
13. I am growing in understanding and wisdom.
14. I am a warm, kind individual.
15. I am relaxed and at ease in all that I do.
16. I give thanks for my good, and I share it with others.
17. I assist the law of evolution by improving myself in every possible way.
18. I am guided and directed in all decisions.
19. I am safe and secure at all times.
20. All fear is dissolved as I am established in complete and secure faith.
21. I do good work today and I have a good time doing it.
22. I live enthusiastically and abundantly.
23. I do only those things which establish, sustain and maintain me in perfect health.
24. I use the energy of life wisely and well.

25. I know who I am and where I am going. I am on my way to bigger and better things.
26. I pray without ceasing, keeping my soul attuned to spiritual inspiration and guidance.
27. I am free from all bondage and limitation. I am free indeed.
28. I praise God from whom all blessings flow.
29. I give thanks for unexpected good, no matter whence it may come.

MARCH

1. I dissolve all effort, as I establish ease and efficiency in all that I do.
2. I relax, let go, and let God work through me all day today.
3. I think only constructive thoughts.
4. I have only affirmative feelings.
5. I do only worthy deeds.
6. I am sincere and honest in all things.
7. I am ever moving onward and upward.
8. I drive carefully, ever aware of the rights of others.
9. Only good can come to me because only good goes out from me.
10. I am pure in heart, mind and soul.
11. I am free in heart, mind and soul.
12. There is nothing I cannot do if I put my mind to it. I put my mind to it.
13. There is nothing I cannot be if I put my heart to it. I put my heart to it.
14. All wonderful things happen to me today and I give thanks for them.
15. I am permanently and irrevocably connected to the Greater Self. I express it in all things.
16. I experience and express perfect order and right action in my daily activities.
17. I expect the best of life today.
18. I give help and happiness to others at every opportunity.
19. My prayers are affirmative, constructive and true.
20. I am in excellent health, spiritually, mentally, emotionally and physically.
21. I prosper in all that I do.
22. I make money easily and use it wisely.
23. I live life abundantly and fully.
24. I am constantly, continuously, constructively, creatively, and profitably employed.

25. I have peace of mind, peace of heart, and peace in my soul.
26. I dissolve all hostility, animosity and resentment as I learn to forgive, understand and love.
27. I am interested in people.
28. I find new ways to be of service to God, country, and mankind.
29. I use my time intelligently, efficiently and well.
30. I endeavor to be an example in all things.
31. I know the Truth and the Truth makes me free.

APRIL

1. I apply myself diligently and well to the business of living.
2. I am a happy, well-adjusted person.
3. I am clear in mind and warm in heart.
4. I love other people and they love me.
5. I look for the best in everyone and in every situation.
6. I make prayer a regular part of my life.
7. I laugh often.
8. I share my good with others.
9. I endeavor to make my life an example which all may follow.
10. I am a healthy person.
11. I am whole and complete in every way.
12. I train my mind and balance my emotions.
13. I take good care of my body by giving it proper diet, exercise and rest.
14. I am vital, alert and energetic.
15. My thoughts are clear and pure; my ideas are noble and good.
16. I speak kindly and considerately at all times.
17. I have deep faith in the wonder and goodness of God.
18. God is the source of my supply.
19. Unlimited abundance flows into every part of my experience.
20. I am a prosperous person.
21. I am a successful person.
22. I am a good person.
23. I am a kind person.
24. I am a useful person.
25. Today I am one step closer to achieving my objective.
26. I use my talents and abilities to the best possible advantage.
27. I make the most of every moment.
28. I use my energies to advantage.
29. I have a good time in everything I do.
30. I think constructively at all times.

MAY

1. I live my life fully and joyously.
2. I seek constantly to improve myself in every possible way.
3. I am interested in everything.
4. My work is God's work. I do it well.
5. I pay particular attention to my family today.
6. I make a masterpiece of this day.
7. I help to make the world a better place to live in.
8. I help my country by being a responsible citizen.
9. My mind is clear and bright.
10. My body is healthy and strong.
11. I am in excellent spirits.
12. I have all the time I need to do whatever I have to do.
13. I give thanks for my possessions and I take good care of them.
14. I have more than enough money to do what I want to do at the moment I want to do it.
15. I have a good time every minute of this day.
16. I am responsible, trustworthy and dependable.
17. I am constantly learning from everyone and everything.
18. I am strengthened as I triumph over all difficulties, and learn the lessons they have to teach me.
19. I learn to love today.
20. My faith is strong and enduring.
21. I see beauty around me everywhere.
22. I am relaxed and easy in all that I do.
23. I am right on the inside, therefore I am right on the outside.
24. I give freely and I receive graciously.
25. I pour my whole self into everything I do.
26. I translate my affirmative attitudes into constructive habits.
27. My goals are clearly in mind and I press forward to victory.
28. I believe in a Power greater than I.
29. I talk things over with God several times today.
30. I am young in heart, mind and deed.
31. I live forever—one day at a time.

JUNE

1. Today is my day. I live it fully.
2. There is no limit to my accomplishment as I realize that Infinite Intelligence is in action through me.

3. God is the inspiration of my life and the strength of my being.
4. The greatness and grandeur of infinite possibility are established in my consciousness.
5. I love my life, and I give thanks for the blessings which are mine.
6. My work is my joyous expression of life.
7. My work is the channel through which I go about my Father's business.
8. Nothing is too great for my capacities or too small for my attention.
9. I bring integrity and intelligence to everything I do.
10. Balance, order and right action characterize my life in every way.
11. Energy and vitality circulate through me and maintain me in perfect health.
12. I am awake to my good and alert to every worthwhile idea and opportunity.
13. I understand the spiritual reality of life.
14. I am renewed in body and exhilarated in mind by the flow of life through me today.
15. I live wisely in the knowledge that great good is mine as I accept it now.
16. Love guides me in all that I do.
17. Divine Power goes before me and makes perfect my way in joy and happiness.
18. Today I accept the fulfillment of every need and the solution to every problem.
19. All fear is dissolved from my consciousness as I immerse myself in steadfast faith in God.
20. All anxiety and tension disappear as I am in contact with the Infinite Healing Presence.
21. I face today with inner calm and confidence.
22. Infinite Wisdom is constantly working through my mind, my body and my affairs.
23. I meet all situations with full realization of the power of Spirit to guide, guard and sustain me.
24. The power within me knows no limitation.
25. I release every problem for right solution into the unlimited creative action of the One Mind.
26. I am inwardly strong and outwardly blessed.
27. Today I get my bloated nothingness out of the way and let the divine circuits flow through.
28. I dissolve all destructive attitudes and affirm all constructive ones.

29. My entire being is renewed by the inspiration of God.
30. I claim and accept the goodness of life, gratefully.

July

1. I know only that which is good, hear only that which is true, and experience only that which is perfect.
2. I forgive and forget the mistakes of the past as I move forward eagerly into this day.
3. I am dynamically attuned to Spiritual Power.
4. I obey the principles of constructive living which make me happy, healthy, wealthy and wise.
5. I give thanks for my emotional stability and for the order and happiness which it brings into my life today.
6. I am an active, self-conscious unit of life.
7. I think, work and live so that God is more visibly expressed through me in terms of his own perfection.
8. Every constructive activity of my life brings prosperity and success to myself and others.
9. I give thanks for the vital healing power of Spirit throughout my entire being.
10. Perfect circulation, perfect assimilation, and perfect elimination are established and maintained in my mind, my body, and my world of experience.
11. The flow of life brings me an abundance of every good thing.
12. Wherever the problem seems to be, the solution already exists.
13. I pass through the door of opportunity and fulfillment today.
14. I measure my success in terms of that which is good, true, beautiful, and of genuine service to myself and others.
15. I eliminate from my life everything that does not have its foundation in God.
16. I forgive myself and others for all wrongs past and present.
17. I experience a new birth of freedom.
18. I give thanks for the lessons of life.
19. I change everything in my life that needs changing.
20. I am in control of my thoughts, feelings and actions.
21. Nothing is too good to be true; nothing is too wonderful to happen.
22. Sound judgment governs my activities and decisions.
23. I am dedicated to the accomplishment of worthwhile goals and purposes.
24. I co-operate with life and life co-operates with me.

25. Powerful ideas flow through me as I open my mind to the influx of Divine Wisdom.
26. I am in partnership with God.
27. I apply myself to learning every lesson in the great school of life.
28. This day brings me one step closer to the realization of the meaning of life.
29. I turn to the Spirit within as I seek to correct those areas of thought and feeling which need correction.
30. I live in the peace and contentment that come from my faith in a Higher Power.
31. I turn my heart Godward, and embrace the goodness of life.

August

1. I experience perfect order and harmony in all that I do.
2. Love and understanding characterize all of my personal relationships.
3. I aim high and I hit the mark.
4. I am guided, guarded and directed throughout this day.
5. I transform my life by controlling my thoughts and balancing my emotions.
6. I receive my inspiration from the inner Source of all knowledge and wisdom.
7. I consciously project and express the wonder and glory of the good life.
8. I put my attention upon one task at a time and see it through to successful completion.
9. I cease all unworthy activities as I dedicate my life to noble purpose and worthwhile activity.
10. I walk as though I own the earth because I surely do.
11. Every moment of my life is filled with beauty.
12. I am a whole person as I am completely and permanently freed from the bondage of lack, limitation, age and disease.
13. My life is filled with happiness, health, abundance and creative self-expression.
14. My way is easy and my burden is light.
15. I accomplish mighty works today and every day throughout my life.
16. I seek to know the Truth and express it in all that I say and do.
17. As one of God's workmen, I create abundantly and well.
18. Since thoughts are things, I choose my thoughts wisely and direct them definitely and positively.

19. I am an individual creative center in the Divine Mind.
20. Since I am not afraid to change, improve and expand my mind, my life is continuously changing and renewing itself.
21. There is no limit to the good that is created within me and expressed through me.
22. I express myself by creatively co-operating with God.
23. Today I move confidently forward along the frontiers of new thought, creating new channels for the flow of fresh and vital experiences.
24. I give good to my fellow men, and I receive good for myself.
25. I change unpleasant conditions by changing myself into a more pleasant person.
26. As I am serene and tranquil amid life's storms, they blow away and disappear.
27. I am free from sorrow and regret as my consciousness expands with joy.
28. I live purposefully and let my light shine before men.
29. The wholeness in my mind produces health in my body and in my entire world of experience.
30. The continuous flow of Spirit enlivens everything in my world today.
31. As confusion, doubt and worry are dissolved, I experience ease, calm and comfort.

SEPTEMBER

1. I am free from all negative influence as I place my faith in God.
2. I am filled with peace, harmony, calm, tranquillity and serenity.
3. I am alert to my opportunities to be a better person and accomplish greater things.
4. Every incident in my daily activities is an adventure in living.
5. Creativity is constantly seeking and finding expression through my consciousness.
6. The door of my mind is open, and I experience the flow of Infinite Intelligence in every phase of my life.
7. Whatever God is, I am. I am the individual action of That which is Perfect.
8. I have faith in unlimited opportunity, and I manifest it in my world.
9. My expectation is great, for my desire is definite and my conviction is firm.

10. Today, in every situation, I make the world a better place in which to live.
11. God knows the answers to my problems, so I look to Him and accept them.
12. I am in the midst of unlimited opportunity.
13. I rise above appearances and conditions as I establish order and harmony in my life.
14. The high state of my consciousness raises the level of thought everywhere.
15. I give thanks for the lessons learned from past shortcomings and mistakes, then I release them and let them go.
16. As I expect only good today, the power of my belief makes good an accomplished fact in my experience.
17. All rigidity of thought and habit is dissolved as my mind becomes an instrument of Infinite Intelligence.
18. Today I claim my affluence, abundance and prosperity.
19. God is the inspiration of my life today.
20. I expand my consciousness so that great ideas can flow abundantly into my mind.
21. I am eternally connected with the unlimited source of Divine Inspiration.
22. I intelligently use my faculties of judgment and discrimination in making right decisions.
23. That within me which is never confused, weary, or afraid, guides me into certainty and right action.
24. I move from darkness into light.
25. I progress from ignorance to understanding.
26. I am growing in understanding and wisdom.
27. I am strong in all my ways.
28. As I deal intelligently with my personal problems, I am more capable of helping others.
29. The vitality and energy of the One Life flow through my mind, my emotions, my body, and my world of affairs.
30. I love.

OCTOBER

1. I change whatever is necessary for me to change in order to be a better person.
2. As I seek to express all that is beautiful and good, my life becomes one of great and glorious adventure.

3. Currents of Divine love flow through me and form my soul in patterns of love.
4. The vital flow of life surges through me in purposeful expression.
5. I thrill to the challenge of life today.
6. I am enveloped and maintained in order, harmony, peace and freedom.
7. I am dynamically filled with a sense of well-being.
8. I am nourished by the rich substance of Spirit.
9. I am motivated by high ideas in everything that I think, plan, and do.
10. I give life the best that is in me.
11. Beauty, purity and wholeness are with me all the days of my life.
12. I obey the laws of life, and they obey me.
13. My inner life unfolds in patterns of integrity, strength and purpose.
14. The light of Divine love flows through me. I am filled with light.
15. I establish and live by a sensible standard of values.
16. I use the power of my thought and the energy of my emotions intelligently and well.
17. I expect the best from everyone and I always get it.
18. My health results from a sense of inner wholeness.
19. No matter what happens, I say, "Father, I do give thanks for this evidence of Thy love for me."
20. I am joyous in my daily activities and in my relations with other people.
21. I embrace the opportunity to live, to learn, to work, to study, to grow, to do the best I can with whatever confronts me on this day.
22. I am enthusiastic about life in general and everything in particular.
23. I organize my life and learn to put first things first.
24. I experience full and satisfying self-expression as I work creatively to complete everything I undertake.
25. I follow the Inner Light which is brightly renewing, cleansing, healing and uplifting me now.
26. All troubles disappear as I realize that that which is within me is greater than any problem, pain or outer condition.
27. I know who I am, where I am going and why. I know what life is all about.
28. My purpose in life is growth, achievement and service.
29. I am filled with Divine inspiration. I see, I perceive, I receive, I know.
30. All good things are working out in my life now and always.
31. The power of God within me is the action of my life today.

NOVEMBER

1. Fear is dissolved. I am filled with faith.
2. Hostility is removed. I learn to love.
3. Anxiety disappears. I experience inner quiet.
4. Worry won't work. I am serene and untroubled.
5. Jealousy is dissolved. Empathy fills my being.
6. I am through with running away. I meet my responsibilities.
7. Confusion is corrected. My life is in order.
8. Rejection is removed. I accept life now.
9. As I let go of my resistance, I learn to co-operate with life.
10. Resistance is overcome. I know the importance of release.
11. I feel no tension. I enjoy perfect relaxation.
12. As I stop condemning myself, I learn the meaning of self-appreciation.
13. I dismiss disappointment in favor of understanding.
14. Irritation is replaced in my consciousness by inner harmony.
15. Agitation ceases. I experience inner and outer tranquillity.
16. Resentment is ruin. I live by compassion.
17. Antagonism is dissolved as I experience the peace that passes all understanding.
18. I am finished with ignorance and stupidity. I grow in knowledge, understanding and wisdom.
19. I am never envious. I am filled with gratitude for my many blessings.
20. Thoughtlessness gives way to the habit of thoughtfulness. I am kind and considerate.
21. All limitation is dissolved as I expand in understanding and the recognition of limitless abundance.
22. Selfishness is dissolved as I learn the true meaning of selflessness.
23. Greed is gone. I am a generous person now.
24. Indecision is conquered. I easily make prompt and intelligent decisions.
25. Perfect love casts out fear. I have a strong and vital faith.
26. I am free from all guilt as I completely forgive myself and others.
27. My nerves are steady and quiet as I experience deep inner calm and quiet.
28. I am safe and secure, protected by the everlasting arms of the Father.
29. I am finished with frustration as I express myself creatively and constructively.
30. All sorrow and grief are dissolved as I live my life joyously and exuberantly.

1. As I conquer all irritation I become pleasant, patient and kind.
2. Instead of complaining, I learn to accept those things I cannot change at the same time I have the courage to change the things I can change, beginning with myself.
3. I do much more good as I dissolve criticism and adopt attitudes of discriminating approval.
4. I heal my grouchiness by approaching all things in high good humor.
5. I display natural good manners at all times.
6. I am thoughtful and considerate of others.
7. I replace gruffness and unpleasantness with tenderness and pleasantness.
8. I eliminate the negative; I accentuate the positive.
9. I stay on the sunny side of the street.
10. I warm up inside and let the radiance of my personality warm and cheer others.
11. I stand aside and let God's will be done through me.
12. I am reasonable and fair in all of my dealings.
13. I enjoy doing things that are good for me and good for others.
14. I cleanse my subconscious of old worn-out ideas and conditionings which no longer belong there and replace them with new ones which do.
15. I am imaginative and creative, eager to embrace new ideas and to do new things.
16. I use the Superior Intelligence within me to solve all problems.
17. I am guided by spiritual intuition in making all decisions.
18. My mind is one with the One Mind.
19. My life is God living through me.
20. I am a channel of love and blessing through which all good things are expressed.
21. I can do all things through the inner awareness of Spirit which strengthens me.
22. I perceive the meaning of life and exult in the glory of its mysteries.
23. I experience peace on earth, good will toward men.
24. My mind and heart proclaim the glad tidings that the kingdom of good is at hand.
25. Christ is born in me today.
26. I reflect upon the great gifts that God has given me.
27. The angels continue to proclaim the good news in every phase of my consciousness.

28. Imagination, intuition and inspiration—the Wise Men within me—guide and direct me throughout my life.
29. Goodness and mercy follow me all the days of my life.
30. I dwell in the house of the Lord forever.
31. I ring out the old; I ring in the new.

MELVIN POWERS SELF-IMPROVEMENT LIBRARY

ASTROLOGY

ASTROLOGY: A FASCINATING HISTORY *P. Naylor*	2.00
ASTROLOGY: HOW TO CHART YOUR HOROSCOPE *Max Heindel*	2.00
ASTROLOGY: YOUR PERSONAL SUN-SIGN GUIDE *Beatrice Ryder*	2.00
ASTROLOGY FOR EVERYDAY LIVING *Janet Harris*	2.00
ASTROLOGY MADE EASY *Astarte*	2.00
ASTROLOGY MADE PRACTICAL *Alexandra Kayhle*	2.00
ASTROLOGY, ROMANCE, YOU AND THE STARS *Anthony Norvell*	3.00
MY WORLD OF ASTROLOGY *Sydney Omarr*	3.00
THOUGHT DIAL *Sydney Omarr*	2.00
ZODIAC REVEALED *Rupert Gleadow*	2.00

BRIDGE & POKER

ADVANCED POKER STRATEGY & WINNING PLAY *A. D. Livingston*	2.00
BRIDGE BIDDING MADE EASY *Edwin Kantar*	5.00
BRIDGE CONVENTIONS *Edwin Kantar*	4.00
COMPLETE DEFENSIVE BRIDGE PLAY *Edwin B. Kantar*	10.00
HOW TO IMPROVE YOUR BRIDGE *Alfred Sheinwold*	2.00
HOW TO WIN AT POKER *Terence Reese & Anthony T. Watkins*	2.00
TEST YOUR BRIDGE PLAY *Edwin B. Kantar*	3.00

BUSINESS STUDY & REFERENCE

CONVERSATION MADE EASY *Elliot Russell*	2.00
EXAM SECRET *Dennis B. Jackson*	2.00
FIX-IT BOOK *Arthur Symons*	2.00
HOW TO DEVELOP A BETTER SPEAKING VOICE *M. Hellier*	2.00
HOW TO MAKE A FORTUNE IN REAL ESTATE *Albert Winnikoff*	3.00
HOW TO MAKE MONEY IN REAL ESTATE *Stanley L. McMichael*	2.00
INCREASE YOUR LEARNING POWER *Geoffrey A. Dudley*	2.00
MAGIC OF NUMBERS *Robert Tocquet*	2.00
PRACTICAL GUIDE TO BETTER CONCENTRATION *Melvin Powers*	2.00
PRACTICAL GUIDE TO PUBLIC SPEAKING *Maurice Forley*	2.00
7 DAYS TO FASTER READING *William S. Schaill*	2.00
SONGWRITERS' RHYMING DICTIONARY *Jane Shaw Whitfield*	3.00
SPELLING MADE EASY *Lester D. Basch & Dr. Milton Finkelstein*	2.00
STUDENT'S GUIDE TO BETTER GRADES *J. A. Rickard*	2.00
TEST YOURSELF — Find Your Hidden Talent *Jack Shafer*	2.00
YOUR WILL & WHAT TO DO ABOUT IT *Attorney Samuel G. Kling*	2.00

CHESS & CHECKERS

BEGINNER'S GUIDE TO WINNING CHESS *Fred Reinfeld*	2.00
BETTER CHESS — How to Play *Fred Reinfeld*	2.00
CHECKERS MADE EASY *Tom Wiswell*	2.00
CHESS IN TEN EASY LESSONS *Larry Evans*	2.00
CHESS MADE EASY *Milton L. Hanauer*	2.00
CHESS MASTERY — A New Approach *Fred Reinfeld*	2.00
CHESS PROBLEMS FOR BEGINNERS *edited by Fred Reinfeld*	2.00
CHESS SECRETS REVEALED *Fred Reinfeld*	2.00
CHESS STRATEGY — An Expert's Guide *Fred Reinfeld*	2.00
CHESS TACTICS FOR BEGINNERS *edited by Fred Reinfeld*	2.00
CHESS THEORY & PRACTICE *Morry & Mitchell*	2.00
HOW TO WIN AT CHECKERS *Fred Reinfeld*	2.00
1001 BRILLIANT WAYS TO CHECKMATE *Fred Reinfeld*	2.00
1001 WINNING CHESS SACRIFICES & COMBINATIONS *Fred Reinfeld*	2.00

COOKERY & HERBS

CULPEPER'S HERBAL REMEDIES *Dr. Nicholas Culpeper*	2.00
FAST GOURMET COOKBOOK *Poppy Cannon*	2.50
HEALING POWER OF HERBS *May Bethel*	2.00
HERB HANDBOOK *Dawn MacLeod*	2.00
HERBS FOR COOKING AND HEALING *Dr. Donald Law*	2.00
HERBS FOR HEALTH How to Grow & Use Them *Louise Evans Doole*	2.00

_____HOME GARDEN COOKBOOK Delicious Natural Food Recipes *Ken Kraft* 3.00
_____NATURAL FOOD COOKBOOK *Dr. Harry C. Bond* 2.00
_____NATURE'S MEDICINES *Richard Lucas* 2.00
_____VEGETABLE GARDENING FOR BEGINNERS *Hugh Wiberg* 2.00
_____VEGETABLES FOR TODAY'S GARDENS *R. Milton Carleton* 2.00
_____VEGETARIAN COOKERY *Janet Walker* 2.00
_____VEGETARIAN COOKING MADE EASY & DELECTABLE *Veronica Vezza* 2.00
_____VEGETARIAN DELIGHTS — A Happy Cookbook for Health *K. R. Mehta* 2.00
_____VEGETARIAN GOURMET COOKBOOK *Joyce McKinnel* 2.00

HEALTH

_____DR. LINDNER'S SPECIAL WEIGHT CONTROL METHOD 1.00
_____GAYELORD HAUSER'S NEW GUIDE TO INTELLIGENT REDUCING 3.00
_____HELP YOURSELF TO BETTER SIGHT *Margaret Darst Corbett* 2.00
_____HOW TO IMPROVE YOUR VISION *Dr. Robert A. Kraskin* 2.00
_____HOW YOU CAN STOP SMOKING PERMANENTLY *Ernest Caldwell* 2.00
_____LSD — THE AGE OF MIND *Bernard Roseman* 2.00
_____MIND OVER PLATTER *Peter G. Lindner, M.D.* 2.00
_____NEW CARBOHYDRATE DIET COUNTER *Patti Lopez-Pereira* 1.00
_____PSYCHEDELIC ECSTASY *William Marshall & Gilbert W. Taylor* 2.00
_____YOU CAN LEARN TO RELAX *Dr. Samuel Gutwirth* 2.00

HOBBIES

_____BLACKSTONE'S MODERN CARD TRICKS *Harry Blackstone* 2.00
_____BLACKSTONE'S SECRETS OF MAGIC *Harry Blackstone* 2.00
_____COIN COLLECTING FOR BEGINNERS *Burton Hobson & Fred Reinfeld* 2.00
_____400 FASCINATING MAGIC TRICKS YOU CAN DO *Howard Thurston* 3.00
_____GOULD'S GOLD & SILVER GUIDE TO COINS *Maurice Gould* 2.00
_____HOW I TURN JUNK INTO FUN AND PROFIT *Sari* 3.00
_____HOW TO WRITE A HIT SONG & SELL IT *Tommy Boyce* 7.00
_____JUGGLING MADE EASY *Rudolf Dittrich* 2.00
_____MAGIC MADE EASY *Byron Wels* 2.00
_____SEW SIMPLY, SEW RIGHT *Mini Rhea & F. Leighton* 2.00
_____STAMP COLLECTING FOR BEGINNERS *Burton Hobson* 2.00
_____STAMP COLLECTING FOR FUN & PROFIT *Frank Cetin* 2.00

HORSE PLAYERS' WINNING GUIDES

_____BETTING HORSES TO WIN *Les Conklin* 2.00
_____HOW TO PICK WINNING HORSES *Bob McKnight* 2.00
_____HOW TO WIN AT THE RACES *Sam (The Genius) Lewin* 2.00
_____HOW YOU CAN BEAT THE RACES *Jack Kavanagh* 2.00
_____MAKING MONEY AT THE RACES *David Barr* 2.00
_____PAYDAY AT THE RACES *Les Conklin* 2.00
_____SMART HANDICAPPING MADE EASY *William Bauman* 2.00

HYPNOTISM

_____ADVANCED TECHNIQUES OF HYPNOSIS *Melvin Powers* 1.00
_____CHILDBIRTH WITH HYPNOSIS *William S. Kroger, M.D.* 2.00
_____HOW TO SOLVE YOUR SEX PROBLEMS
    WITH SELF-HYPNOSIS *Frank S. Caprio, M.D.* 2.00
_____HOW TO STOP SMOKING THRU SELF-HYPNOSIS *Leslie M. LeCron* 2.00
_____HOW TO USE AUTO-SUGGESTION EFFECTIVELY *John Duckworth* 2.00
_____HOW YOU CAN BOWL BETTER USING SELF-HYPNOSIS *Jack Heise* 2.00
_____HOW YOU CAN PLAY BETTER GOLF USING SELF-HYPNOSIS *Heise* 2.00
_____HYPNOSIS AND SELF-HYPNOSIS *Bernard Hollander, M.D.* 2.00
_____HYPNOTISM (Originally published in 1893) *Carl Sextus* 3.00
_____HYPNOTISM & PSYCHIC PHENOMENA *Simeon Edmunds* 2.00
_____HYPNOTISM MADE EASY *Dr. Ralph Winn* 2.00
_____HYPNOTISM MADE PRACTICAL *Louis Orton* 2.00
_____HYPNOTISM REVEALED *Melvin Powers* 1.00
_____HYPNOTISM TODAY *Leslie LeCron & Jean Bordeaux, Ph.D.* 2.00
_____MODERN HYPNOSIS *Lesley Kuhn & Salvatore Russo, Ph.D.* 3.00

_____ NEW CONCEPTS OF HYPNOSIS *Bernard C. Gindes, M.D.* 3.00
_____ POST-HYPNOTIC INSTRUCTIONS *Arnold Furst* 2.00
     How to give post-hypnotic suggestions for therapeutic purposes.
_____ PRACTICAL GUIDE TO SELF-HYPNOSIS *Melvin Powers* 2.00
_____ PRACTICAL HYPNOTISM *Philip Magonet, M.D.* 1.00
_____ SECRETS OF HYPNOTISM *S. J. Van Pelt, M.D.* 2.00
_____ SELF-HYPNOSIS *Paul Adams* 2.00
_____ SELF-HYPNOSIS Its Theory, Technique & Application *Melvin Powers* 2.00
_____ SELF-HYPNOSIS A Conditioned-Response Technique *Laurance Sparks* 3.00
_____ THERAPY THROUGH HYPNOSIS *edited by Raphael H. Rhodes* 3.00

JUDAICA

_____ HOW TO LIVE A RICHER & FULLER LIFE *Rabbi Edgar F. Magnin* 2.00
_____ MODERN ISRAEL *Lily Edelman* 2.00
_____ OUR JEWISH HERITAGE *Rabbi Alfred Wolf & Joseph Gaer* 2.00
_____ ROMANCE OF HASSIDISM *Jacob S. Minkin* 2.50
_____ SERVICE OF THE HEART *Evelyn Garfield, Ph.D.* 3.00
_____ STORY OF ISRAEL IN COINS *Jean & Maurice Gould* 2.00
_____ STORY OF ISRAEL IN STAMPS *Maxim & Gabriel Shamir* 1.00
_____ TONGUE OF THE PROPHETS *Robert St. John* 3.00
_____ TREASURY OF COMFORT *edited by Rabbi Sidney Greenberg* 3.00

MARRIAGE, SEX & PARENTHOOD

_____ ABILITY TO LOVE *Dr. Allan Fromme* 3.00
_____ ENCYCLOPEDIA OF MODERN SEX & LOVE TECHNIQUES *Macandrew* 2.00
_____ GUIDE TO SUCCESSFUL MARRIAGE *Drs. Albert Ellis & Robert Harper* 3.00
_____ HOW TO RAISE AN EMOTIONALLY HEALTHY, HAPPY CHILD, *A. Ellis* 2.00
_____ IMPOTENCE & FRIGIDITY *Edwin W. Hirsch, M.D.* 2.00
_____ NEW APPROACHES TO SEX IN MARRIAGE *John E. Eichenlaub, M.D.* 2.00
_____ PSYCHOSOMATIC GYNECOLOGY *William S. Kroger, M.D.* 10.00
_____ SEX WITHOUT GUILT *Albert Ellis, Ph.D.* 2.00
_____ SEXUALLY ADEQUATE FEMALE *Frank S. Caprio, M.D.* 2.00
_____ SEXUALLY ADEQUATE MALE *Frank S. Caprio, M.D.* 2.00
_____ YOUR FIRST YEAR OF MARRIAGE *Dr. Tom McGinnis* 2.00

METAPHYSICS & OCCULT

_____ BOOK OF TALISMANS, AMULETS & ZODIACAL GEMS *William Pavitt* 3.00
_____ CONCENTRATION—A Guide to Mental Mastery *Mouni Sadhu* 2.00
_____ DREAMS & OMENS REVEALED *Fred Gettings* 2.00
_____ EXTRASENSORY PERCEPTION *Simeon Edmunds* 2.00
_____ FORTUNE TELLING WITH CARDS *P. Foli* 2.00
_____ HANDWRITING ANALYSIS MADE EASY *John Marley* 2.00
_____ HANDWRITING TELLS *Nadya Olyanova* 3.00
_____ HOW TO UNDERSTAND YOUR DREAMS *Geoffrey A. Dudley* 2.00
_____ ILLUSTRATED YOGA *William Zorn* 2.00
_____ IN DAYS OF GREAT PEACE *Mouni Sadhu* 2.00
_____ KING SOLOMON'S TEMPLE IN THE MASONIC TRADITION *Alex Horne* 5.00
_____ MAGICIAN — His training and work *W. E. Butler* 2.00
_____ MEDITATION *Mouni Sadhu* 3.00
_____ MODERN NUMEROLOGY *Morris C. Goodman* 2.00
_____ NUMEROLOGY—ITS FACTS AND SECRETS *Ariel Yvon Taylor* 2.00
_____ PALMISTRY MADE EASY *Fred Gettings* 2.00
_____ PALMISTRY MADE PRACTICAL *Elizabeth Daniels Squire* 2.00
_____ PALMISTRY SECRETS REVEALED *Henry Frith* 2.00
_____ PRACTICAL YOGA *Ernest Wood* 2.00
_____ PROPHECY IN OUR TIME *Martin Ebon* 2.50
_____ PSYCHOLOGY OF HANDWRITING *Nadya Olyanova* 2.00
_____ SEEING INTO THE FUTURE *Harvey Day* 2.00
_____ SUPERSTITION — Are you superstitious? *Eric Maple* 2.00
_____ TAROT *Mouni Sadhu* 4.00
_____ TAROT OF THE BOHEMIANS *Papus* 3.00
_____ TEST YOUR ESP *Martin Ebon* 2.00

_____WAYS TO SELF-REALIZATION *Mouni Sadhu*	2.00
_____WITCHCRAFT, MAGIC & OCCULTISM—A Fascinating History *W. B. Crow*	3.00
_____WITCHCRAFT — THE SIXTH SENSE *Justine Glass*	2.00
_____WORLD OF PSYCHIC RESEARCH *Hereward Carrington*	2.00
_____YOU CAN ANALYZE HANDWRITING *Robert Holder*	2.00

SELF-HELP & INSPIRATIONAL

_____ACT YOUR WAY TO SUCCESSFUL LIVING *Neil & Margaret Rau*	2.00
_____CYBERNETICS WITHIN US *Y. Saparina*	3.00
_____DAILY POWER FOR JOYFUL LIVING *Dr. Donald Curtis*	2.00
_____DOCTOR PSYCHO-CYBERNETICS *Maxwell Maltz, M.D.*	3.00
_____DYNAMIC THINKING *Melvin Powers*	1.00
_____GREATEST POWER IN THE UNIVERSE *U. S. Andersen*	4.00
_____GROW RICH WHILE YOU SLEEP *Ben Sweetland*	2.00
_____GROWTH THROUGH REASON *Albert Ellis, Ph.D.*	3.00
_____GUIDE TO DEVELOPING YOUR POTENTIAL *Herbert A. Otto, Ph.D.*	3.00
_____GUIDE TO HAPPINESS *Dr. Maxwell S. Cagan*	2.00
_____GUIDE TO LIVING IN BALANCE *Frank S. Caprio, M.D.*	2.00
_____GUIDE TO RATIONAL LIVING *Albert Ellis, Ph.D. & R. Harper, Ph.D.*	2.00
_____HELPING YOURSELF WITH APPLIED PSYCHOLOGY *R. Henderson*	2.00
_____HELPING YOURSELF WITH PSYCHIATRY *Frank S. Caprio, M.D.*	2.00
_____HOW TO ATTRACT GOOD LUCK *A. H. Z. Carr*	2.00
_____HOW TO CONTROL YOUR DESTINY *Norvell*	2.00
_____HOW TO DEVELOP A WINNING PERSONALITY *Martin Panzer*	2.00
_____HOW TO DEVELOP AN EXCEPTIONAL MEMORY *Young & Gibson*	3.00
_____HOW TO OVERCOME YOUR FEARS *M. P. Leahy, M.D.*	2.00
_____HOW YOU CAN HAVE CONFIDENCE AND POWER *Les Giblin*	2.00
_____HUMAN PROBLEMS & HOW TO SOLVE THEM *Dr. Donald Curtis*	2.00
_____I WILL *Ben Sweetland*	2.00
_____LEFT-HANDED PEOPLE *Michael Barsley*	3.00
_____MAGIC IN YOUR MIND *U. S. Andersen*	3.00
_____MAGIC OF THINKING BIG *Dr. David J. Schwartz*	2.00
_____MAGIC POWER OF YOUR MIND *Walter M. Germain*	3.00
_____MENTAL POWER THRU SLEEP SUGGESTION *Melvin Powers*	1.00
_____ORIENTAL SECRETS OF GRACEFUL LIVING *Boye De Mente*	1.00
_____PRACTICAL GUIDE TO SUCCESS & POPULARITY *C. W. Bailey*	2.00
_____PSYCHO-CYBERNETICS *Maxwell Maltz, M.D.*	2.00
_____SCIENCE OF MIND IN DAILY LIVING *Dr. Donald Curtis*	2.00
_____SECRET OF SECRETS *U. S. Andersen*	3.00
_____STUTTERING AND WHAT YOU CAN DO ABOUT IT *W. Johnson, Ph.D.*	2.00
_____SUCCESS-CYBERNETICS *U. S. Andersen*	2.00
_____10 DAYS TO A GREAT NEW LIFE *William E. Edwards*	2.00
_____THINK AND GROW RICH *Napoleon Hill*	3.00
_____THREE MAGIC WORDS *U. S. Andersen*	3.00
_____TREASURY OF THE ART OF LIVING *Sidney S. Greenberg*	3.00
_____YOU ARE NOT THE TARGET *Laura Huxley*	3.00
_____YOUR SUBCONSCIOUS POWER *Charles M. Simmons*	3.00
_____YOUR THOUGHTS CAN CHANGE YOUR LIFE *Dr. Donald Curtis*	2.00

SPORTS

_____ARCHERY — An Expert's Guide *Don Stamp*	2.00
_____BICYCLING FOR FUN AND GOOD HEALTH *Kenneth E. Luther*	2.00
_____CAMPING-OUT 101 Ideas & Activities *Bruno Knobel*	2.00
_____COMPLETE GUIDE TO FISHING *Vlad Evanoff*	2.00
_____HOW TO WIN AT POCKET BILLIARDS *Edward D. Knuchell*	3.00
_____MOTORCYCLING FOR BEGINNERS *I. G. Edmonds*	2.00

The books listed above can be obtained from your book dealer or directly from Melvin Powers. When ordering, please remit 25c per book postage & handling.
Send 25c for our illustrated catalog of self-improvement books.

Melvin Powers
12015 Sherman Road, No. Hollywood, California 91605